Clashes of Culture

Clashes of Culture

The Great Books Foundation

A nonprofit educational organization

Published and distributed by

 The Great Books Foundation
A nonprofit educational organization

35 East Wacker Drive, Suite 2300
Chicago, IL 60601-2298

First Printing
9 8 7 6 5 4 3 2 1 0

Library of Congress Cataloging-in-Publication Data
Clashes of culture.
     p. cm. — (50th anniversary series)
   Contents: Deep play: notes on the Balinese cockfight / Clifford Geertz —
The two shores / Carlos Fuentes — The souls of black folk (selection) / W. E. B.
Du Bois — The antheap / Doris Lessing — A voyage to the country of the
houyhnhnms / Jonathan Swift — Poetry / Derek Walcott — Questions for
A passage to India (E. M. Forster) — Questions for Wide sargasso sea (Jean Rhys)
   ISBN 1-880323-83-4
   1. Literature — Collections. 2. Group reading. 3. Reader-response
criticism. I. Great Books Foundation (U.S.) II. Series: Great Books Foundation
50th anniversary series.
PN6014.C535 1998
808.8—DC21   98-24339

CONTENTS

PREFACE

"So that's what Geertz means when he describes
cockfighting as a form of literature!" "Why is sexuality often the
focus of racial conflict?" "Have we achieved the 'frank and fair'
discussion of race relations that Du Bois envisions?"

Anyone who has been in a book discussion group has experienced the joy of new insight. Sometimes an idea or question occurs to us during the group meeting. Often, it is afterward—sometimes much later—that an idea we had overlooked unexpectedly strikes us with new force. A good group becomes a community of minds. We share perspectives, questions, insights, and surprises. Our fellow readers challenge and broaden our thinking as we probe deeply into characters and ideas. They help us resolve questions, and raise new ones, in a creative process that connects literature with life.

It is this kind of experience that makes book discussion groups worthwhile, and that the Great Books Foundation fosters for thousands of readers around the world.

The Great Books Foundation is a pioneer of book discussion groups that bring together dedicated readers who wish to continue to learn throughout their lives. The literature anthologies published by the Foundation have been the focus of many enlightening discussions among people of all educational backgrounds and walks of life. And the *shared inquiry* method practiced by Great Books groups has proven to be a powerful approach to literature that solves many practical concerns of new discussion groups: How can we maintain a flow of ideas? What kinds of questions should we discuss? How can we keep the discussion focused on the reading so that we use our time together to really get at the heart of a work—to learn from it and each other?

With the publication of its 50th Anniversary Series, the Great Books Foundation continues and expands upon its tradition of helping all readers engage in a meaningful exchange of ideas about outstanding works of literature.

ABOUT CLASHES OF CULTURE

The reading selections in *Clashes of Culture* have been chosen to stimulate lively shared inquiry discussions. This collection brings together works from around the world that speak to each other on a theme of universal human significance. In this volume you will find classic works by W. E. B. Du Bois and Jonathan Swift, a selection from the contemporary cultural anthropologist Clifford Geertz, fiction by Doris Lessing and Carlos Fuentes, and poetry by Derek Walcott.

These are carefully crafted works that readers will interpret in different ways. They portray characters whose lives and motivations are complex, embody concepts that go beyond simple analysis, and raise many questions to inspire extended reflection.

As an aid to reading and discussion, open-ended *interpretive questions* are included with each selection in the volume, and also for the recommended novels *A Passage to India* by E. M. Forster and *Wide Sargasso Sea* by Jean Rhys. A fundamental or *basic* interpretive question about the meaning of the selection is printed in boldface, followed by a list of related questions that will help you fully discuss the issue raised by the basic question. Passages for *textual analysis* that you may want to look at closely during discussion are suggested for each set of questions. Questions under the heading "For Further Reflection" can be used at the end of discussion to help your group consider the reading selection in a broader context.

ABOUT SHARED INQUIRY

The success of Great Books discussions depends not only on thought-provoking literature, but also on the shared inquiry method of discussion. A shared inquiry discussion begins with a basic interpretive question—a genuine question about the meaning of the selection that continues to be puzzling even after careful reading. As participants offer different possible answers to this question, the discussion leader or members of the group follow up on the ideas that are voiced, asking questions about how responses relate to the original question or to new ideas, and probing what specifically in the text prompted the response.

In shared inquiry discussion, readers think for themselves about the selection, and do not rely on critical or biographical sources outside the text for ideas about its meaning. Discussion remains focused on the text. Evidence for opinions is found in the selection. Because interpretive questions have no single "correct answer," participants are encouraged to entertain a range of ideas. The exchange of ideas is open and spontaneous, a common search for understanding that leads to closer, more illuminating reading.

Shared inquiry fosters a habit of critical questioning and thinking. It encourages patience in the face of complexity, and a respect for the opinions of others. As participants explore the work in depth, they try out ideas, reconsider simple answers, and synthesize interpretations. Over time, shared inquiry engenders a profound experience of intellectual intimacy as your group searches together for meaning in literature.

IMPROVING YOUR DISCUSSIONS

The selections in *Clashes of Culture* will support six meetings of your discussion group, with each selection and the two poems being the focus of a single meeting. Discussions usually last about two hours, and are guided by a member of the group who acts as leader. Since the leader has no special knowledge or qualification beyond a genuine curiosity about the text, any member of the group may lead discussion. The leader carefully prepares the interpretive questions that he or she wants to explore with the group, and is primarily responsible for continuing the process of questioning that maintains the flow of ideas.

To ensure a successful discussion, we encourage you to make it a policy to read the selection twice. A first reading will familiarize you with the plot and ideas of a selection; on a second reading you will read more reflectively and discover many aspects of the work that deepen your thinking about it. Allowing a few days to pass between your readings will also help you approach a second reading with greater insight.

Read the selection actively. Make marginal comments that you might want to refer to in discussion. While our interpretive questions can help you think about different aspects of the work, jotting down your own questions as you read is the best way to engage with the selection and bring a wealth of ideas and meaningful questions to discussion.

During discussion, expect a variety of answers to the basic question. Follow up carefully on these different ideas. Refer to and read from the text often—by way of explaining your answer, and to see if the rest of the group understands the author's words the same way you do. (You will often be surprised!) As your group looks closely at the text, many new ideas will arise.

While leaders in shared inquiry discussion strive to keep comments focused on the text and on the basic interpretive question the group is discussing, the entire group can share responsibility for politely refocusing comments that wander from the text into personal anecdotes or issues that begin to sidetrack discussion.

Remember that during shared inquiry discussion you are investigating differing perspectives on the reading. Talk should focus foremost on characters in the story, not on participants' daily lives and concerns or current social topics. By maintaining this focus, each discussion will be new and interesting, with each participant bringing a different perspective to bear on the text. After the work has been explored thoroughly on its own terms, your thinking about important issues of the day or in your own life will be enhanced. We have found that it is best to formally set aside a time—perhaps the last half-hour of discussion or over coffee afterward—for members of the group to share personal experiences and opinions that go beyond a discussion of the selection.

Discussing the Poetry Selections

Many book groups shy away from the challenge of discussing poetry, but the shared inquiry method will enable you to make poetry a very satisfying part of your discussion group. Poetry, by its very nature, communicates ideas through suggestion, allusion, and resonance. Because meaning in poetry resides in the interaction between author and reader, and is brought to light through the pooling of different perspectives and readers' responses, poems are ideal for shared inquiry discussion.

It is helpful to read each poem, or parts of it, aloud before beginning discussion. Because poetry is usually more densely constructed than prose and highly selective in detail, it often lends itself to what we call *textual analysis*—looking closely at particular lines, words, and images as an entryway to discussing the whole work. Having readers share their different associations with a word or image can often help broaden interpretations.

DISCUSSING THE NOVELS

Many novels might come to mind that relate to the theme of clashes of culture. We have recommended *A Passage to India* and *Wide Sargasso Sea* as particularly enriching novels on this theme, and have provided interpretive questions that can be a significant aid to the reader. Even readers familiar with these novels will find a shared inquiry discussion of them a fresh and rewarding experience.

Most shared inquiry groups discuss a novel at a single discussion; some prefer to spread the discussion over more than one session, especially for longer novels. Since it is usually not realistic to expect participants to read a novel twice in full before discussion, we recommend that you at least reread parts of the novel that seemed especially important to you or that raised a number of questions in your mind. Our passages for textual analysis suggest parts of the novel where reading twice might be most valuable. You might even begin your discussion, after posing a basic question, by looking closely at one or two short passages to get people talking about central ideas and offering a variety of opinions that can be probed and expanded into a discussion of the whole work.

HOW THE GREAT BOOKS FOUNDATION CAN HELP YOU

The Great Books Foundation can be a significant resource for you and your discussion group. Our staff conducts shared inquiry workshops throughout the country that will help you or your entire group conduct better discussions. Thousands of people—from elementary school teachers and college professors to those who just love books and ideas—have found our workshops to be an enjoyable experience that changes forever how they approach literature.

The Foundation publishes a variety of reading series that might interest you. We invite you to call us at 1-800-222-5870 or visit our Web site at http://www.greatbooks.org. We can help you start a book group, put you in touch with established Great Books groups in your area, or give you information about many special events—such as poetry weekends or week-long discussion institutes—sponsored by Great Books groups around the country.

Finally, we invite you to inquire about Junior Great Books for students in kindergarten through high school, to learn how you can help develop the next generation of book lovers and shared inquiry participants.

We hope you enjoy *Clashes of Culture* and that it inaugurates many years of exciting discussions for your group. Great Books programs—for children as well as adults—are founded on the idea that readers discussing together can achieve insight and great pleasure from literature. We look forward, with you, to cultivating this idea through the next century.

Footnotes by the author are not bracketed; footnotes by
the Great Books Foundation, an editor,
or a translator are [bracketed].

Deep Play:
Notes on the
Balinese Cockfight

Clifford Geertz

CLIFFORD GEERTZ (1926–   ) was born
in San Francisco. He has taught at Harvard,
the University of California–Berkeley, the
University of Chicago, and, since 1970,
the Institute for Advanced Study in Princeton.
Geertz has called himself an interpretive
anthropologist and is known for his theory
of culture as a system of symbols. In his
writing, Geertz draws upon a broad range
of disciplines—history, philosophy,
psychology, and literary criticism—and
his work has found a wide readership
among general readers as well as scholars.
He has won a number of important honors,
including the social science prize from the
American Academy of Arts and Sciences,
the Huxley Medal from the Royal
Anthropological Institute, and the National
Book Critics Circle Award. "Deep Play"
appears in *The Interpretation of Cultures,*
for which Geertz won the Sorokin Prize
from the American Sociological Association
in 1974.

NOTE: Scholarly citations have been omitted
from the selection.

THE RAID

Early in April of 1958, my wife and I arrived, malarial and diffident, in a Balinese village we intended, as anthropologists, to study. A small place, about five hundred people, and relatively remote, it was its own world. We were intruders, professional ones, and the villagers dealt with us as Balinese seem always to deal with people not part of their life who yet press themselves upon them: as though we were not there. For them, and to a degree for ourselves, we were non-persons, specters, invisible men.

We moved into an extended family compound (that had been arranged before through the provincial government) belonging to one of the four major factions in village life. But except for our landlord and the village chief, whose cousin and brother-in-law he was, everyone ignored us in a way only a Balinese can do. As we wandered around, uncertain, wistful, eager to please, people seemed to look right through us with a gaze focused several yards behind us on some more actual stone or tree. Almost nobody greeted us; but nobody scowled or said anything unpleasant to us either, which would have been almost as satisfactory. If we ventured to approach someone (something one is powerfully inhibited from doing in such an atmosphere), he moved, negligently but definitely, away. If, seated or leaning against a wall, we had him trapped, he said nothing at all, or mumbled what for the Balinese is the ultimate nonword—"yes." The indifference, of course, was studied; the villagers were watching every move we made, and they had an enormous amount of quite accurate information about who we were and what we were going to be doing. But they acted as if we simply did not exist, which, in fact, as this behavior was designed to inform us, we did not, or anyway not yet.

This is, as I say, general in Bali. Everywhere else I have been in Indonesia, and more latterly in Morocco, when I have gone into a new village, people have poured out from all sides to take a very close look at me, and often an all-too-probing feel as well. In Balinese villages, at least those away from the tourist circuit, nothing happens at all. People go on pounding, chatting, making offerings, staring into space, carrying baskets about while one drifts around feeling vaguely disembodied. And the same thing is true on the individual level. When you first meet a Balinese, he seems virtually not to relate to you at all; he is, in the term Gregory Bateson and Margaret Mead made famous, "away." Then—in a day, a week, a month (with some people the magic moment never comes)—he decides, for reasons I have never quite been able to fathom, that you *are* real, and then he becomes a warm, gay, sensitive, sympathetic, though, being Balinese, always precisely controlled person. You have crossed, somehow, some moral or metaphysical shadow line. Though you are not exactly taken as a Balinese (one has to be born to that), you are at least regarded as a human being rather than a cloud or a gust of wind. The whole complexion of your relationship dramatically changes to, in the majority of cases, a gentle, almost affectionate one—a low-keyed, rather playful, rather mannered, rather bemused geniality.

My wife and I were still very much in the gust-of-wind stage, a most frustrating, and even, as you soon begin to doubt whether you are really real after all, unnerving one, when, ten days or so after our arrival, a large cockfight was held in the public square to raise money for a new school.

Now, a few special occasions aside, cockfights are illegal in Bali under the Republic (as, for not altogether unrelated reasons, they were under the Dutch), largely as a result of the pretensions to puritanism radical nationalism tends to bring with it. The elite, which is not itself so very puritan, worries about the poor, ignorant peasant gambling all his money away, about what foreigners will think, about the waste of time better devoted to building up the country. It sees cockfighting as "primitive," "backward," "unprogressive," and generally unbecoming an ambitious nation. And, as with those other embarrassments— opium smoking, begging, or uncovered breasts—it seeks, rather unsystematically, to put a stop to it.

Of course, like drinking during Prohibition or, today, smoking marihuana, cockfights, being a part of "The Balinese Way of Life," nonetheless go on happening, and with extraordinary frequency. And, as with Prohibition or marihuana, from time to time the police (who, in 1958 at least, were almost all not Balinese but Javanese) feel called upon to make a raid, confiscate the cocks and spurs, fine a few people, and even now and then expose some of them in the tropical sun for a day as object lessons which never, somehow, get learned, even though occasionally, quite occasionally, the object dies.

As a result, the fights are usually held in a secluded corner of a village in semisecrecy, a fact which tends to slow the action a little—not very much, but the Balinese do not care to have it slowed at all. In this case, however, perhaps because they were raising money for a school that the government was unable to give them, perhaps because raids had been few recently, perhaps, as I gathered from subsequent discussion, there was a notion that the necessary bribes had been paid, they thought they could take a chance on the central square and draw a larger and more enthusiastic crowd without attracting the attention of the law.

They were wrong. In the midst of the third match, with hundreds of people, including, still transparent, myself and my wife, fused into a single body around the ring, a superorganism in the literal sense, a truck full of policemen armed with machine guns roared up. Amid great screeching cries of "pulisi! pulisi!" from the crowd, the policemen jumped out, and, springing into the center of the ring, began to swing their guns around like gangsters in a motion picture, though not going so far as actually to fire them. The superorganism came instantly apart as its components scattered in all directions. People raced down the road, disappeared headfirst over walls, scrambled under platforms, folded themselves behind wicker screens, scuttled up coconut trees. Cocks armed with steel spurs sharp enough to cut off a finger or run a hole through a foot were running wildly around. Everything was dust and panic.

On the established anthropological principle "When in Rome," my wife and I decided, only slightly less instantaneously than everyone else, that the thing to do was run too. We ran down the main village street, northward, away from where we were living, for we were on that side of the ring. About halfway down another fugitive ducked suddenly into a compound—his own, it turned out—and we, seeing nothing ahead of us but rice fields, open country, and a very high volcano, followed him. As the three of us came tumbling into the courtyard, his wife, who had apparently been through this sort of thing before, whipped out a table, a tablecloth, three chairs, and three cups of tea, and we all, without any explicit communication whatsoever, sat down, commenced to sip tea, and sought to compose ourselves.

A few moments later, one of the policemen marched importantly into the yard, looking for the village chief. (The chief had not only been at the fight, he had arranged it. When the truck drove up he ran to the river, stripped off his sarong, and plunged in so he could say, when at length they found him sitting there pouring water over his head, that he had been away bathing when the whole affair had occurred and was ignorant of it. They did not believe him and fined him three hundred rupiah, which the village raised collectively.) Seeing me and my wife, "White Men," there in the yard, the policeman performed a classic double take. When he found his voice again he asked, approximately, what in the devil did we think we were doing there. Our host of five minutes leaped instantly to our defense, producing an impassioned description of who and what we were, so detailed and so accurate that it was my turn, having barely communicated with a living human being save my landlord and the village chief for more than a week, to be astonished. We had a perfect right to be there, he said, looking the Javanese upstart in the eye. We were American professors; the government had cleared us; we were there to study culture; we were going to write a book to tell Americans about Bali. And we had all been there drinking tea and talking about cultural matters all afternoon and did not know anything about any cockfight. Moreover, we had not seen the village chief all day; he must have gone to town. The policeman retreated in rather total disarray. And, after a decent interval, bewildered but relieved to have survived and stayed out of jail, so did we.

The next morning the village was a completely different world for us. Not only were we no longer invisible, we were suddenly the center of all attention, the object of a great outpouring of warmth, interest, and most especially, amusement. Everyone in the village knew we had fled like everyone else. They asked us about it again and again (I must have told the story, small detail by small detail, fifty times by the end of the day), gently, affectionately, but quite insistently teasing us: "Why didn't you just stand there and tell the police who you were?" "Why didn't you just say you were only watching and not betting?" "Were you really afraid of those little guns?" As always, kinesthetically minded and, even when fleeing for their lives (or, as happened eight years later, surrendering them), the world's most poised people, they gleefully mimicked, also over and over again, our graceless style of running and what they claimed were our panic-stricken facial expressions. But above all, everyone was extremely pleased and even more surprised that we had not simply "pulled out our papers" (they knew about those too) and asserted our Distinguished Visitor status, but had instead demonstrated our solidarity with what were now our covillagers. (What we had actually demonstrated was our cowardice, but there is fellowship in that too.) Even the Brahmana priest, an old, grave, halfway-to-heaven type who because of its associations with the underworld would never be involved, even distantly, in a cockfight, and was difficult to approach even to other Balinese, had us called into his court-yard to ask us about what had happened, chuckling happily at the sheer extraordinariness of it all.

In Bali, to be teased is to be accepted. It was the turning point so far as our relationship to the community was concerned, and we were quite literally "in." The whole village opened up to us, probably more than it ever would have otherwise (I might actu-ally never have gotten to that priest, and our accidental host became one of my best informants), and certainly very much faster. Getting caught, or almost caught, in a vice raid is perhaps not a very generalizable recipe for achieving that mysterious necessity of anthropological field work, rapport, but for me it worked very well. It led to a sudden and unusually complete acceptance into a society extremely difficult for outsiders to pen-etrate. It gave me the kind of immediate, inside-view grasp of an aspect of "peasant mentality" that anthropologists not fortunate enough to flee headlong with their subjects from armed author-ities normally do not get. And, perhaps most important of all, for the other things might have come in other ways, it put me very quickly on to a combination emotional explosion, status war, and philosophical drama of central significance to the society whose inner nature I desired to understand. By the time I left I had spent about as much time looking into cockfights as into witchcraft, irrigation, caste, or marriage.

OF COCKS AND MEN

Bali, mainly because it is Bali, is a well-studied place. Its mythology, art, ritual, social organization, patterns of child rearing, forms of law, even styles of trance, have all been microscopically examined for traces of that elusive substance Jane Belo called "The Balinese Temper." But, aside from a few passing remarks, the cockfight has barely been noticed, although as a popular obsession of consuming power it is at least as important a revelation of what being a Balinese "is really like" as these more celebrated phenomena. As much of America surfaces in a ballpark, on a golf links, at a racetrack, or around a poker table, much of Bali surfaces in a cock ring. For it is only apparently cocks that are fighting there. Actually, it is men.

To anyone who has been in Bali any length of time, the deep psychological identification of Balinese men with their cocks is unmistakable. The double entendre here is deliberate. It works in exactly the same way in Balinese as it does in English, even to producing the same tired jokes, strained puns, and uninventive obscenities. Bateson and Mead have even suggested that, in line with the Balinese conception of the body as a set of separately animated parts, cocks are viewed as detachable, self-operating penises, ambulant genitals with a life of their own.[1] And while I do not have the kind of unconscious material either to confirm or disconfirm this intriguing notion, the fact that they are masculine symbols par excellence is about as indubitable, and to the Balinese about as evident, as the fact that water runs downhill.

---

1. The cockfight is unusual within Balinese culture in being a single-sex public activity from which the other sex is totally and expressly excluded. Sexual differentiation is culturally extremely played down in Bali and most activities, formal and informal, involve the participation of men and women on equal ground, commonly as linked couples. From religion, to politics, to economics, to kinship, to dress, Bali is a rather "unisex" society, a fact both its customs and its symbolism clearly express. Even in contexts where women do not in fact play much of a role—music, painting, certain agricultural activities—their absence, which is only relative in any case, is more a mere matter of fact than socially enforced. To this general pattern, the cockfight, entirely of, by, and for men (women—at least *Balinese* women—do not even watch), is the most striking exception.

The language of everyday moralism is shot through, on the male side of it, with roosterish imagery. *Sabung,* the word for cock (and one which appears in inscriptions as early as A.D. 922), is used metaphorically to mean "hero," "warrior," "champion," "man of parts," "political candidate," "bachelor," "dandy," "lady-killer," or "tough guy." A pompous man whose behavior presumes above his station is compared to a tailless cock who struts about as though he had a large, spectacular one. A desperate man who makes a last, irrational effort to extricate himself from an impossible situation is likened to a dying cock who makes one final lunge at his tormentor to drag him along to a common destruction. A stingy man, who promises much, gives little, and begrudges that, is compared to a cock which, held by the tail, leaps at another without in fact engaging him. A marriageable young man still shy with the opposite sex or someone in a new job anxious to make a good impression is called "a fighting cock caged for the first time." Court trials, wars, political contests, inheritance disputes, and street arguments are all compared to cockfights. Even the very island itself is perceived from its shape as a small, proud cock, poised, neck extended, back taut, tail raised, in eternal challenge to large, feckless, shapeless Java.[2]

But the intimacy of men with their cocks is more than metaphorical. Balinese men, or anyway a large majority of Balinese men, spend an enormous amount of time with their favorites, grooming them, feeding them, discussing them, trying them out against one another, or just gazing at them with a mixture of rapt admiration and dreamy self-absorption. Whenever you see a group of Balinese men squatting idly in the council shed or along the road in their hips down, shoulders forward, knees up fashion, half or more of them will have a rooster in his hands, holding it between his thighs, bouncing it

---

2. There is indeed a legend to the effect that the separation of Java and Bali is due to the action of a powerful Javanese religious figure who wished to protect himself against a Balinese culture hero (the ancestor of two Kshatriya castes) who was a passionate cockfighting gambler.

gently up and down to strengthen its legs, ruffling its feathers with abstract sensuality, pushing it out against a neighbor's rooster to rouse its spirit, withdrawing it toward his loins to calm it again. Now and then, to get a feel for another bird, a man will fiddle this way with someone else's cock for a while, but usually by moving around to squat in place behind it, rather than just having it passed across to him as though it were merely an animal.

In the houseyard, the high-walled enclosures where the people live, fighting cocks are kept in wicker cages moved frequently about so as to maintain the optimum balance of sun and shade. They are fed a special diet, which varies somewhat according to individual theories but which is mostly maize, sifted for impurities with far more care than it is when mere humans are going to eat it, and offered to the animal kernel by kernel. Red pepper is stuffed down their beaks and up their anuses to give them spirit. They are bathed in the same ceremonial preparation of tepid water, medicinal herbs, flowers, and onions in which infants are bathed, and for a prize cock just about as often. Their combs are cropped, their plumage dressed, their spurs trimmed, and their legs massaged, and they are inspected for flaws with the squinted concentration of a diamond merchant. A man who has a passion for cocks, an enthusiast in the literal sense of the term, can spend most of his life with them, and even those, the overwhelming majority, whose passion though intense has not entirely run away with them, can and do spend what seems not only to an outsider, but also to themselves, an inordinate amount of time with them. "I am cock crazy," my landlord, a quite ordinary afficionado by Balinese standards, used to moan as he went to move another cage, give another bath, or conduct another feeding. "We're all cock crazy."

The madness has some less visible dimensions, however, because although it is true that cocks are symbolic expressions or magnifications of their owner's self, the narcissistic male ego writ out in Aesopian terms, they are also expressions—and rather more immediate ones—of what the Balinese regard as the direct inversion, aesthetically, morally, and metaphysically, of human status: animality.

The Balinese revulsion against any behavior regarded as animal-like can hardly be overstressed. Babies are not allowed to crawl for that reason. Incest, though hardly approved, is a much less horrifying crime than bestiality. (The appropriate punishment for the second is death by drowning; for the first, being forced to live like an animal.)[3] Most demons are represented—in sculpture, dance, ritual, myth—in some real or fantastic animal form. The main puberty rite consists in filing the child's teeth so they will not look like animal fangs. Not only defecation but eating is regarded as a disgusting, almost obscene activity, to be conducted hurriedly and privately, because of its association with animality. Even falling down or any form of clumsiness is considered to be bad for these reasons. Aside from cocks and a few domestic animals—oxen, ducks—of no emotional significance, the Balinese are aversive to animals and treat their large number of dogs not merely callously but with a phobic cruelty. In identifying with his cock, the Balinese man is identifying not just with his ideal self, or even his penis, but also, and at the same time, with what he most fears, hates, and, ambivalence being what it is, is fascinated by—"The Powers of Darkness."

The connection of cocks and cockfighting with such Powers, with the animalistic demons that threaten constantly to invade the small, cleared-off space in which the Balinese have so carefully built their lives and devour its inhabitants, is quite explicit. A cockfight, any cockfight, is in the first instance a blood sacrifice offered, with the appropriate chants and oblations, to the demons in order to pacify their ravenous, cannibal hunger. No temple festival should be conducted until one is made. (If it is omitted, someone will inevitably fall into a trance and command with the voice of an angered spirit that the oversight be

---

3. An incestuous couple is forced to wear pig yokes over their necks and crawl to a pig trough and eat with their mouths there.

immediately corrected.) Collective responses to natural evils—illness, crop failure, volcanic eruptions—almost always involve them. And that famous holiday in Bali, "The Day of Silence" (*Njepi*), when everyone sits silent and immobile all day long in order to avoid contact with a sudden influx of demons chased momentarily out of hell, is preceded the previous day by large-scale cockfights (in this case legal) in almost every village on the island.

In the cockfight, man and beast, good and evil, ego and id, the creative power of aroused masculinity and the destructive power of loosened animality fuse in a bloody drama of hatred, cruelty, violence, and death. It is little wonder that when, as is the invariable rule, the owner of the winning cock takes the carcass of the loser—often torn limb from limb by its enraged owner—home to eat, he does so with a mixture of social embarrassment, moral satisfaction, aesthetic disgust, and cannibal joy. Or that a man who has lost an important fight is sometimes driven to wreck his family shrines and curse the gods, an act of metaphysical (and social) suicide. Or that in seeking earthly analogues for heaven and hell the Balinese compare the former to the mood of a man whose cock has just won, the latter to that of a man whose cock has just lost.

THE FIGHT

Cockfights (*tetadjen; sabungan*) are held in a ring about fifty feet square. Usually they begin toward late afternoon and run three or four hours until sunset. About nine or ten separate matches (*sehet*) comprise a program. Each match is precisely like the others in general pattern: there is no main match, no connection between individual matches, no variation in their format, and each is arranged on a completely ad hoc basis. After a fight has ended and the emotional debris is cleaned away—the bets have been paid, the curses cursed, the carcasses possessed—seven, eight, perhaps even a dozen men slip negligently into the ring with a cock and seek to find there a logical opponent for it. This process, which rarely takes less than ten minutes, and often a good deal longer, is conducted in a very subdued, oblique, even dissembling manner. Those not immediately involved give it at best but disguised, sidelong attention; those who, embarrassedly, are, attempt to pretend somehow that the whole thing is not really happening.

A match made, the other hopefuls retire with the same deliberate indifference, and the selected cocks have their spurs (*tadji*) affixed—razor-sharp, pointed steel swords, four or five inches long. This is a delicate job which only a small proportion of men, a half-dozen or so in most villages, know how to do properly. The man who attaches the spurs also provides them, and if the rooster he assists wins, its owner awards him the spur-leg of the victim. The spurs are affixed by winding a long length of string around the foot of the spur and the leg of the cock. For reasons I shall come to presently, it is done somewhat differently from case to case, and is an obsessively deliberate affair. The lore about spurs is extensive—they are sharpened only at eclipses and the dark of the moon, should be kept out of the sight of women, and so forth. And they are handled, both in use and out, with the same curious combination of fussiness and sensuality the Balinese direct toward ritual objects generally.

The spurs affixed, the two cocks are placed by their handlers (who may or may not be their owners) facing one another in the center of the ring.[4] A coconut pierced with a small hole is placed in a pail of water, in which it takes about twenty-one seconds to

---

4. Except for unimportant, small-bet fights (on the question of fight "importance," see below) spur affixing is usually done by someone other than the owner. Whether the owner handles his own cock or not more or less depends on how skilled he is at it, a consideration whose importance is again relative to the importance of the fight. When spur affixers and cock handlers are someone other than the owner, they are almost always a quite close relative—a brother or cousin—or a very intimate friend of his. They are thus almost extensions of his personality, as the fact that all three will refer to the cock as "mine," say "I" fought So-and-So, and so on, demonstrates. Also, owner-handler-affixer triads tend to be fairly fixed, though individuals may participate in several and often exchange roles within a given one.

sink, a period known as a *tjeng* and marked at beginning and end by the beating of a slit gong. During these twenty-one seconds the handlers (*pengangkeb*) are not permitted to touch their roosters. If, as sometimes happens, the animals have not fought during this time, they are picked up, fluffed, pulled, prodded, and otherwise insulted, and put back in the center of the ring and the process begins again. Sometimes they refuse to fight at all, or one keeps running away, in which case they are imprisoned together under a wicker cage, which usually gets them engaged.

Most of the time, in any case, the cocks fly almost immediately at one another in a wing-beating, head-thrusting, leg-kicking explosion of animal fury so pure, so absolute, and in its own way so beautiful, as to be almost abstract, a Platonic concept of hate. Within moments one or the other drives home a solid blow with his spur. The handler whose cock has delivered the blow immediately picks it up so that it will not get a return blow, for if he does not the match is likely to end in a mutually mortal tie as the two birds wildly hack each other to pieces. This is particularly true if, as often happens, the spur sticks in its victim's body, for then the aggressor is at the mercy of his wounded foe.

With the birds again in the hands of their handlers, the coconut is now sunk three times after which the cock which has landed the blow must be set down to show that he is firm, a fact he demonstrates by wandering idly around the ring for a coconut sink. The coconut is then sunk twice more and the fight must recommence.

During this interval, slightly over two minutes, the handler of the wounded cock has been working frantically over it, like a trainer patching a mauled boxer between rounds, to get it in shape for a last, desperate try for victory. He blows in its mouth, putting the whole chicken head in his own mouth and sucking and blowing, fluffs it, stuffs its wounds with various sorts of medicines, and generally tries anything he can think of to arouse the last ounce of spirit which may be hidden somewhere within it. By the time he is forced to put it back down he is usually drenched in chicken blood, but, as in prize-fighting, a good handler is worth his weight in gold. Some of them can virtually make the dead walk, at least long enough for the second and final round.

In the climactic battle (if there is one; sometimes the wounded cock simply expires in the handler's hands or immediately as it is placed down again), the cock who landed the first blow usually proceeds to finish off his weakened opponent. But this is far from an inevitable outcome, for if a cock can walk, he can fight, and if he can fight, he can kill, and what counts is which cock expires first. If the wounded one can get a stab in and stagger on until the other drops, he is the official winner, even if he himself topples over an instant later.

Surrounding all this melodrama—which the crowd packed tight around the ring follows in near silence, moving their bodies in kinesthetic sympathy with the movement of the animals, cheering their champions on with wordless hand motions, shiftings of the shoulders, turnings of the head, falling back en masse as the cock with the murderous spurs careens toward one side of the ring (it is said that spectators sometimes lose eyes and fingers from being too attentive), surging forward again as they glance off toward another—is a vast body of extraordinarily elaborate and precisely detailed rules.

These rules, together with the developed lore of cocks and cockfighting which accompanies them, are written down in palm-leaf manuscripts (*lontar; rontal*) passed on from generation to generation as part of the general legal and cultural tradition of the villages. At a fight, the umpire (*saja komong; djuru kembar*)— the man who manages the coconut—is in charge of their application and his authority is absolute. I have never seen an umpire's judgment questioned on any subject, even by the more despondent losers, nor have I ever heard, even in private, a charge of unfairness directed against one, or, for that matter, complaints about umpires in general. Only exceptionally well-trusted, solid, and, given the complexity of the code, knowledgeable citizens perform this job, and in fact men will bring their cocks only to fights presided over by such men. It is also the umpire to whom accusations of cheating, which, though rare in the extreme, occasionally arise, are referred; and it is he who in the not infrequent cases where the cocks expire virtually together decides which (if either, for, though the Balinese do not care for such an outcome, there can be ties) went first. Likened to a judge, a king, a priest, and a policeman, he is all of these, and under his assured direction the animal passion of the fight proceeds within the civic certainty of the law. In the dozens of cockfights I saw in Bali, I never once saw an altercation about rules. Indeed, I never saw an open altercation, other than those between cocks, at all.

This crosswise doubleness of an event which, taken as a fact of nature, is rage untrammeled and, taken as a fact of culture, is form perfected, defines the cockfight as a sociological entity. A cockfight is what, searching for a name for something not vertebrate enough to be called a group and not structureless enough to be called a crowd, Erving Goffman has called a "focused gathering"—a set of persons engrossed in a common flow of activity and relating to one another in terms of that flow. Such gatherings meet and disperse; the participants in them fluctuate; the activity that focuses them is discrete—a particulate process that reoccurs rather than a continuous one that endures. They take their form from the situation that evokes them, the floor on which they are placed, as Goffman puts it; but it is a form, and an articulate one, nonetheless. For the situation, the floor is itself created, in jury deliberations, surgical operations, block meetings, sit-ins, cockfights, by the cultural preoccupations—here, as we shall see, the celebration of status rivalry—which not only specify the focus but, assembling actors and arranging scenery, bring it actually into being.

In classical times (that is to say, prior to the Dutch invasion of 1908), when there were no bureaucrats around to improve popular morality, the staging of a cockfight was an explicitly societal matter. Bringing a cock to an important fight was, for an adult male, a compulsory duty of citizenship; taxation of fights, which were usually held on market day, was a major source of public revenue; patronage of the art was a stated responsibility of princes; and the cock ring, or *wantilan,* stood in the center of the village near those other monuments of Balinese civility—the council house, the origin temple, the marketplace, the signal tower, and the banyan tree. Today, a few special occasions aside, the newer rectitude makes so open a statement of the connection between the excitements of collective life and those of blood sport impossible, but, less directly expressed, the connection itself remains intimate and intact. To expose it, however, it is necessary to turn to the aspect of cockfighting around which all the others pivot, and through which they exercise their force, an aspect I have thus far studiously ignored. I mean, of course, the gambling.

ODDS AND EVEN MONEY

The Balinese never do anything in a simple way that they can contrive to do in a complicated one, and to this generalization cockfight wagering is no exception.

In the first place, there are two sorts of bets, or *toh.*[5] There is the single axial bet in the center between the principals (*toh ketengah*), and there is the cloud of peripheral ones around the ring between members of the audience (*toh kesasi*). The first is typically large; the second typically small. The first is collective, involving coalitions of bettors clustering around the owner; the second is individual, man to man. The first is a matter of deliberate, very quiet, almost furtive arrangement by the coalition members and the umpire huddled like conspirators in the center of the ring; the second is a matter of impulsive shouting, public

---

5. This word, which literally means an indelible stain or mark, as in a birthmark or a vein in a stone, is used as well for a deposit in a court case, for a pawn, for security offered in a loan, for a stand-in for someone else in a legal or ceremonial context, for an earnest advanced in a business deal, for a sign placed in a field to indicate its ownership is in dispute, and for the status of an unfaithful wife from whose lover her husband must gain satisfaction or surrender her to him.

offers, and public acceptances by the excited throng around its edges. And most curiously, and as we shall see most revealingly, *where the first is always, without exception, even money, the second, equally without exception, is never such.* What is a fair coin in the center is a biased one on the side.

The center bet is the official one, hedged in again with a web-work of rules, and is made between the two cock owners, with the umpire as overseer and public witness.[6] This bet, which, as I say, is always relatively and sometimes very large, is never raised simply by the owner in whose name it is made, but by him together with four or five, sometimes seven or eight, allies—kin, village mates, neighbors, close friends. He may, if he is not especially well-to-do, not even be the major contributor; though, if only to show that he is not involved in any chicanery, he must be a significant one.

Of the fifty-seven matches for which I have exact and reliable data on the center bet, the range is from fifteen ringgits to five hundred, with a mean at eighty-five and with the distribution being rather noticeably trimodal: small fights (15 ringgits either side of 35) accounting for about 45 percent of the total number; medium ones (20 ringgits either side of 70) for about 25 percent; and large (75 ringgits either side of 175) for about 20 percent, with a few very small and very large ones out at the extremes. In a society where the normal daily wage of a manual laborer—a brickmaker, an ordinary farmworker, a market porter—was about three ringgits a day, and considering the fact that fights were held on the average about every two-and-a-half days in the immediate area I studied, this is clearly serious gambling, even if the bets are pooled rather than individual efforts.

The side bets are, however, something else altogether. Rather than the solemn, legalistic pactmaking of the center, wagering

---

6. The center bet must be advanced in cash by both parties prior to the actual fight. The umpire holds the stakes until the decision is rendered and then awards them to the winner, avoiding, among other things, the intense embarrassment both winner and loser would feel if the latter had to pay off personally following his defeat. About 10 percent of the winner's receipts are subtracted for the umpire's share and that of the fight sponsors.

takes place rather in the fashion in which the stock exchange used to work when it was out on the curb. There is a fixed and known odds paradigm which runs in a continuous series from ten-to-nine at the short end to two-to-one at the long: 10–9, 9–8, 8–7, 7–6, 6–5, 5–4, 4–3, 3–2, 2–1. The man who wishes to back the *underdog cock* (leaving aside how favorites, *kebut,* and underdogs, *ngai,* are established for the moment) shouts the short-side number indicating the odds he wants *to be given.* That is, if he shouts *gasal,* "five," he wants the underdog at five-to-four (or, for him, four-to-five); if he shouts "four," he wants it at four-to-three (again, he putting up the "three"); if "nine," at nine-to-eight, and so on. A man backing the favorite, and thus considering giving odds if he can get them short enough, indicates the fact by crying out the color-type of that cock—"brown," "speckled," or whatever.[7]

As odds-takers (backers of the underdog) and odds-givers (backers of the favorite) sweep the crowd with their shouts, they begin to focus in on one another as potential betting pairs, often from far across the ring. The taker tries to shout the giver into

---

7. Actually, the typing of cocks, which is extremely elaborate (I have collected more than twenty classes, certainly not a complete list), is not based on color alone, but on a series of independent, interacting dimensions, which include—besides color—size, bone thickness, plumage, and temperament. (But *not* pedigree. The Balinese do not breed cocks to any significant extent, nor, so far as I have been able to discover, have they ever done so. The *asil,* or jungle cock, which is the basic fighting strain everywhere the sport is found, is native to southern Asia, and one can buy a good example in the chicken section of almost any Balinese market for anywhere from four or five ringgits up to fifty or more.) The color element is merely the one normally used as the type name, except when the two cocks of different types—as on principle they must be—have the same color, in which case a secondary indication from one of the other dimensions ("large speckled" v. "small speckled," etc.) is added. The types are coordinated with various cosmological ideas which help shape the making of matches, so that, for example, you fight a small, headstrong, speckled brown-on-white cock with flat-lying feathers and thin legs from the east side of the ring on a certain day of the complex Balinese calendar, and a large, cautious, all-black cock with tufted feathers and stubby legs from the north side on another day, and so on. All this is again recorded in palm-leaf manuscripts and endlessly discussed by the Balinese (who do not all have identical systems), and a full-scale componential-cum-symbolic analysis of cock classifications would be extremely valuable both as an adjunct to the description of the cockfight and in itself. But my data on the subject, though extensive and varied, do not seem to be complete and systematic enough to attempt such an analysis here.

longer odds, the giver to shout the taker into shorter ones.[8] The taker, who is the wooer in this situation, will signal how large a bet he wishes to make at the odds he is shouting by holding a number of fingers up in front of his face and vigorously waving them. If the giver, the wooed, replies in kind, the bet is made; if he does not, they unlock gazes and the search goes on.

The side betting, which takes place after the center bet has been made and its size announced, consists then in a rising crescendo of shouts as backers of the underdog offer their propositions to anyone who will accept them, while those who are backing the favorite but do not like the price being offered shout equally frenetically the color of the cock to show they too are desperate to bet but want shorter odds.

Almost always, odds-calling, which tends to be very consensual in that at any one time almost all callers are calling the same thing, starts off toward the long end of the range—five-to-four or four-to-three—and then moves, also consensually, toward the short end with greater or lesser speed and to a greater or lesser degree. Men crying "five" and finding themselves answered only with cries of "brown" start crying "six," either drawing the other callers fairly quickly with them or retiring from the scene as their too-generous offers are snapped up. If the change is made and partners are still scarce, the procedure is repeated in a move to "seven," and so on, only rarely, and in the very largest fights, reaching the ultimate "nine" or "ten" levels. Occasionally, if the cocks are clearly mismatched, there may be no upward movement at all, or even a movement down the scale to four-to-three, three-to-two, very, very rarely two-to-one, a shift which is accompanied by a declining number of bets as a shift upward is accompanied by an increasing number. But

---

8. For purposes of ethnographic completeness, it should be noted that it is possible for the man backing the favorite—the odds-giver—to make a bet in which he wins if his cock wins or there is a tie, a slight shortening of the odds (I do not have enough cases to be exact, but ties seem to occur about once every fifteen or twenty matches). He indicates his wish to do this by shouting *sapih* ("tie") rather than the cock-type, but such bets are in fact infrequent.

the general pattern is for the betting to move a shorter or longer distance up the scale toward the, for sidebets, nonexistent pole of even money, with the overwhelming majority of bets falling in the four-to-three to eight-to-seven range.[9]

As the moment for the release of the cocks by the handlers approaches, the screaming, at least in a match where the center bet is large, reaches almost frenzied proportions as the remaining unfulfilled bettors try desperately to find a last-minute partner at a price they can live with. (Where the center bet is small, the opposite tends to occur: betting dies off, trailing into silence, as odds lengthen and people lose interest.) In a large-bet, well-made match—the kind of match the Balinese regard as "real cockfighting"—the mob scene quality, the sense that sheer chaos is about to break loose, with all those waving, shouting, pushing, clambering men, is quite strong, an effect which is only heightened by the intense stillness that falls with instant suddenness, rather as if someone had turned off the current, when the slit gong sounds, the cocks are put down, and the battle begins.

When it ends, anywhere from fifteen seconds to five minutes later, *all bets are immediately paid.* There are absolutely no IOUs, at least to a betting opponent. One may, of course, borrow from a friend before offering or accepting a wager, but to offer or accept it you must have the money already in hand and, if you lose, you must pay it on the spot, before the next match begins. This is an

---

9. The precise dynamics of the movement of the betting is one of the most intriguing, most complicated, and, given the hectic conditions under which it occurs, most difficult to study, aspects of the fight. Motion-picture recording plus multiple observers would probably be necessary to deal with it effectively. Even impressionistically—the only approach open to a lone ethnographer caught in the middle of all this—it is clear that certain men lead both in determining the favorite (that is, making the opening cock-type calls which always initiate the process) and in directing the movement of the odds, these "opinion leaders" being the more accomplished cockfighters-cum-solid-citizens to be discussed below. If these men begin to change their calls, others follow; if they begin to make bets, so do others and—though there are always a large number of frustrated bettors crying for shorter or longer odds to the end—the movement more or less ceases. But a detailed understanding of the whole process awaits what, alas, it is not very likely ever to get: a decision theorist armed with precise observations of individual behavior.

iron rule, and as I have never heard of a disputed umpire's decision (though doubtless there must sometimes be some), I have also
never heard of a welshed bet, perhaps because in a worked-up
cockfight crowd the consequences might be, as they are reported
to be sometimes for cheaters, drastic and immediate.

It is, in any case, this formal asymmetry between balanced
center bets and unbalanced side ones that poses the critical ana-
lytical problem for a theory which sees cockfight wagering
as the link connecting the fight to the wider world of Balinese
culture. It also suggests the way to go about solving it and
demonstrating the link.

The first point that needs to be made in this connection is
that the higher the center bet, the more likely the match will in
actual fact be an even one. Simple considerations of rationality
suggest that. If you are betting fifteen ringgits on a cock, you
might be willing to go along with even money even if you feel
your animal somewhat the less promising. But if you are betting
five hundred you are very, very likely to be loathe to do so.
Thus, in large-bet fights, which of course involve the better animals, tremendous care is taken to see that the cocks are about
as evenly matched as to size, general condition, pugnacity, and
so on as is humanly possible. The different ways of adjusting the
spurs of the animals are often employed to secure this. If one
cock seems stronger, an agreement will be made to position his
spur at a slightly less advantageous angle—a kind of handicap-
ping, at which spur affixers are, so it is said, extremely skilled.
More care will be taken, too, to employ skillful handlers and to
match them exactly as to abilities.

In short, in a large-bet fight the pressure to make the match a
genuinely fifty-fifty proposition is enormous, and is consciously
felt as such. For medium fights the pressure is somewhat less,
and for small ones less yet, though there is always an effort to
make things at least approximately equal, for even at fifteen
ringgits (five days' work) no one wants to make an even money
bet in a clearly unfavorable situation. And, again, what statistics
I have tend to bear this out. In my fifty-seven matches, the

favorite won thirty-three times overall, the underdog twenty-four, a 1.4: 1 ratio. But if one splits the figures at sixty-ringgit center bets, the ratios turn out to be 1.1: 1 (twelve favorites, eleven underdogs) for those above this line, and 1.6: 1 (twenty-one and thirteen) for those below it. Or, if you take the extremes, for very large fights, those with center bets over a hundred ringgits, the ratio is 1: 1 (seven and seven); for very small fights, those under forty ringgits, it is 1.9: 1 (nineteen and ten).[10]

Now, from this proposition—that the higher the center bet the more exactly a fifty-fifty proposition the cockfight is—two things more or less immediately follow: (1) the higher the center bet is, the greater the pull on the side betting toward the short-odds end of the wagering spectrum, and vice versa; (2) the higher the center bet is, the greater the volume of side betting, and vice versa.

The logic is similar in both cases. The closer the fight is in fact to even money, the less attractive the long end of the odds will appear and, therefore, the shorter it must be if there are to be takers. That this is the case is apparent from mere inspection, from the Balinese's own analysis of the matter, and from what more systematic observations I was able to collect. Given the difficulty of making precise and complete recordings of side betting, this argument is hard to cast in numerical form, but in all my cases the odds-giver, odds-taker consensual point, a quite pronounced mini-max saddle where the bulk (at a guess, two-thirds to three-quarters in most cases) of the bets are actually made, was three or four points further along the scale toward

---

10. Assuming only binomial variability, the departure from a fifty-fifty expectation in the sixty-ringgits-and-below case is 1.38 standard deviations, or (in a one-direction test) an eight-in-one-hundred possibility by chance alone; for the below-forty-ringgits case it is 1.65 standard deviations, or about five in one hundred. The fact that these departures though real are not extreme merely indicates, again, that even in the smaller fights the tendency to match cocks at least reasonably evenly persists. It is a matter of relative relaxation of the pressures toward equalization, not their elimination. The tendency for high-bet contests to be coin-flip propositions is, of course, even more striking, and suggests the Balinese know quite well what they are about.

the shorter end for the large-center-bet fights than for the small ones, with medium ones generally in between. In detail, the fit is not, of course, exact, but the general pattern is quite consistent: the power of the center bet to pull the side bets toward its own even-money pattern is directly proportional to its size, because its size is directly proportional to the degree to which the cocks are in fact evenly matched. As for the volume question, total wagering is greater in large-center-bet fights because such fights are considered more "interesting," not only in the sense that they are less predictable, but, more crucially, that more is at stake in them—in terms of money, in terms of the quality of the cocks, and consequently, as we shall see, in terms of social prestige.[11]

The paradox of fair coin in the middle, biased coin on the outside is thus a merely apparent one. The two betting systems, though formally incongruent, are not really contradictory to one another, but are part of a single larger system in which the center bet is, so to speak, the "center of gravity," drawing, the larger it is the more so, the outside bets toward the short-odds end of the scale. The center bet thus "makes the game," or perhaps better, defines it, signals what, following a notion of Jeremy Bentham's, I am going to call its "depth."

The Balinese attempt to create an interesting, if you will, "deep," match by making the center bet as large as possible so

---

11. The reduction in wagering in smaller fights (which, of course, feeds on itself; one of the reasons people find small fights uninteresting is that there is less wagering in them, and contrariwise for large ones) takes place in three mutually reinforcing ways. First, there is a simple withdrawal of interest as people wander off to have a cup of coffee or chat with a friend. Second, the Balinese do not mathematically reduce odds, but bet directly in terms of stated odds as such. Thus, for a nine-to-eight bet, one man wagers nine ringgits, the other eight; for five-to-four, one wagers five, the other four. For any given currency unit, like the ringgit, therefore, 6.3 times as much money is involved in a ten-to-nine bet as in a two-to-one bet, for example, and, as noted, in small fights betting settles toward the longer end. Finally, the bets which are made tend to be one- rather than two-, three-, or in some of the very largest fights, four- or five-finger ones. (The fingers indicate the *multiples* of the stated bet odds at issue, not absolute figures. Two fingers in a six-to-five situation means a man wants to wager ten ringgits on the underdog against twelve, three in an eight-to-seven situation, twenty-one against twenty-four, and so on.)

that the cocks matched will be as equal and as fine as possible, and the outcome, thus, as unpredictable as possible. They do not always succeed. Nearly half the matches are relatively trivial, relatively uninteresting—in my borrowed terminology, "shallow"—affairs. But that fact no more argues against my interpretation than the fact that most painters, poets, and playwrights are mediocre argues against the view that artistic effort is directed toward profundity and, with a certain frequency, approximates it. The image of artistic technique is indeed exact: the center bet is a means, a device, for creating "interesting," "deep" matches, *not* the reason, or at least not the main reason, *why* they are interesting, the source of their fascination, the substance of their depth. The question of why such matches are interesting—indeed, for the Balinese, exquisitely absorbing— takes us out of the realm of formal concerns into more broadly sociological and social-psychological ones, and to a less purely economic idea of what "depth" in gaming amounts to.[12]

---

12. Besides wagering there are other economic aspects of the cockfight, especially its very close connection with the local market system, which, though secondary both to its motivation and to its function, are not without importance. Cockfights are open events to which anyone who wishes may come, sometimes from quite distant areas, but well over 90 percent, probably over 95, are very local affairs, and the locality concerned is defined not by the village, nor even by the administrative district, but by the rural market system. Bali has a three-day market week with the familiar "solar system"–type rotation. Though the markets themselves have never been very highly developed, small morning affairs in a village square, it is the microregion such rotation rather generally marks out—ten or twenty square miles, seven or eight neighboring villages (which in contemporary Bali is usually going to mean anywhere from five to ten or eleven thousand people) from which the core of any cockfight audience, indeed virtually all of it, will come. Most of the fights are in fact organized and sponsored by small combines of petty rural merchants under the general premise, very strongly held by them and indeed by all Balinese, that cockfights are good for trade because "they get money out of the house, they make it circulate." Stalls selling various sorts of things as well as assorted sheer-chance gambling games (see below) are set up around the edge of the area so that this even takes on the quality of a small fair. This connection of cockfighting with markets and market sellers is very old, as, among other things, their conjunction in inscriptions indicates. Trade has followed the cock for centuries in rural Bali, and the sport has been one of the main agencies of the island's monetization.

PLAYING WITH FIRE

Bentham's concept of "deep play" is found in his *The Theory of Legislation.* By it he means play in which the stakes are so high that it is, from his utilitarian standpoint, irrational for men to engage in it at all. If a man whose fortune is a thousand pounds (or ringgits) wages five hundred of it on an even bet, the marginal utility of the pound he stands to win is clearly less than the marginal disutility of the one he stands to lose. In genuine deep play, this is the case for both parties. They are both in over their heads. Having come together in search of pleasure they have entered into a relationship which will bring the participants, considered collectively, net pain rather than net pleasure. Bentham's conclusion was, therefore, that deep play was immoral from first principles and, a typical step for him, should be prevented legally.

But more interesting than the ethical problem, at least for our concerns here, is that despite the logical force of Bentham's analysis men do engage in such play, both passionately and often, and even in the face of law's revenge. For Bentham and those who think as he does (nowadays mainly lawyers, economists, and a few psychiatrists), the explanation is, as I have said, that such men are irrational—addicts, fetishists, children, fools, savages, who need only to be protected against themselves. But for the Balinese, though naturally they do not formulate it in so many words, the explanation lies in the fact that in such play, money is less a measure of utility, had or expected, than it is a symbol of moral import, perceived or imposed.

It is, in fact, in shallow games, ones in which smaller amounts of money are involved, that increments and decrements of cash are more nearly synonyms for utility and disutility, in the ordinary, unexpanded sense—for pleasure and pain, happiness and unhappiness. In deep ones, where the amounts of money are great, much more is at stake than material gain: namely, esteem, honor, dignity, respect—in a word, though in Bali a profoundly freighted word, status.[13] It is at stake symbolically, for (a few cases of ruined addict gamblers aside) no one's status is actually altered by the outcome of a cockfight; it is only, and that momentarily, affirmed or insulted. But for the Balinese, for whom nothing is more pleasurable than an affront obliquely delivered or more painful than one obliquely received—particularly when mutual acquaintances, undeceived by surfaces, are watching—such appraisive drama is deep indeed.

This, I must stress immediately, is *not* to say that the money does not matter, or that the Balinese is no more concerned about losing five hundred ringgits than fifteen. Such a conclusion would be absurd. It is because money *does,* in this hardly unmaterialistic society, matter and matter very much that the more of it one risks, the more of a lot of other things, such as one's pride, one's poise, one's dispassion, one's masculinity, one also risks, again only momentarily but again very publicly as well. In deep cockfights, an owner and his collaborators, and, as we shall see, to a lesser but still quite real extent, also their backers on the outside, put their money where their status is.

It is in large part *because* the marginal disutility of loss is so great at the higher levels of betting that to engage in such betting is to lay one's public self, allusively and metaphorically, through the medium of one's cock, on the line. And though to a Benthamite this might seem merely to increase the irrationality of the enterprise that much further, to the Balinese what it mainly increases is the meaningfulness of it all. And as (to follow Weber rather than Bentham) the imposition of meaning on life is the major end and primary condition of human existence, that access of significance more than compensates for the economic

---

13. Of course, even in Bentham, utility is not normally confined as a concept to monetary losses and gains, and my argument here might be more carefully put in terms of a denial that for the Balinese, as for any people, utility (pleasure, happiness . . .) is merely identifiable with wealth. But such terminological problems are in any case secondary to the essential point: the cockfight is not roulette.

costs involved.[14] Actually, given the even-money quality of the larger matches, important changes in material fortune among those who regularly participate in them seem virtually nonexistent, because matters more or less even out over the long run. It is, actually, in the smaller, shallow fights, where one finds the handful of more pure, addict-type gamblers involved—those who *are* in it mainly for the money—that "real" changes in social position, largely downward, are affected. Men of this sort, plungers, are highly dispraised by "true cockfighters" as fools who do not understand what the sport is all about, vulgarians who simply miss the point of it all. They are, these addicts, regarded as fair game for the genuine enthusiasts, those who do understand, to take a little money away from—something that is easy enough to do by luring them, through the force of their greed, into irrational bets on mismatched cocks. Most of them do indeed manage to ruin themselves in a remarkably short time, but there always seems to be one or two of them around, pawning their land and selling their clothes in order to bet, at any particular time.[15]

---

14. There is nothing specifically Balinese, of course, about deepening significance with money, as Whyte's description of corner boys in a working-class district of Boston demonstrates: "Gambling plays an important role in the lives of Cornerville people. Whatever game the corner boys play, they nearly always bet on the outcome. When there is nothing at stake, the game is not considered a real contest. This does not mean that the financial element is all-important. I have frequently heard men say that the honor of winning was much more important than the money at stake. The corner boys consider playing for money the real test of skill and, unless a man performs well when money is at stake, he is not considered a good competitor." W. F. Whyte, *Street Corner Society,* 2d ed. (Chicago, 1955), 140.

15. The extremes to which this madness is conceived on occasion to go—and the fact that it is considered madness—is demonstrated by the Balinese folk tale *I Tuhung Kuning.* A gambler becomes so deranged by his passion that, leaving on a trip, he orders his pregnant wife to take care of the prospective newborn if it is a boy but to feed it as meat to his fighting cocks if it is a girl. The mother gives birth to a girl, but rather than giving the child to the cocks she gives them a large rat and conceals the girl with her own mother. When the husband returns, the cocks, crowing a jingle, inform him of the deception and, furious, he sets out to kill the child. A goddess descends from heaven and takes the girl up to the skies with her. The cocks die from the food given them, the owner's sanity is restored, the goddess brings the girl back to the father, who reunites him with his wife.

This graduated correlation of "status gambling" with deeper fights and, inversely, "money gambling" with shallower ones is in fact quite general. Bettors themselves form a sociomoral hierarchy in these terms. As noted earlier, at most cockfights there are, around the very edges of the cockfight area, a large number of mindless, sheer-chance-type gambling games (roulette, dice throw, coin-spin, pea-under-the-shell) operated by concessionaires. Only women, children, adolescents, and various other sorts of people who do not (or not yet) fight cocks—the extremely poor, the socially despised, the personally idiosyncratic—play at these games, at, of course, penny-ante levels. Cockfighting men would be ashamed to go anywhere near them. Slightly above these people in standing are those who, though they do not themselves fight cocks, bet on the smaller matches around the edges. Next, there are those who fight cocks in small or, occasionally, medium matches, but have not the status to join in the large ones, though they may bet from time to time on the side in those. And finally, there are those, the really substantial members of the community, the solid citizenry around whom local life revolves, who fight in the larger fights and bet on them around the side. The focusing element in these focused gatherings, these men generally dominate and define the sport as they dominate and define the society. When a Balinese male talks, in that almost venerative way, about "the true cockfighter," the *bebatoh* ("bettor") or *djuru kurung* ("cage keeper"), it is this sort of person, not those who bring the mentality of the pea-and-shell game into the quite different, inappropriate context of the cockfight, the driven gambler (*potét,* a word which has the secondary meaning of thief or reprobate), and the wistful hanger-on, that they mean. For such a man, what is really going on in a match is something rather closer to an *affaire d'honneur* (though, with the Balinese talent for practical fantasy, the blood that is spilled is only figuratively human) than to the stupid, mechanical crank of a slot machine.

What makes Balinese cockfighting deep is thus not money in itself, but what, the more of it that is involved the more so, money causes to happen: the migration of the Balinese status hierarchy into the body of the cockfight. Psychologically an Aesopian representation of the ideal/demonic, rather narcissistic, male self, sociologically it is an equally Aesopian representation of the complex fields of tension set up by the controlled, muted, ceremonial, but, for all that, deeply felt interaction of those selves in the context of everyday life. The cocks may be surrogates for their owners' personalities, animal mirrors of psychic form, but the cockfight is—or more exactly, deliberately is made to be—a simulation of the social matrix, the involved system of cross-cutting, overlapping, highly corporate groups— villages, kin groups, irrigation societies, temple congregations, "castes"—in which its devotees live. And as prestige, the necessity to affirm it, defend it, celebrate it, justify it, and just plain bask in it (but not, given the strongly ascriptive character of Balinese stratification, to seek it), is perhaps the central driving force in the society, so also—ambulant penises, blood sacrifices, and monetary exchanges aside—is it of the cockfight. This apparent amusement and seeming sport is, to take another phrase from Erving Goffman, "a status bloodbath."

The easiest way to make this clear, and at least to some degree to demonstrate it, is to invoke the village whose cock-fighting activities I observed the closest—the one in which the raid occurred and from which my statistical data are taken.

Like all Balinese villages, this one—Tihingan, in the Klungkung region of southeast Bali—is intricately organized, a labyrinth of alliances and oppositions. But, unlike many, two sorts of corporate groups, which are also status groups, particularly stand out, and we may concentrate on them, in a part-for-whole way, without undue distortion.

First, the village is dominated by four large, patrilineal, partly endogamous descent groups which are constantly vying with one another and form the major factions in the village. Sometimes they group two and two, or rather the two larger ones versus the two smaller ones plus all the unaffiliated people; sometimes they operate independently. There are also subfactions within them, subfactions within the subfactions, and so on to rather fine levels of distinction. And second, there is the village itself, almost entirely endogamous, which is opposed to all the other villages round about in its cockfight circuit (which, as explained, is the market region), but which also forms alliances with certain of these neighbors against certain others in various supravillage political and social contexts. The exact situation is thus, as everywhere in Bali, quite distinctive; but the general pattern of a tiered hierarchy of status rivalries between highly corporate but various based groupings (and, thus, between the members of them) is entirely general.

Consider, then, as support of the general thesis that the cockfight, and especially the deep cockfight, is fundamentally a dramatization of status concerns, the following facts, which to avoid extended ethnographic description I shall simply pronounce to be facts—though the concrete evidence, examples, statements, and numbers that could be brought to bear in support of them, is both extensive and unmistakable:

1. A man virtually never bets against a cock owned by a member of his own kin group. Usually he will feel obliged to bet for it, the more so the closer the kin tie and the deeper the fight. If he is certain in his mind that it will not win, he may just not bet at all, particularly if it is only a second cousin's bird or if the fight is a shallow one. But as a rule he will feel he must support it and, in deep games, nearly always does. Thus the great majority of the people calling "five" or "speckled" so demonstratively are expressing their allegiance to their kinsman, not their evaluation of his bird, their understanding of probability theory, or even their hopes of unearned income.

2. This principle is extended logically. If your kin group is not involved you will support an allied kin group against an unallied one in the same way, and so on through the very involved networks of alliances which, as I say, make up this, as any other, Balinese village.

3. So, too, for the village as a whole. If an outsider cock is fighting any cock from your village, you will tend to support the local one. If, what is a rarer circumstance but occurs every now and then, a cock from outside your cockfight circuit is fighting one inside it, you will also tend to support the "home bird."

4. Cocks which come from any distance are almost always favorites, for the theory is the man would not have dared to bring it if it was not a good cock, the more so the further he has come. His followers are, of course, obliged to support him, and when the more grand-scale legal cockfights are held (on holidays, and so on) the people of the village take what they regard to be the best cocks in the village, regardless of ownership, and go off to support them, although they will almost certainly have to give odds on them and to make large bets to show that they are not a cheapskate village. Actually, such "away games," though infrequent, tend to mend the ruptures between village members that the constantly occurring "home games," where village factions are opposed rather than united, exacerbate.

5. Almost all matches are sociologically relevant. You seldom get two outsider cocks fighting, or two cocks with no particular group backing, or with group backing which is mutually unrelated in any clear way. When you do get them, the game is very shallow, betting very slow, and the whole thing very dull, with no one save the immediate principals and an addict gambler or two at all interested.

6. By the same token, you rarely get two cocks from the same group, even more rarely from the same subfaction, and virtually never from the same sub-subfaction (which would be in most cases one extended family) fighting. Similarly, in outside village fights two members of the village will rarely fight against one another, even though, as bitter rivals, they would do so with enthusiasm on their home grounds.

7. On the individual level, people involved in an institutional-ized hostility relationship, called *puik,* in which they do not speak or otherwise have anything to do with each other (the causes of this formal breaking of relations are many: wife-capture, inheritance arguments, political differences) will bet very heavily, sometimes almost maniacally, against one another in what is a frank and direct attack on the very mas-culinity, the ultimate ground of his status, of the opponent.

8. The center bet coalition is, in all but the shallowest games, *always* made up by structural allies—no "outside money" is involved. What is "outside" depends upon the context, of course, but given it, no outside money is mixed in with the main bet; if the principals cannot raise it, it is not made. The center bet, again especially in deeper games, is thus the most direct and open expression of social opposition, which is one of the reasons why both it and matchmaking are surrounded by such an air of unease, furtiveness, embarrassment, and so on.

9. The rule about borrowing money—that you may borrow *for* a bet but not *in* one—stems (and the Balinese are quite conscious of this) from similar considerations: you are never at the *economic* mercy of your enemy that way. Gambling debts, which can get quite large on a rather short-term basis, are always to friends, never to enemies, structurally speaking.

10. When two cocks are structurally irrelevant or neutral so far as *you* are concerned (though, as mentioned, they almost never are to each other) you do not even ask a relative or a friend whom he is betting on, because if you know how he is betting and he knows you know, and you go the other way, it will lead to strain. This rule is explicit and rigid; fairly elaborate, even rather artificial precautions are taken to avoid breaking it. At the very least you must pretend not to notice what he is doing, and he what you are doing.

11. There is a special word for betting against the grain, which is also the word for "pardon me" (*mpura*). It is considered a bad thing to do, though if the center bet is small it is some-

times all right as long as you do not do it too often. But the larger the bet and the more frequently you do it, the more the "pardon me" tack will lead to social disruption.

12. In fact, the institutionalized hostility relation, *puik,* is often formally initiated (though its causes always lie elsewhere) by such a "pardon me" bet in a deep fight, putting the symbolic fat in the fire. Similarly, the end of such a relationship and resumption of normal social intercourse is often signalized (but, again, not actually brought about) by one or the other of the enemies supporting the other's bird.

13. In sticky, cross-loyalty situations, of which in this extraordinarily complex social system there are of course many, where a man is caught between two more or less equally balanced loyalties, he tends to wander off for a cup of coffee or something to avoid having to bet, a form of behavior reminiscent of that of American voters in similar situations.

14. The people involved in the center bet are, especially in deep fights, virtually always leading members of their group— kinship, village, or whatever. Further, those who bet on the side (including these people) are, as I have already remarked, the more established members of the village—the solid citizens. Cockfighting is for those who are involved in the everyday politics of prestige as well, not for youth, women, subordinates, and so forth.

15. So far as money is concerned, the explicitly expressed attitude toward it is that it is a secondary matter. It is not, as I have said, of no importance; Balinese are no happier to lose several weeks' income than anyone else. But they mainly look on the monetary aspects of the cockfight as self-balancing, a matter of just moving money around, circulating it among a fairly well-defined group of serious cockfighters. The really important wins and losses are seen mostly in other terms, and the general attitude toward wagering is not any hope of cleaning up, of making a killing (addict gamblers again excepted), but that of the horseplayer's prayer: "Oh, God,

please let me break even." In prestige terms, however, you do not want to break even, but, in a momentary, punctuate sort of way, win utterly. The talk (which goes on all the time) is about fights against such-and-such a cock of So-and-So which your cock demolished, not on how much you won, a fact people, even for large bets, rarely remember for any length of time, though they will remember the day they did in Pan Loh's finest cock for years.

16. You must bet on cocks of your own group aside from mere loyalty considerations, for if you do not people generally will say, "What! Is he too proud for the likes of us? Does he have to go to Java or Den Pasar [the capital town] to bet, he is such an important man?" Thus there is a general pressure to bet not only to show that you are important locally, but that you are not so important that you look down on every-one else as unfit even to be rivals. Similarly, home team people must bet against outside cocks or the outsiders will accuse them—a serious charge—of just collecting entry fees and not really being interested in cockfighting, as well as again being arrogant and insulting.

17. Finally, the Balinese peasants themselves are quite aware of all this and can and, at least to an ethnographer, do state most of it in approximately the same terms as I have. Fighting cocks, almost every Balinese I have ever discussed the subject with has said, is like playing with fire only not getting burned. You activate village and kin group rivalries and hostilities, but in "play" form, coming dangerously and entrancingly close to the expression of open and direct inter-personal and intergroup aggression (something which, again, almost never happens in the normal course of ordinary life), but not quite, because, after all, it is "only a cockfight."

More observations of this sort could be advanced, but perhaps the general point is, if not made, at least well-delineated, and the whole argument thus far can be usefully summarized in a formal paradigm:

THE MORE A MATCH IS . . .

1. Between near status equals (and / or personal enemies)
2. Between high-status individuals

THE DEEPER THE MATCH.

THE DEEPER THE MATCH . . .

1. The closer the identification of cock and man (or, more properly, the deeper the match the more the man will advance his best, most closely-identified-with cock).
2. The finer the cocks involved and the more exactly they will be matched.
3. The greater the emotion that will be involved and the more the general absorption in the match.
4. The higher the individual bets center and outside, the shorter the outside bet odds will tend to be, and the more betting there will be overall.
5. The less an "economic" and the more a "status" view of gaming will be involved, and the "solider" the citizens who will be gaming.[16]

Inverse arguments hold for the shallower the fight, culminating, in a reversed-signs sense, in the coin-spinning and dice-throwing amusements. For deep fights there are no absolute upper limits, though there are of course practical ones, and there are a great many legendlike tales of great Duel-in-the-Sun combats between lords and princes in classical times (for cockfighting has always been as much an elite concern as a popular one), far deeper than anything anyone, even aristocrats, could produce today anywhere in Bali.

Indeed, one of the great culture heroes of Bali is a prince, called after his passion for the sport, "The Cockfighter," who

---

16. As this is a formal paradigm, it is intended to display the logical, not the causal, structure of cockfighting. Just which of these considerations leads to which, in what order, and by what mechanisms, is another matter—one I have attempted to shed some light on in the general discussion.

happened to be away at a very deep cockfight with a neighboring prince when the whole of his family—father, brothers, wives, sisters—were assassinated by commoner usurpers. Thus spared, he returned to dispatch the upstart, regain the throne, reconstitute the Balinese high tradition, and build its most powerful, glorious, and prosperous state. Along with everything else that the Balinese see in fighting cocks—themselves, their social order, abstract hatred, masculinity, demonic power—they also see the archetype of status virtue, the arrogant, resolute, honormad player with real fire, the Kshatriya prince.[17]

---

17. In another of Hooykaas-van Leeuwen Boomkamp's folk tales ("De Gast," *Sprookjes en Verhalen van Bali*, 172–180), a low caste *Sudra*, a generous, pious, and carefree man who is also an accomplished cockfighter, loses, despite his accomplishment, fight after fight until he is not only out of money but down to his last cock. He does not despair, however—"I bet," he says, "upon the Unseen World."

His wife, a good and hard-working woman, knowing how much he enjoys cockfighting, gives him her last "rainy day" money to go and bet. But, filled with misgivings due to his run of ill luck, he leaves his own cock at home and bets merely on the side. He soon loses all but a coin or two and repairs to a food stand for a snack, where he meets a decrepit, odorous, and generally unappetizing old beggar leaning on a staff. The old man asks for food, and the hero spends his last coins to buy him some. The old man then asks to pass the night with the hero, which the hero gladly invites him to do. As there is no food in the house, however, the hero tells his wife to kill the last cock for dinner. When the old man discovers this fact, he tells the hero he has three cocks in his own mountain hut and says the hero may have one of them for fighting. He also asks for the hero's son to accompany him as a servant, and, after the son agrees, this is done.

The old man turns out to be Siva and, thus, to live in a great palace in the sky, though the hero does not know this. In time, the hero decides to visit his son and collect the promised cock. Lifted up into Siva's presence, he is given the choice of three cocks. The first crows: "I have beaten fifteen opponents." The second crows, "I have beaten twenty-five opponents." The third crows, "I have beaten the king." "That one, the third, is my choice," says the hero, and returns with it to earth.

When he arrives at the cockfight, he is asked for an entry fee and replies, "I have no money; I will pay after my cock has won." As he is known never to win, he is let in because the king, who is there fighting, dislikes him and hopes to enslave him when he loses and cannot pay off. In order to insure that this happens, the king matches his finest cock against the hero's. When the cocks are placed down, the hero's flees, and the crowd, led by the arrogant king, hoots in laughter. The hero's cock then flies at the king himself, killing him with a spur stab in the throat. The hero flees. His house is encircled by the king's men. The cock changes into a Garuda, the great mythic bird of Indic legend, and carries the hero and his wife to safety in the heavens.

When the people see this, they make the hero king and his wife queen and they return as such to earth. Later their son, released by Siva, also returns and the hero-king announces his intention to enter a hermitage. ("I will fight no more cockfights. I have bet on the Unseen and won.") He enters the hermitage and his son becomes king.

FEATHERS, BLOOD, CROWDS, AND MONEY

"Poetry makes nothing happen," Auden says in his elegy of Yeats, "it survives in the valley of its saying . . . a way of happening, a mouth." The cockfight too, in this colloquial sense, makes nothing happen. Men go on allegorically humiliating one another and being allegorically humiliated by one another, day after day, glorying quietly in the experience if they have triumphed, crushed only slightly more openly by it if they have not. *But no one's status really changes.* You cannot ascend the status ladder by winning cockfights; you cannot, as an individual, really ascend it at all. Nor can you descend it that way.[18] All you can do is enjoy and savor, or suffer and withstand, the concocted sensation of drastic and momentary movement along an aesthetic semblance of that ladder, a kind of behind-the-mirror status jump which has the look of mobility without its actuality.

Like any art form—for that, finally, is what we are dealing with—the cockfight renders ordinary, everyday experience comprehensible by presenting it in terms of acts and objects which have had their practical consequences removed and been reduced (or, if you prefer, raised) to the level of sheer appearances, where their meaning can be more powerfully articulated and more exactly perceived. The cockfight is "really real" only to the cocks—it does not kill anyone, castrate anyone, reduce anyone to animal status, alter the hierarchical relations among people, or refashion the hierarchy; it does not even redistribute income in any significant way. What it does is what, for other peoples with other temperaments and other conventions, *Lear* and *Crime and Punishment* do; it catches up these themes— death, masculinity, rage, pride, loss, beneficence, chance—and, ordering them into an encompassing structure, presents them in

---

18. Addict gamblers are really less declassed (for their status is, as everyone else's, inherited) than merely impoverished and personally disgraced. The most prominent addict gambler in my cockfight circuit was actually a very high caste *satria* who sold off most of his considerable lands to support his habit. Though everyone privately regarded him as a fool and worse (some, more charitable, regarded him as sick), he was publicly treated with the elaborate deference and politeness due his rank.

such a way as to throw into relief a particular view of their essential nature. It puts a construction on them, makes them, to those historically positioned to appreciate the construction, meaningful—visible, tangible, graspable—"real," in an ideational sense. An image, fiction, a model, a metaphor, the cockfight is a means of expression; its function is neither to assuage social passions nor to heighten them (though, in its playing-with-fire way it does a bit of both), but, in a medium of feathers, blood, crowds, and money, to display them.

The question of how it is that we perceive qualities in things—paintings, books, melodies, plays—that we do not feel we can assert literally to be there has come, in recent years, into the very center of aesthetic theory. Neither the sentiments of the artist, which remain his, nor those of the audience, which remain theirs, can account for the agitation of one painting or the serenity of another. We attribute grandeur, wit, despair, exuberance to strings of sounds; lightness, energy, violence, fluidity to blocks of stone. Novels are said to have strength, buildings eloquence, plays momentum, ballets repose. In this realm of eccentric predicates, to say that the cockfight, in its perfected cases at least, is "disquietful" does not seem at all unnatural, merely, as I have just denied it practical consequence, somewhat puzzling.

The disquietfulness arises, "somehow," out of a conjunction of three attributes of the fight: its immediate dramatic shape; its metaphoric content; and its social context. A cultural figure against a social ground, the fight is at once a convulsive surge of animal hatred, a mock war of symbolical selves, and a formal simulation of status tensions, and its aesthetic power derives from its capacity to force together these diverse realities. The reason it is disquietful is not that it has material effects (it has some, but they are minor); the reason that it is disquietful is that, joining pride to selfhood, selfhood to cocks, and cocks to destruction, it brings to imaginative realization a dimension of Balinese experience normally well-obscured from view. The transfer of a sense of gravity into what is in itself a rather blank and unvarious spectacle, a commotion of beating wings and throbbing legs, is effected by interpreting it as expressive of something unsettling in the way its authors and audience live, or, even more ominously, what they are.

As a dramatic shape, the fight displays a characteristic that does not seem so remarkable until one realizes that it does not have to be there: a radically atomistical structure.[19] Each match is a world unto itself, a particulate burst of form. There is the matchmaking, there is the betting, there is the fight, there is the result—utter triumph and utter defeat—and there is the hurried, embarrassed passing of money. The loser is not consoled. People drift away from him, look around him, leave him to assimilate his momentary descent into nonbeing, reset his face, and return, scarless and intact, to the fray. Nor are winners congratulated, or events rehashed; once a match is ended the crowd's attention turns totally to the next, with no looking back. A shadow of the experience no doubt remains with the principals, perhaps even with some of the witnesses of a deep fight, as it remains with us when we leave the theater after seeing a powerful play well performed; but it quite soon fades to become at most a schematic memory—a diffuse glow or an abstract shudder—and usually not even that. Any expressive form lives only in its own present— the one it itself creates. But, here, that present is severed into a string of flashes, some more bright than others, but all of them disconnected, aesthetic quanta. Whatever the cockfight says, it says in spurts.

---

19. British cockfights (the sport was banned there in 1840) indeed seem to have lacked it, and to have generated, therefore, a quite different family of shapes. Most British fights were "mains," in which a preagreed number of cocks were aligned into two teams and fought serially. Score was kept and wagering took place both on the individual matches and on the main as a whole. There were also "battle Royales," both in England and on the Continent, in which a large number of cocks were let loose at once with the one left standing at the end the victor. And in Wales, the so-called Welsh main followed an elimination pattern, along the lines of a present-day tennis tournament, winners proceeding to the next round. As a genre, the cockfight has perhaps less compositional flexibility than, say, Latin comedy, but it is not entirely without any.

But, as I have argued lengthily elsewhere, the Balinese live in spurts. Their life, as they arrange it and perceive it, is less a flow, a directional movement out of the past, through the present, toward the future, than an on-off pulsation of meaning and vacuity, an arhythmic alternation of short periods when "something" (that is, something significant) is happening, and equally short ones where "nothing" (that is, nothing much) is—between what they themselves call "full" and "empty" times, or, in another idiom, "junctures" and "holes." In focusing activity down to a burning-glass dot, the cockfight is merely being Balinese in the same way in which everything from the monadic encounters of everyday life, through the clanging pointillism of gamelan music, to the visiting-day-of-the-gods temple celebrations are. It is not an imitation of the punctuateness of Balinese social life, nor a depiction of it, nor even an expression of it; it is an example of it, carefully prepared.

If one dimension of the cockfight's structure, its lack of temporal directionality, makes it seem a typical segment of the general social life, however, the other, its flat out, head-to-head (or spur-to-spur) aggressiveness, makes it seem a contradiction, a reversal, even a subversion of it. In the normal course of things, the Balinese are shy to the point of obsessiveness of open conflict. Oblique, cautious, subdued, controlled, masters of indirection and dissimulation—what they call *alus,* "polished," "smooth"—they rarely face what they can turn away from, rarely resist what they can evade. But here they portray themselves as wild and murderous, with manic explosions of instinctual cruelty. A powerful rendering of life as the Balinese most deeply do not want it (to adapt a phrase Frye has used of Gloucester's blinding) is set in the context of a sample of it as they do in fact have it. And, because the context suggests that the rendering, if less than a straightforward description, is nonetheless more than an idle fancy; it is here that the disquietfulness—the disquietfulness of the *fight,* not (or, anyway, not necessarily) its patrons, who seem in fact rather thoroughly to enjoy it—emerges. The slaughter in the cock ring is not a depiction of how things literally are among men, but, what is almost worse, of how, from a particular angle, they imaginatively are.[20]

The angle, of course, is stratificatory. What, as we have already seen, the cockfight talks most forcibly about is status relationships, and what it says about them is that they are matters of life and death. That prestige is a profoundly serious business is apparent everywhere one looks in Bali—in the village, the family, the economy, the state. A peculiar fusion of Polynesian title ranks and Hindu castes, the hierarchy of pride is the moral backbone of the society. But only in the cockfight are the sentiments upon which that hierarchy rests revealed in their natural colors. Enveloped elsewhere in a haze of etiquette, a thick cloud of euphemism and ceremony, gesture and allusion, they are here expressed in only the thinnest disguise of an animal mask, a mask which in fact demonstrates them far more effectively than it conceals them. Jealousy is as much a part of Bali as poise, envy as grace, brutality as charm; but without the cockfight the Balinese would have a much less certain understanding of them, which is, presumably, why they value it so highly.

Any expressive form works (when it works) by disarranging semantic contexts in such a way that properties conventionally

---

20. There are two other Balinese values and disvalues which, connected with punctuate temporality on the one hand and unbridled aggressiveness on the other, reinforce the sense that the cockfight is at once continuous with ordinary social life and a direct negation of it: what the Balinese call *ramé*, and what they call *paling*. *Ramé* means crowded, noisy, and active, and is a highly sought-after social state: crowded markets, mass festivals, busy streets are all *ramé*, as, of course, is, in the extreme, a cockfight. *Ramé* is what happens in the "full" times (its opposite, *sepi*, "quiet," is what happens in the "empty" ones). *Paling* is social vertigo, the dizzy, disoriented, lost, turned-around feeling one gets when one's place in the coordinates of social space is not clear, and it is a tremendously disfavored, immensely anxiety-producing state. Balinese regard the exact maintenance of spatial orientation ("not to know where north is" is to be crazy), balance, decorum, status relationships, and so forth, as fundamental to ordered life (*krama*) and *paling*, the sort of whirling confusion of position the scrambling cocks exemplify, as its profoundest enemy and contradiction.

ascribed to certain things are unconventionally ascribed to others, which are then seen actually to possess them. To call the wind a cripple, as Stevens does, to fix tone and manipulate timbre, as Schoenberg does, or, closer to our case, to picture an art critic as a dissolute bear, as Hogarth does, is to cross conceptual wires; the established conjunctions between objects and their qualities are altered, and phenomena—fall weather, melodic shape, or cultural journalism—are clothed in signifiers which normally point to other referents.[21] Similarly, to connect—and connect, and connect—the collision of roosters with the divisiveness of status is to invite a transfer of perceptions from the former to the latter, a transfer which is at once a description and a judgment. (Logically, the transfer could, of course, as well go the other way; but, like most of the rest of us, the Balinese are a great deal more interested in understanding men than they are in understanding cocks.)

What sets the cockfight apart from the ordinary course of life, lifts it from the realm of everyday practical affairs, and surrounds it with an aura of enlarged importance is not, as functionalist sociology would have it, that it reinforces status discriminations (such reinforcement is hardly necessary in a society where every act proclaims them), but that it provides a metasocial commentary upon the whole matter of assorting human beings into fixed hierarchical ranks and then organizing the major part of collective existence around that assortment. Its function, if you want to call it that, is interpretive: it is a Balinese reading of Balinese experience, a story they tell themselves about themselves.

---

21. The Stevens reference is to his "The Motive for Metaphor" ("You like it under the trees in autumn, / Because everything is half dead. / The wind moves like a cripple among the leaves / And repeats words without meaning").

SAYING SOMETHING OF SOMETHING

To put the matter this way is to engage in a bit of metaphorical refocusing of one's own, for it shifts the analysis of cultural forms from an endeavor in general parallel to dissecting an organism, diagnosing a symptom, deciphering a code, or ordering a system—the dominant analogies in contemporary anthropology—to one in general parallel with penetrating a literary text. If one takes the cockfight, or any other collectively sustained symbolic structure, as a means of "saying something of something" (to invoke a famous Aristotelian tag), then one is faced with a problem not in social mechanics but social semantics. For the anthropologist, whose concern is with formulating sociological principles, not with promoting or appreciating cockfights, the question is, what does one learn about such principles from examining culture as an assemblage of texts?

Such an extension of the notion of a text beyond written material, and even beyond verbal, is, though metaphorical, not, of course, all that novel. The *interpretatio naturae* tradition of the middle ages, which, culminating in Spinoza, attempted to read nature as Scripture, the Nietzschean effort to treat value systems as glosses on the will to power (or the Marxian one to treat them as glosses on property relations), and the Freudian replacement of the enigmatic text of the manifest dream with the plain one of the latent, all offer precedents, if not equally recommendable ones. But the idea remains theoretically undeveloped; and the more profound corollary, so far as anthropology is concerned, that cultural forms can be treated as texts, as imaginative works built out of social materials, has yet to be systematically exploited.[22]

---

22. Lévi-Strauss' "structuralism" might seem an exception. But it is only an apparent one, for, rather than taking myths, totem rites, marriage rules, or whatever as texts to interpret, Lévi-Strauss takes them as ciphers to solve, which is very much not the same thing. He does not seek to understand symbolic forms in terms of how they function in concrete situations to organize perceptions (meanings, emotions, concepts, attitudes); he seeks to understand them entirely in terms of their internal structure, *independent de tout sujet, de tout objet, et de toute contexte.*

In the case at hand, to treat the cockfight as a text is to bring out a feature of it (in my opinion, the central feature of it) that treating it as a rite or a pastime, the two most obvious alternatives, would tend to obscure: its use of emotion for cognitive ends. What the cockfight says it says in a vocabulary of sentiment—the thrill of risk, the despair of loss, the pleasure of triumph. Yet what it says is not merely that risk is exciting, loss depressing, or triumph gratifying, banal tautologies of affect, but that it is of these emotions, thus exampled, that society is built and individuals are put together. Attending cockfights and participating in them is, for the Balinese, a kind of sentimental education. What he learns there is what his culture's ethos and his private sensibility (or, anyway, certain aspects of them) look like when spelled out externally in a collective text; that the two are near enough alike to be articulated in the symbolics of a single such text; and—the disquieting part—that the text in which this revelation is accomplished consists of a chicken hacking another mindlessly to bits.

Every people, the proverb has it, loves its own form of violence. The cockfight is the Balinese reflection on theirs: on its look, its uses, its force, its fascination. Drawing on almost every level of Balinese experience, it brings together themes—animal savagery, male narcissism, opponent gambling, status rivalry, mass excitement, blood sacrifice—whose main connection is their involvement with rage and the fear of rage, and, binding them into a set of rules which at once contains them and allows them play, builds a symbolic structure in which, over and over again, the reality of their inner affiliation can be intelligibly felt. If, to quote Northrop Frye again, we go to see *Macbeth* to learn what a man feels like after he has gained a kingdom and lost his soul, Balinese go to cockfights to find out what a man, usually composed, aloof, almost obsessively self-absorbed, a kind of moral autocosm, feels like when, attacked, tormented, challenged, insulted, and driven in result to the extremes of fury, he has totally triumphed or been brought totally low. The whole passage, as it takes us back to Aristotle (though to the *Poetics* rather than the *Hermeneutics*), is worth quotation:

> But the poet [as opposed to the historian], Aristotle says, never makes any real statements at all, certainly no particular or specific ones. The poet's job is not to tell you what happened, but what happens: not what did take place, but the kind of thing that always does take place. He gives you the typical, recurring, or what Aristotle calls universal event. You wouldn't go to *Macbeth* to learn about the history of Scotland—you go to it to learn what a man feels like after he's gained a kingdom and lost his soul. When you meet such a character as Micawber in Dickens, you don't feel that there must have been a man Dickens knew who was exactly like this: you feel that there's a bit of Micawber in almost everybody you know, including yourself. Our impressions of human life are picked up one by one, and remain for most of us loose and disorganized. But we constantly find things in literature that suddenly coordinate and bring into focus a great many such impressions, and this is part of what Aristotle means by the typical or universal human event.

It is this kind of bringing of assorted experiences of everyday life to focus that the cockfight, set aside from that life as "only a game" and reconnected to it as "more than a game," accomplishes, and so creates what, better than typical or universal, could be called a paradigmatic human event—that is, one that tells us less what happens than the kind of thing that would happen if, as is not the case, life were art and could be as freely shaped by styles of feeling as *Macbeth* and *David Copperfield* are.

Enacted and re-enacted, so far without end, the cockfight enables the Balinese, as, read and reread, *Macbeth* enables us, to see a dimension of his own subjectivity. As he watches fight after fight, with the active watching of an owner and a bettor (for cockfighting has no more interest as a pure spectator sport than does croquet or dog racing), he grows familiar with it and what it has to say to him, much as the attentive listener to string quartets or the absorbed viewer of still life grows slowly more familiar with them in a way which opens his subjectivity to himself.[23]

Yet, because—in another of those paradoxes, along with painted feelings and unconsequenced acts, which haunt aesthetics—that subjectivity does not properly exist until it is thus organized, art forms generate and regenerate the very subjectivity they pretend only to display. Quartets, still lifes, and cockfights are not merely reflections of a pre-existing sensibility analogically represented; they are positive agents in the creation and maintenance of such a sensibility. If we see ourselves as a pack of Micawbers, it is from reading too much Dickens (if we see ourselves as unillusioned realists, it is from reading too little); and similarly for Balinese, cocks, and cockfights. It is in such a way, coloring experience with the light they cast it in, rather than through whatever material effects they may have, that the arts play their role, as arts, in social life.[24]

In the cockfight, then, the Balinese forms and discovers his temperament and his society's temper at the same time. Or, more exactly, he forms and discovers a particular facet of them. Not only are there a great many other cultural texts providing

---

23. The use of the, to Europeans, "natural" visual idiom for perception—"see," "watches," and so forth—is more than usually misleading here, for the fact that, as mentioned earlier, Balinese follow the progress of the fight as much (perhaps, as fighting cocks are actually rather hard to see except as blurs of motion, more) with their bodies as with their eyes, moving their limbs, heads, and trunks in gestural mimicry of the cocks' maneuvers, means that much of the individual's experience of the fight is kinesthetic rather than visual. If ever there was an example of Kenneth Burke's definition of a symbolic act as "the dancing of an attitude" [*The Philosophy of Literary Form*, rev. ed. (New York, 1957), 9] the cockfight is it.

24. All this coupling of the occidental great with the oriental lowly will doubtless disturb certain sorts of aestheticians as the earlier efforts of anthropologists to speak of Christianity and totemism in the same breath disturbed certain sorts of theologians. But as ontological questions are (or should be) bracketed in the sociology of religion, judgmental ones are (or should be) bracketed in the sociology of art. In any case, the attempt to deprovincialize the concept of art is but part of the general anthropological conspiracy to deprovincialize all important social concepts—marriage, religion, law, rationality—and though this is a threat to aesthetic theories which regard certain works of art as beyond the reach of sociological analysis, it is no threat to the conviction, for which Robert Graves claims to have been reprimanded at his Cambridge tripos, that some poems are better than others.

commentaries on status hierarchy and self-regard in Bali, but there are a great many other critical sectors of Balinese life besides the stratificatory and the agonistic that receive such commentary. The ceremony consecrating a Brahmana priest, a matter of breath control, postural immobility, and vacant concentration upon the depths of being, displays a radically different, but to the Balinese equally real, property of social hierarchy—its reach toward the numinous transcendent. Set not in the matrix of the kinetic emotionality of animals, but in that of the static passionlessness of divine mentality, it expresses tranquillity, not disquiet. The mass festivals at the village temples, which mobilize the whole local population in elaborate hostings of visiting gods—songs, dances, compliments, gifts— assert the spiritual unity of village mates against their status inequality and project a mood of amity and trust. The cockfight is not the master key to Balinese life, any more than bullfighting is to Spanish. What it says about that life is not unqualified nor even unchallenged by what other equally eloquent cultural statements say about it. But there is nothing more surprising in this than in the fact that Racine and Molière were contemporaries, or that the same people who arrange chrysanthemums cast swords.[25]

The culture of a people is an ensemble of texts, themselves ensembles, which the anthropologist strains to read over the

---

25. That what the cockfight has to say about Bali is not altogether without perception, and that the disquiet it expresses about the general pattern of Balinese life is not wholly without reason, is attested by the fact that in two weeks of December 1965, during the upheavals following the unsuccessful coup in Djakarta, between forty thousand and eighty thousand Balinese (in a population of about two million) were killed, largely by one another—the worst outburst in the country. This is not to say, of course, that the killings were caused by the cockfight, could have been predicted on the basis of it, or were some sort of enlarged version of it with real people in the place of the cocks—all of which is nonsense. It is merely to say that if one looks at Bali not just through the medium of its dances, its shadow plays, its sculpture, and its girls, but—as the Balinese themselves do— also through the medium of its cockfight, the fact that the massacre occurred seems, if no less appalling, less like a contradiction to the laws of nature. As more than one real Gloucester has discovered, sometimes people actually get life precisely as they most deeply do not want it.

shoulders of those to whom they properly belong. There are enormous difficulties in such an enterprise, methodological pitfalls to make a Freudian quake, and some moral perplexities as well. Nor is it the only way that symbolic forms can be sociologically handled. Functionalism lives, and so does psychologism. But to regard such forms as "saying something of something," and saying it to somebody, is at least to open up the possibility of an analysis which attends to their substance rather than to reductive formulas professing to account for them.

As in more familiar exercises in close reading, one can start anywhere in a culture's repertoire of forms and end up anywhere else. One can stay, as I have here, within a single, more or less bounded form, and circle steadily within it. One can move between forms in search of broader unities or informing contrasts. One can even compare forms from different cultures to define their character in reciprocal relief. But whatever the level at which one operates, and however intricately, the guiding principle is the same: societies, like lives, contain their own interpretations. One has only to learn how to gain access to them. ∿

Interpretive Questions for Discussion

According to Geertz, why are the Balinese crazy about cockfighting—"a bloody drama of hatred, cruelty, violence, and death"?

1. Why does Geertz say it is men, not cocks, that are fighting in the ring? (9) Why do Balinese men, through their cocks, identify so strongly with what they most hate—"the direct inversion, aesthetically, morally, and metaphysically, of human status: animality"? (11–12)

2. Why in Balinese culture are the fighting cocks the focus of extreme tenderness as well as extreme violence? If the men acknowledge that they are "cock crazy," why don't they feel inclined to change their behavior? (10–11)

3. Why are the Balinese fascinated by the fusion of opposites in the cockfight, of "man and beast, good and evil, ego and id, the creative power of aroused masculinity and the destructive power of loosened animality"? (13)

4. Why, as an "invariable rule," does the owner of the winning cock eat the carcass of the loser, with "a mixture of social embarrassment, moral satisfaction, aesthetic disgust, and cannibal joy"? (13)

5. If the cockfight is merely sublimated or symbolic aggression, why do losers sometimes commit metaphysical and social "suicide"? Why does the symbolic meaning of the fight sometimes spill over into real life? (13)

6. Why does winning a cockfight increase one's social prestige when the competitions are made as even—and therefore as unpredictable and unrelated to skill—as possible? (23–25)

7. Why are the Balinese attracted to "deep play"—play in which the stakes are so high that it is irrational to engage in it at all? Why does Geertz insist that the "appraisive drama" of the cockfight is "deep indeed," even though no one's status actually changes, either socially or financially? (27–29)

8. What does Geertz mean when he says that money causes the Balinese status hierarchy to migrate into the body of the cockfight? (30–31) Why isn't it necessary for a cock to survive the fight in order to win it? (15–16)

9. Why do the Balinese think of cockfighting as "playing with fire only not getting burned"? Why, despite the societal forces displayed in a match, will the Balinese ultimately acknowledge that "after all, it is 'only a cockfight' "? (36)

10. Does the obsession with cockfights suggest that the Balinese are dissatisfied with their society?

Suggested textual analysis
Pages 9–13 (Of Cocks and Men)

Why does the "disquieting" cockfight serve as a cohesive force in Balinese society?

1. Why, when you first meet a Balinese, is he or she "away"? Why do the Balinese ignore the author and his wife, even while watching them closely? (3–4)

2. Why, after their encounter with the police, do the author and his wife stop being invisible and become the center of attention in the village? (6–8) Why does everyone ask about the incident and tease them about it—even the Brahmana priest, who "would never be involved, even distantly, in a cockfight"?

3. Why do the men bring their fighting birds along whenever they gather socially? (10–11)

4. Why is the Balinese cockfight extensively governed by rules and lore that are carefully written down and passed on from generation to generation? Why is it important to the Balinese to combine "the animal passion of the fight" with "the civic certainty of the law"? (17)

5. Why do people strictly observe the rules of the cockfight, without ever disputing them? (16–17) Why are the debts to opponents always paid immediately? (22, 34)

6. Why is status rivalry something the Balinese celebrate in "focused gatherings" rather than in continuous, enduring processes? (17) Why does the cockfight have "a radically atomistical structure"? (17, 41)

7. Why does Geertz describe the cockfight as "a powerful rendering of life as the Balinese most deeply do not want it . . . set in the context of a sample of it as they do in fact have it"? (42)

8. Why do the majority of people betting on the side express "their allegiance to their kinsman, not their evaluation of his bird, their understanding of probability theory, or even their hopes of unearned income"? (32) Why is "betting against the grain" considered a "bad thing to do"? (34–35)

9. Why does the Balinese cockfight reveal "in their natural colors" the sentiments upon which the "moral backbone of the society" rests? (43)

10. Why is the function of the cockfight "interpretive"? Why do the Balinese experience cockfighting as "a metasocial commentary upon the whole matter of assorting human beings into fixed hierarchical ranks"? (44)

Suggested textual analysis
Pages 39–44 (Feathers, Blood, Crowds, and Money)

According to Geertz, what does the anthropologist learn from "examining culture as an assemblage of texts"?

1. Although Bali has been "microscopically examined," why is Geertz the only anthropologist to take notice of the cockfight? (9)

2. Why does Geertz look upon a cockfight as a text? Why is it helpful to think of the analysis of cultural forms as being more like "penetrating a literary text" than diagnosing a symptom, deciphering a code, or ordering a system? (45)

3. If cockfighting is a form of literature—an imaginative work "built out of social materials"—why does it need real blood to be effective? (45–46)

4. What does Geertz mean when he says that the cockfight uses "emotion for cognitive ends"—that it provides "a kind of sentimental education"? (46)

5. Why does it benefit the Balinese to learn through the cockfight that his private sensibility and his culture's ethos are alike, and that both are well-expressed symbolically by one chicken hacking another chicken mindlessly to bits? What is the Balinese supposed to do with or gain from this knowledge? (46)

6. What does Geertz mean when he says that the cockfight is a paradigmatic rather than a typical or universal human event? (47)

7. Why does the cockfight enable the Balinese "to see a dimension of his own subjectivity"? (47) What does Geertz mean when he says that the cockfight, like the arts generally, "generate and regenerate the very subjectivity they pretend only to display"? (48)

8. According to Geertz, why is the culture of a people "an ensemble of texts" rather than a single text with many parts? (49) Why is there no one definitive text?

9. Why does Geertz state that "societies, like lives, contain their own interpretations"? Why can one start anywhere in a culture's repertoire of forms and end up anywhere else? (50)

10. Why does regarding symbolic forms as "saying something of something" and "saying it to somebody" make possible an analysis that "attends to their substance rather than to reductive formulas professing to account for them"? (50)

Suggested textual analysis
Pages 45–50 (Saying Something of Something)

FOR FURTHER REFLECTION

1. Does cockfighting serve essentially the same function in Balinese society that great literature does in ours? Is it fair to compare *Macbeth* to a cockfight?

2. Does Balinese cockfighting meet your criteria for civilized behavior? Were the authorities right to outlaw cockfighting, despite its meaning to the indigenous Balinese?

3. Is "deep play" a significant aspect of American culture?

4. Is there a universal human nature that transcends differences among cultures, or does culture determine our essence?

5. Should cultures be judged according to how well people are able to find meaning in life? Is American culture a success or failure by this standard?

6. Do sports such as football, horseracing, or boxing mean the same to an American as cockfighting means to a Balinese, or is the comparison too simple-minded? How would Geertz interpret the metaphorical meaning of unaggressive pastimes such as golf or baseball?

THE TWO SHORES

Carlos Fuentes

CARLOS FUENTES (1928–   ), Mexico's best-known modern novelist, was born in Mexico City. After studying law at the University of Mexico, Fuentes pursued a career as a diplomat while simultaneously editing a number of literary and political journals. Since 1959 he has devoted himself to writing; his novels, short stories, essays, political journalism, and screenplays all deal with the interpretation of Mexican culture and history. Fuentes' left-wing politics and identification with the militant social conscience of Mexico eventually earned him the hostility of the Mexican establishment and made him for a time *persona non grata* in the United States. Fuentes has taught at Columbia, Harvard, Princeton, Brown, and other American universities, and has also served as Mexico's ambassador to France. In 1987 he received the Cervantes Prize, the highest award bestowed on a Spanish-language writer.

Like the planets in their orbits, the world of ideas
tends toward circularity.

—Amos Oz, *Late Love*

Combien de royaumes nous ignorent!

—Pascal, *Pensées*

[10]

ALL THIS I saw. The fall of the great Aztec city in
the moan of the conch shells, the clash of steel against flint, and
the fire of Castilian cannon. I saw the burnt water of the lake where
stood this Great Tenochtitlán, two times the size of Córdoba.

The temples fell, the standards, the trophies. The very gods
themselves fell. And the day after the defeat, using the stones of
the Indian temples, we began to build the Christian churches.
Anyone curious—or who happens to be a mole—will find at the
base of the columns of the Cathedral of Mexico the magic
emblems of the God of Night, the smoking mirror of Tezcatlipoca.
How long will the new mansions of our one God, built on the
ruins of the not one but thousand gods last? Perhaps as long as
the name of these: Rain, Water, Wind, Fire, Garbage . . .

To tell the truth, I don't know. I just died of buboes. A horrible
death, painful, incurable. A bouquet of plagues bestowed upon
me by my own Indian brothers in exchange for the evils we
Spaniards visited on them. I am shocked to see this city of

Mexico populated by faces scarred by smallpox, as devastated as the causeways of the conquered city—all in the twinkling of an eye. The water of the lake heaves, boiling; the walls have contracted an incurable leprosy; the faces have forever lost their dark beauty, their perfect profile: for all time, Europe has marked the face of this New World, which, in fact, is older than the European face. Although to tell the truth, from this Olympian vantage point death has given me, I see everything that's happened as the meeting of two old worlds, both millenarian—the stones we've found here are as old as those of Egypt, and the destiny of all empires was written for all time on the wall at Balthazar's feast.

I saw it all. I'd like to tell it all. But my appearances in history are rigorously limited to what's been said about me. The chronicler Bernal Díaz del Castillo mentions me fifty-eight times in his *True History of the Conquest of New Spain*. The last thing known about me is that I was already dead when Hernán Cortés, our commander, embarked on his ill-fated expedition to Honduras in October of 1524. That's how the chronicler describes it, and he soon forgets about me.

True, I do reappear in the final parade of ghosts, when Bernal Díaz lists the fates of the comrades of the conquest. The writer possesses a prodigious memory: he remembers every name, doesn't forget a single horse or who rode it. Perhaps he had no other recourse but memory to save himself from death. Or from something worse: disillusion and sadness. Let's not fool ourselves. No one escaped unscathed from this venture of discovery and conquest—neither the conquered, who witnessed the destruction of their world, nor the conquerors, who never achieved the total satisfaction of their ambitions, suffering instead endless injustices and disenchantments. Both should have built a new world after their shared defeat. I can know that because I've already died; the chronicler from Medina del Campo didn't know it very well when he wrote his fabulous history, which is why he's got more than enough memory and not enough imagination.

Not a single comrade of the conquest is missing from his list. But the vast majority are dispatched with a laconic epitaph: *He died his death*. It's true that some, very few, are singled out because they died "in the power of the Indians." The most interesting are those who had a singular, almost always violent, fate.

Glory and abjection are equally evident in this affair of the conquest. Cortés sentenced Pedro Escudero and Juan Cermeño to the gallows because they tried to escape to Cuba on a boat, while he only ordered their pilot, Gonzalo de Umbría, to have his toes cut off. Maimed and all, this Umbría had the effrontery to appear before the King and complain, obtaining thereby rents paid in gold and Indian townships. Cortés must have regretted not having hanged him as well. Observe then, readers, listeners, penitents, or whatever you are as you approach my tomb, how decisions are made when time presses and history suppresses. Things could always have happened exactly opposite to the way the chronicle records them. Always.

But it also tells you that in this undertaking there was a bit of everything, from the personal pleasures of a certain Morón who was a great musician, a man named Porras with bright red hair who was a great singer, or an Ortiz who was a great cittern player and dancing master, to the disasters of Enrique something-or-other, a native of Palencia, who drowned from fatigue, the weight of his weapons, and the heat they caused him.

There are crossed destinies: Cortés marries Alfonso de Grado to no less a personage than Doña Isabel, daughter of the Aztec emperor Moctezuma; at the same time, a certain Xuárez, called the Old Man, ends up killing his wife with a corn-grinding stone. Who wins, who loses in a war of conquest? Juan Sedeño came with a fortune—merely his own ship, a mare and a black to serve him, bacon, a good supply of cassava bread—and made more here. A certain Burguillos, on the other hand, acquired wealth and good Indians, but he gave it all up to become a Franciscan. Most returned from the conquest or stayed on in Mexico without saving a single *maravedí*.

So what can one more destiny—my own—matter in this parade of glory and misery? I'll merely say that in this matter of destinies, I think that the wisest of all of us was the man called Solís, "Behind-the-Door," who spent his time in his house behind the door watching the others pass by in the street, not meddling with anyone and not being meddled with by anyone. Now I think that in death we're all like Solís: behind the door, watching people pass by without being seen, and reading what's said about us in the chronicles written by the survivors.

About me, then, this is the final statement:

> Another soldier, whose name was Jerónimo de Aguilar, passed; I include Aguilar in this account because he was the man we found at Catoche Point, who was being held by Indians and who became our translator. He died crippled with buboes.

[9]

I have many final impressions of the great business of the conquest of Mexico, in which fewer than six hundred valiant Spaniards subdued an empire nine times larger than Spain in territory and three times larger in population. To say nothing of the fabulous treasure we found here, which, shipped to Cádiz and Seville, made the fortune not only of Spain but of the whole of Europe, for all time, right until today.

I, Jerónimo de Aguilar, look at the New World before closing my eyes forever, and the last thing I see is the coast of Veracruz and the ships setting sail filled with Mexican treasure, guided by the most trustworthy of compasses: a sun of gold and a moon of silver, both simultaneously hanging over a blue-black sky that is stormy on high but bloody as soon as it touches the surface of the water.

I want to bid farewell to the world with this image of power and riches in the background of my vision: five well-stocked ships, a large number of soldiers, and many horses, shot, shotguns, crossbows, and all sorts of weapons, piled up to the masts and stored in the holds as ballast; eighty thousand pesos in gold and silver, infinite jewels, and the entire wardrobe of Moctezuma and Guatemuz, the last Mexican kings. A clean conquest operation, justified by the treasure a bold captain in the service of the Crown sends to His Majesty, King Charles.

But my eyes don't manage to close in peace, thinking above all about the abundance of protection, arms, men, and horses that accompanied the gold and silver of Mexico back to Spain— a cruel contrast to the insecurity, slim resources, and small number of soldiers with which Cortés and his men came from Cuba in the first moment of this dubious exploit. And yet, just look at the ironies of history.

Quiñones, captain of Cortés' personal guard, sent to protect the treasure, crossed the Bahamas but stopped at the island of Terceira with the booty of Mexico. He fell in love with a woman there, and was stabbed to death because of it; while Alonso de Dávila, who led the expedition, crossed the path of the French pirate Jean Fleury, whose nickname among us is Juan Florín, who stole the gold and silver and imprisoned Dávila in France, where King Francis I had declared again and again, "Show me the clause in Adam's testament in which the king of Spain is given half the world," to which his corsairs answered in chorus: "When God created the sea, he gave it to all of us without exception." And as a moral to the story: Florín or Fleury was himself captured on the high seas by Basques (Valladolid, Burgos, the Basque Country: the Discovery and Conquest finally united and mobilized all Spain!) and hanged in the port of Pico . . .

And the thing doesn't end there, because a certain Cárdenas, a pilot born in the Triana district of Seville and a member of our expedition, denounced Cortés in Castile, saying that he'd never seen a land where there were two kings as there were in New Spain, since Cortés took for himself, without any right to it, as much as he sent to His Majesty. For his declaration, the King gave this man from Triana a thousand pesos in rents and a parcel of Indians.

The bad thing is that he was right. We were all witnesses to the way our commander took the lion's share and promised us soldiers rewards at the end of the war. May it be long in coming! So we were left, after sweating our teeth out, without a pot to piss in . . . Cortés was sentenced and deprived of power; his captains lost their lives, their freedom, and, what's worse, the treasure, which ended up scattered to the four corners of Europe . . .

Is there any justice, I ask myself, in all this? Did we do nothing more than give the gold of the Aztecs a better destiny by pulling it out of its sterile occupation and spreading it around, distributing it, conferring on it an economic purpose instead of an ornamental or sacred one, putting it into circulation, melting it down the better to see it melt away?

[8]

From my grave, I try to judge things calmly; but one image forces itself on my thoughts again and again. I see before me a young man, about twenty-two years old, of clear, dark complexion, of a very noble disposition, both in body and in facial features.

He was married to one of Moctezuma's nieces. He was called Guatemuz or Guatimozín and had a cloud of blood in his eyes. Whenever he felt his vision blur, he lowered his eyelids, and I saw them: one was gold and the other silver. He was the last emperor of the Aztecs, after his uncle Moctezuma was stoned to death by the disillusioned mob. We Spaniards killed something more than the power of the Indians: we killed the magic that surrounded it. Moctezuma did not fight. Guatemuz—let it be said to his honor—fought like a hero.

Captured with his captains and brought before Cortés on August 13, at the hour of vespers on Saint Hippolytus Day in the year 1521, Guatemuz said that in the defense of his people and vassals he'd done everything he was obliged to do out of honor and (he added) also out of passion, strength, and conviction. "And since I've been brought by force, a prisoner," he said then to Cortés, "before your person and power. Take that dagger you wear on your belt and kill me with it."

This young, valiant Indian, the last emperor of the Aztecs, began to weep, but Cortés answered him that for being so brave he should come in peace to the fallen city and govern in Mexico and in its provinces as he had before.

I know all this because I was the translator of the interview between Cortés and Guatemuz, who could not understand each other alone. I translated as I pleased. I didn't communicate to the conquered prince what Cortés really said, but put into the mouth of our leader a threat: "You will be my prisoner; today I will torture you by burning your feet and those of your comrades until you confess where the rest of your uncle Moctezuma's treasure is (the part that didn't end up in the hands of French pirates)."

I added, inventing on my own and mocking Cortés: "You'll never be able to walk again, but you'll accompany me on future conquests, crippled and weeping, as a symbol of continuity and the source of legitimacy for my enterprise, whose banners, raised on high, are gold and fame, power and religion."

I translated, I betrayed, I invented. Right then and there, Guatemuz' tears dried, and instead of tears, down one cheek ran gold and down the other silver, cutting a furrow in them as a knife would, leaving a permanent wound in them which, may it please God, death has healed.

Since my own death, I remember that vespers of Saint Hippolytus, recorded by Bernal Díaz as an eternal night of rain and lightning, and I reveal myself before posterity as a falsifier, a traitor to my commander Cortés, who instead of making a peace offering to the fallen prince offered him cruelty, continued oppression without mercy, and eternal shame for the conquered.

But since things happened as I'd said, my false words becoming reality, wasn't I right to translate the commander backwards and tell the truth with my lies to the Aztec? Or were my words

perhaps a mere exchange and I nothing more than the intermediary (the translator), the mainspring of a fatal destiny that
transformed trick into truth?

On that Saint Hippolytus night, playing the role of translator
between the conquistador and the conquered, I merely confirmed the power of words: I used them to say the opposite of
what Cortés said only to express what he actually did. I'd
acquired a knowledge of the soul of my commander, Hernán
Cortés, a dazzling mix of reason and folly, will and weakness,
skepticism and fantastic naïveté, good luck and bad, gallantry
and jest, virtue and malice—all those things went into the man
from Estremadura, the conqueror of Mexico whom I'd followed
from Yucatán to Moctezuma's court.

The powers of folly and foolishness or malice and good fortune when they're not in harmony, when they're only words,
can turn our intentions upside down. The story of the last Aztec
king, Guatemuz, ended with him not in the place of power
promised by Cortés, not in the honor with which the Indian
surrendered, but in a cruel comedy, the very one I'd invented
and made inevitable with my lies. The young emperor was the
king of fools, dragged without feet by the victor's chariot,
crowned with cactus, and finally hanged upside down from the
branches of a sacred silk-cotton tree like a hunted-down animal.
What happened was exactly what I had lyingly invented.

For that reason I don't sleep in peace. Possibilities not carried
out, the alternatives of freedom all rob me of sleep.

A woman was to blame.

[7]

Among all the prodigies produced by my captain Don Hernán
Cortés to impress the Indians—fire from harquebuses, steel
swords, glass beads—none was so important as the horses of the
conquest. A shotgun blast fades in smoke; a Spanish blade can
be overcome by a two-handed Indian sword; glass may fool people, an emerald as well. But the horse exists, stands there, has a

life of its own, moves, possesses the combined power of nerve, gloss, muscle, foaming mouth, and hooves. Those hooves, links to the earth, makers of thunder, twins of steel. Hypnotic eyes. The rider who gets on and off adds to the perpetual metamorphosis of the beast seen now but never before imagined, not, certainly, by the Indians, not even by a single one of their gods.

Could the horse be the dream of a god who never communicated his secret nightmare to us?

An Indian could never overcome an armed Castilian on horseback, and this is the true secret of the conquest, not any dream or prophecy. Cortés exploited his meager cavalry to the limit, not only in attacks or fights in open country but in specially prepared seaside cavalcades where the chargers seemed to shake the waves—so much so that even we Spaniards imagined that if the horses were not there, these coasts would be as calm as a mirror of water.

We stared in astonishment at the unthought-of fraternity between the sea foam and the foam on their dewlaps.

And in Tabasco, when Captain Cortés wanted to astonish the envoys of the Great Moctezuma, he paired off a stallion with a mare in heat and hid them, instructing me to make them whinny at the right moment. The king's envoys had never heard that sound and succumbed in shock to the powers of the *Teúl*, or Spanish God, as the Indians called Cortés from that moment on.

The truth is that neither I nor anyone else had ever before heard such a whinny come out of the silence, devoid of a body, and reveal animal desire, bestial lust, with such crude force. My captain's theatrics far surpassed his intentions and even shocked us Spaniards. It made all of us feel a bit like beasts . . .

But the emissaries of the Great Moctezuma had also seen all the portents of that year prophesied by their magicians concerning the return of their blond and bearded god. Our marvels—the horses, the cannon—only confirmed what they already carried in their eyes: comets at midday, water in flames, fallen towers, nocturnal shrieking of wandering women, children carried away by the wind . . .

And lo and behold, Don Hernán Cortés arrives at that precise moment, as white as winters in the Gredos mountains, as hard as the earth in Medellín and Trujillo, and with a beard older than he was. So they wait for the return of the gods and instead get people like the hunchback Rodrigo Jara or Juan Pérez, who killed his wife, known as the Cowherd's Daughter, or Pedro Perón de Toledo, of turbulent descendancy, or a certain Izquierdo from Castromocho. Some gods! Even in the grave I cackle to think of it.

One image cuts off my laughter. The horse.

Even Valladolid, "the Fat Man," looked good on horseback; I mean he inspired respect and awe. The mortality of the man was saved by the immortality of the horse. Cortés was right when he told us from the first moment: "We shall bury the dead at night and in secret. That way our enemies will think us immortal."

The rider fell; never the charger. Never; not Cortés' bay, not Alonso Hernández's silver-gray mare that ran so well, not Montejo's sorrel, not even Morán's splayfooted, spotted nag. So it wasn't just men who entered the Great Tenochtitlán on November 3, 1520, but centaurs: mythological beings with two heads and six feet, armed with thunder and dressed in stone. And besides, thanks to the coincidences of the calendar, we'd been confused with the returning god, Quetzalcoatl.

Appropriately, Moctezuma received us on foot, halfway along the causeway that linked the valley to the city built on a lake, saying: "Welcome. You are home. Now rest."

No one among us had ever seen a city more splendid than Moctezuma's capital, neither in the Old World nor in the New: the canals, the canoes, the towers and wide plazas, the well-stocked markets and the novel things to be seen there, things never seen by us, things not mentioned in the Bible: tomatoes, turkeys, chili, chocolate, maize, potatoes, tobacco, agave beer, emeralds, jade, gold and silver in abundance, featherwork, and soft, mournful chanting . . .

Beautiful women, well-swept rooms, patios full of birds, and cages stuffed with tigers; gardens and albino dwarfs to serve us. Like Alexander in Capua, we were threatened by the delights of triumph. We were rewarded for our efforts. The horses were well taken care of.

Until one morning. Moctezuma, the great king who had received us with such hospitality in his city and in his palace, was in a royal chamber surrounded by all of us, when something happened that changed the course of our enterprise.

Cortés' lieutenant, Pedro de Alvarado, bold and gallant, cruel and shameless, had red hair and a red beard, which made the Indians call him *Tonantío,* which means the Sun. Likable and brazen, Tonantío had been amusing King Moctezuma with a game of dice—another novelty for these Indians—and for the moment the monarch was distracted, incapable of guessing his fortune beyond the next toss of the dice, even when he was being cheated, as he was at that moment by the irrepressible Alvarado. The king looked irritated, because he usually changed clothes several times a day, and either his serving maids were late or his tunic smelled or itched, who knows what . . .

Just at that moment, four *tamemes,* or Indian bearers, walk into the chamber followed by the usual din of our guards, and with impassive expressions drop in front of Cortés and the emperor the severed head of a horse.

It was then that the conquistador's second translator, an enslaved princess from Tabasco baptized Doña Marina but nicknamed La Malinche, quickly interpreted the messengers who'd come from the coast with news of an uprising of Mexicans in Veracruz against the garrison left there by Cortés. The Aztec troops had killed Juan de Escalante, head constable of the port, and six Spaniards.

Most important, they'd killed the horse. Here was the proof.

I noticed that Alvarado stood stock-still with his hand filled with dice in the air, staring at the half-open, glassy eyes of the horse as if he'd seen himself in them and as if in the flint-cut neck, slashed as if in rage, the enraged and red-haired captain had seen his own end.

Moctezuma lost interest in the game, shrugging his shoulders a bit, and stared fixedly at the horse's head. His eloquent eyes, however, silently told us Spaniards, "So you're gods? Well then, behold the mortality of your powers."

Cortés, on the other hand, stood staring at Moctezuma with such a face of betrayal that I could only read in it what our captain wanted to see in the king's countenance.

I have never felt that so many things were said without a word being spoken. Moctezuma, approaching the horse's head in a devout, almost humiliated fashion, said, without saying anything, that just as the horse died so could the Spaniards die if he decreed it. And he would decree it, if the foreigners did not withdraw in peace.

Without saying a word, Cortés warned the king that it would not be advisable for him to start a war that would ultimately destroy both him and his city.

Pedro de Alvarado, who knew nothing of subtle discourses, spoken or unspoken, violently threw the dice against the face of the horrifying divinity that presided over the chamber, the goddess named for her skirt of serpents. Before Moctezuma could say anything, Cortés stepped forward and ordered the king to abandon his palace and come to live in the one occupied by the Spaniards.

"If you sound an alarm or shout, you will be killed by my captains," Cortés said in an even tone, impressing Moctezuma more by that than Alvarado had with his physical fury. Nevertheless, after his initial shock and dismay, the King responded by removing from his arm and wrist the seal of Huichilobos, the god of war, as if he were going to order our slaughter.

But all he did was excuse himself: "I never ordered the attack in Veracruz. I shall punish my captains for having done it."

The handmaidens entered with the fresh clothes. They seemed flustered by the low tavern brawl they'd stumbled upon. Moctezuma recovered his dignity and said he would not leave his palace.

Alvarado then confronted Cortés: "Why are you wasting so many words? Either we take him prisoner or we run him through."

Once again, it was the interpreter Doña Marina who decided the struggle, forcefully advising the king: "Lord Moctezuma, what I recommend is that you go with them now to their dwelling without making a sound. I know they will honor you as the great lord you are. If you do otherwise, you will be put to death."

You understand that the woman said these things to the emperor on her own initiative, not translating Cortés but speaking Moctezuma's Mexican language fluently. The king looked like a cornered animal, but instead of shifting around on four legs he staggered on his own two feet. He offered his sons as hostages. He repeated these words several times: "Do not dishonor me in this way. What will my principal men say if they see me taken prisoner? Anything but this dishonor."

Was this pusillanimous creature the great lord who had subjugated all the tribes from Xalisco to Nicaragua through terror? Was this the cruel despot who one day ordered that those who dreamed about the end of his reign be put to death so that the dreams would die with the dreamers? I can only understand the enigma of Moctezuma's weakness before the Spaniards by using words as an explanation. Called *Tlatoani,* or Lord of the Great Voice, Moctezuma was slowly but surely losing his control over words—more than his control over men. I think that novelty disconcerted him, and Doña Marina had just proven, by arguing with him face-to-face, that the words of the king were no longer sovereign. Therefore, neither was he. Others, the foreigners, but also this treacherous woman from Tabasco, owned a vocabulary forbidden to Moctezuma.

In this second opportunity that stood between things said, things done, and the unforeseeable consequences of both, I saw my own opportunity. That night, under a mantle of secrecy, I spoke to the king in Mexican and told him privately about the dangers threatening the Spaniards. Did Moctezuma know that the governor of Cuba had sent an expedition to arrest Cortés, whom he considered a vile rebel who acted without authorization and who was worthy of being imprisoned instead of making a prisoner of such a great lord as Moctezuma, the equal only of another king, Don Carlos, whom Cortés, with no credentials, sought to represent?

I repeat these words as I said them, in one rush, without taking a breath, with no shade of meaning, no subtlety, hating myself for my betrayal but, above all, for my inferiority in the arts of dissimulation, trickery, and dramatic pauses, in which my rivals, Cortés and La Malinche, were masters.

I ended as abruptly as I'd begun, getting, as they say, right to the point: "This expedition against Cortés is led by Pánfilo de Narváez, a captain as bold as Cortés himself, but with five times as many men."

"Are they also Christians?" asked Moctezuma.

I said they were, and that they represented King Carlos, from whom Cortés was fleeing.

Moctezuma patted my hand and offered me a ring as green as a parrot. I gave it back and told him that my love for his people was reward enough. The king looked at me without understanding, as if he himself had never understood that he led a group of human beings. I asked myself then and I ask myself now, what kind of power did Moctezuma think he had and over whom? Perhaps he was only acting out some pantomime in front of the gods, wearing himself out in an effort to hear them and to be heard by them. But what was exchanged there was neither jewels nor pats on the hand but words, words that could give Moctezuma more power than all the horses and harquebuses the Spaniards possessed, if the Aztec king would only decide to speak to his men, his people, instead of speaking to the gods, his pantheon.

I told the king the secret of Cortés' weakness, just as Doña Marina had given Cortés the secret of Aztec weakness, the discord, the envy, the struggle between brothers, which affected Spain just as much as Mexico: one half of the country perpetually dying of the other half.

[6]

Thus I associated myself with the hope of an Indian victory. All my acts, you've already guessed and I can tell you right from my intangible shroud, were directed toward that goal: the triumph of the Indians over the Spaniards. Once again, Moctezuma let opportunity slip through his fingers. He got ahead of events, boasting in the presence of Cortés that he knew Cortés was threatened by Narváez instead of hastening to join forces with Narváez against Cortés, to defeat the man from Estremadura, and then to turn the Aztec nation against the fatigued regiment of Narváez. In that way, Mexico would have been saved . . .

I must say at this point that Moctezuma's vanity was always stronger than his cunning, although even stronger than his vanity was his feeling that everything was foretold, which was why the king had only to carry out the role set for him by religious and political ceremonial. In the soul of the king, fidelity to forms was its own reward. It had always happened that way, wasn't that the truth?

I didn't know how to say it wasn't, to argue with him. Perhaps my Mexican vocabulary was insufficient, and I didn't know the subtlest forms of Aztec philosophic and moral reasoning. What I did want was to frustrate the fatal plan, if such a thing existed, by means of words, imagination, lies. But when words, imagination, and lies jumble together, the result is the truth . . .

The Aztec king was hoping Cortés would be beaten by the punitive expedition sent by the governor of Cuba, but he did nothing to hasten the defeat of our captain. His certainty was understandable. If Cortés, with only five hundred men, had defeated the chiefs of Tabasco and Zempoala as well as the fierce Tlaxcaltecs, wouldn't more than two thousand Spaniards also armed with fire and horses defeat him?

But the cunning Cortés, accompanied by his new Indian allies, defeated Narváez' people and captured their leader.

Observe the irony of this matter: now we had two prisoners of importance, one Aztec and the other Spanish, Moctezuma and Narváez. Was there any limit to the number of our victories?

"The truth is, I don't understand you," the Great Moctezuma, sequestered but quite at his ease being bathed by his beautiful handmaidens, said to us.

But did we understand him?

This question, reader, obliges me to pause and reflect before events once again rush to their conclusion, always more swiftly than the pen of the narrator, although this time he writes from death.

Moctezuma: Did we understand exactly how alien to him treacherous political machinations were, and how natural, by contrast, was the proximity of a religious world impenetrable to Europeans? Impenetrable for having been forgotten: our contact with God and His primary emanations had been lost for a long, long time. In that, Moctezuma and his people were indeed alike, though neither knew it: the clay of creation, the nearness of the gods, still moistened them.

Did we understand him, sheltered as he was in another time, the time of origins, which for him was current, immediate time, portentous as both refuge and threat?

I compared him to a cornered animal. Instead, this refined man seems to me, now that death has made us equal, not only like the scrupulous individual of infinite courtesies we met when we entered Mexico but like the first man, always the first, amazed that the world exists and that the light advances every day before fading into the cruelty of every night. His obligation consisted in always being, in the name of all, the first man to ask: "Will the sun come up again?"

This was a more urgent question for Moctezuma and the Aztecs than knowing whether Narváez defeated Cortés, Cortés defeated Narváez, the Tlaxcaltecs defeated Cortés, or if Moctezuma would fall before all of them: as long as he didn't fall before the gods.

Would it rain again, would the maize grow again, the river run, the beasts roar?

All the power, the elegance, the very distance of Moctezuma was the disguise of a man recently arrived at the regions of the dawn. He was a witness to the first shout and the first terror. Fear of being and gratitude for being were mixed within him, behind the paraphernalia of plumed headpieces and collars, handmaidens, tiger knights, and bloody priests.

It was a woman, Marina, an Indian like him, from his own land, who actually defeated him, although she did use two tongues. It was she who revealed to Cortés that the Aztec empire was divided, that the peoples subjugated by Moctezuma hated him and hated each other as well, and that the Spaniards could grasp opportunity by the forelock; it was she who understood the secret uniting our two lands: fratricidal hatred, division—I've already said it: two nations, each one dying of the other . . .

Too late. I communicated to Moctezuma that Cortés was also hated and beset on all sides from an imperia; Spain as contentious as the Mexican empire he was conquering.

I forgot two things.

Cortés listened to Marina not only as an interpreter but as a lover. And as translator and lover, she paid attention to the human voices of this land. Moctezuma listened only to the gods; I wasn't one of them, so the attention he paid me was one more manifestation of his courtesy, as rich as an emerald but as evanescent as the voice of a parrot.

I, who also possessed the two voices, European and American, had been defeated. I had two homelands, which perhaps was more my weakness than my strength. Marina, La Malinche, bore the deep pain and rancor but also the hope of her condition; she had to risk everything to save her life and have descendants. Her weapon was the same as mine: her tongue. But I found myself divided between Spain and the New World. I knew both shores.

Marina didn't; she could give herself entirely to the New World, not to her subjugated past, true enough, but to her ambiguous, uncertain, and therefore unconquered future. Perhaps I deserved my defeat. I could not save the poor king of my adoptive country, Mexico, by telling him a secret, a truth, an infidelity.

Then came the defeat I've already told of.

[5]

Doña Marina and I fought, truly fought, in the drama of Cholula. I didn't always possess the Mexican language. My initial advantage was knowing Spanish and Maya after the long time I spent among the Indians in Yucatán. Doña Marina—La Malinche— spoke only Maya and Mexican when she was given to Cortés as a slave. So for a while I was the only one who could translate into the language of Castile. The Mayas of the coast told me the things I would translate into Spanish or say them to La Malinche, but she depended on me to communicate them to Cortés. Sometimes, the Mexicans would tell the woman things she would say to me in Maya and I would translate them into Spanish. And although in those instances she had an advantage—she could invent whatever she wanted in passing from Nahuatl to Maya—I went on being the master of language. The Castilian translation that reached the ears of the conquistador was always mine.

Then we reached Cholula, after the vicissitudes of the coast, the founding of Veracruz, the taking of Zempoala and its fat chieftain, who revealed to us, huffing and puffing from his litter, that the conquered peoples would unite with us against Moctezuma. We arrived after our fight against the haughty Tlaxcaltecs, who, even though they were mortal enemies of Moctezuma, did not want to exchange the power of Mexico for the new oppression of the Spaniards.

For centuries, people have said that the Tlaxcaltecs are to blame for everything; pride and betrayal can be faithful companions, each one covering up for the other. The fact is that

when we—Cortés and our small band of Spaniards, along with
the battalions of fierce Tlaxcaltec warriors—drew up outside
the gates of Cholula, we were stopped by the priests of those
holy places, because Cholula was the pantheon of all the gods
of these lands. As in Rome, they were all admitted, with no
distinctions made about their origin, into the great, collective
temple of divinities. To that end, the people of Cholula erected
the greatest pyramid of all, a honeycomb of seven structures one
inside the other, all linked together by deep labyrinths of red
and yellow reverberations.

I already knew that in this land everything is governed by the
stars, the Sun and Moon, Venus, who is her own precious twin
at dawn and dusk, and a calendar that provides a precise
account of the agricultural year and its 360 bountiful days plus
5 unlucky days: the masked days.

It must have been on one of those days that we Spaniards
arrived here, because after sending the Tlaxcaltec host ahead we
ran into a blockade of popes, priests dressed in black—black
tunics, black hair, black skin, all as black as the night wolves of
these lands, with one single flash emblazoned on their hair, eyes,
and togas: the shine of the blood, like a sticky, brilliant sweat,
that was proper to their office.

Loud and firmly did these priests speak, forbidding admittance to the violent Tlaxcaltecs. Cortés yielded to their demand,
on condition that the Cholulans quickly abandon their idols.

"They haven't even entered, and they're already asking us to
betray the gods!" exclaimed the popes in a tone difficult to
define, between a lament and a challenge, between sigh and
fury, between fatality and dissimulation, as if they were ready to
die for their divinities, but resigning themselves at the same time
to give them up for lost.

All this did La Malinche translate from Mexican into
Spanish, while I, Jerónimo de Aguilar, the first of all the inter-
preters, remained in a kind of limbo, waiting for my turn to
translate into Castilian, until I realized, perhaps stupefied by the
unbearable stench of muddy blood and incense, shit from

Andalusian horses, excessive sweat from the soldiers, conflictive cooking of chili and bacon, of garlic and turkey, all indistinguishable from the sacrificial cooking that wafted its smoke and chanting from the pyramid, I realized that Jerónimo de Aguilar was no longer needed. The diabolical female was translating everything, this bitch of a Marina, this whore who learned to speak Spanish. This scoundrel, this trickster, this expert in sucking, the conquistador's concubine, had stolen my professional singularity away from me, the function where there was no substitute for me, my—to coin a word—my *monopoly* over the Castilian language . . . La Malinche had pulled the Spanish language out of Cortés' sex, she'd sucked it out of him, she'd castrated him of it without his knowing it, by disguising mutilation as pleasure . . .

This language was no longer mine alone. Now it belonged to her, and that night I tortured myself in my own sheltered solitude within the clamor of Cholula, whose people had crowded into the streets and onto the terraces to watch us pass with our horses and shotguns and helmets and beards; I tortured myself imagining the nights of love of the man from Estremadura and his whore, her body, hairless and cinnamon-hued, with the excitable nipples these women use to attack and the secret and deep sex they hide, sparse in hair, abundant in juices, between their wide hips. I imagined the incomparable smoothness of the thighs of Indian women, used to having water flow over them to wash away the crusts of time, the past, and the pain that clot between the legs of our Spanish mothers. Female smoothness, I imagined her in my solitude, hidden holes in which my lord Hernán Cortés has poked his fingers, tongue, phallus, his fingers adorned with festive rings and wrapped in gauntlets when time came for war: the hands of the conquistador, between jewels and steel, metal nails, fingertips of blood, and lines of fire—luck, love, intelligence in flames, guiding toward the perfumed medlar of the Indian woman first his sex sheathed in a pubic beard which must be as ascetic as the vegetation of

Estremadura, and a pair of balls which I imagine tense, as hard as the shot of our harquebuses.

But Cortés' sex was ultimately less sexual than his mouth and beard, that beard which seemed too old for a thirty-five-year-old man, as if he'd inherited it from the times of Viriatus and his fields of hay set afire against the Roman invaders, from the times of the besieged city of Numantia and its squadrons dressed in mourning, from the times of Pelayo and his lances made from pure Asturian mist: a beard older than the man on whose jaws it grew. Perhaps the Mexicans were right, and a beardless Cortés wore, borrowed, the extremely long beard of that very same god Quetzalcoatl, with whom these natives confused him . . .

The most terrible, the most shocking thing was not Cortés' sex, but that from the depth of the forest, from the mourning, from the mist, would emerge his tongue, which was the conqueror's true sex, and that he would stick it into the Indian woman's mouth with more power, more seed, and more pregnancy—my God, I'm delirious! I'm suffering, Lord!—with more fecundity than his sex. Tongue-phallus-whip, thrashing, hard, and ductile at the same time: poor me, Jerónimo de Aguilar, dead all this time, with my tongue split up the middle, fork-tongued like the plumed serpent. Who am I, of what use am I?

[4]

The Cholulans said we could enter without the Tlaxcaltecs. They could not renounce their gods, but they would obey the King of Spain with pleasure. They said it through La Malinche, who translated it from Mexican into Spanish while I stood there like a royal ninny, mulling over what my next step would be to recover my tattered dignity. (I'm not going far enough: language was more than dignity, it was power; and more than power, it was the very life that animated my plans, my own program of discovery, unique, surprising, unrepeatable . . .)

But since I couldn't go to bed with Cortés, I thought I'd be better off giving the devil her due and decided that at least for now there was no sense crying over spilt milk.

During the first days, the Cholulans gave us abundant food and feed. But soon enough they began to stint on the food. Then they grew obstinate and remiss, and I started looking at Doña Marina with suspicion, while she stared back at me, immutable, firmly supported by her carnal intimacy with our captain.

A perpetual cloud ominously hung over the sacred city; the smoke became so thick we couldn't see the tops of the temples or the stones under our feet. Cholula's head and feet dissolved in mist, though it was impossible to know if it came, as I said when we arrived, from the different levels of the pyramid, from the horses' assholes, or from the bowels of the mountains. The strange thing is that Cholula stands on level ground, but now nothing was level here and instead seemed unfathomable and craggy.

Observe how words transformed even the landscape: Cholula's new landscape was nothing more than the reflection of the sinuous struggle of words, sometimes as deep as a ravine, at other times craggy, like a mountain of thorns; whispering and soothing like a great river, or stirred up and raucous like an ocean dragging loose stones: a shrieking of mermaids wounded by the tide.

I told the popes: "I lived in Yucatán for eight years. That's where I have my true friends. If I abandoned them, it was to follow these white gods and find out their secrets, because they have not come to be your brothers but to conquer this land and smash your gods.

"Listen carefully to me," I said to the priests. "These foreigners really are gods, but they are enemies of your gods."

I said to Cortés: "There is no danger. They're convinced we're gods and honor us as gods."

Cortés said: "Why then are they refusing us food and fodder?"

Marina told Cortés: "The city is full of sharpened stakes to kill your horses if you use them to attack; take care, sir; the roofs are piled high with stones, they've built protective screens of adobe bricks, and the streets are blocked with thick logs."

I told the popes: "They are evil gods, but they are gods. They don't have to eat."

The popes replied: "How can it be they do not eat? What kind of gods can they be? The *teúles* eat. They demand sacrifices."

I insisted: "They are different *teúles*. They don't want sacrifices."

I said it and bit my tongue because I saw in my argument a justification of the Christian religion I hadn't noticed before. The popes exchanged looks, and a chill ran down my spine. They realized what I realized. The Aztec gods demanded the sacrifice of men. The Christian God, nailed to the cross, sacrificed himself. The popes stared at the crucifix raised at the entrance to the house taken over by the Spaniards and felt their minds collapse. In that moment, I would have been delighted to change places with the crucified Jesus, accepting His wounds if this nation did not make the invincible exchange between a religion that demanded human sacrifice and another that allowed divine sacrifice.

"There is no danger," I said to Cortés, knowing there was danger.

"There is danger," Marina said to Cortés, knowing there was none.

I wanted to destroy the conquistador so he would never reach the gates of the Great Tenochtitlán: I wanted Cholula to be his tomb, the end of his daring exploits.

Marina wanted to make an example of Cholula to preclude future betrayals. She had to invent the danger. As proof, she brought in an old woman and her son who swore that a great ambush was being prepared against the Spaniards and that the Indians had prepared their cooking pots with salt, chili, and tomatoes to boil us so they could stuff themselves with our flesh. Is it true, or did Doña Marina invent as much as I did?

"There is no danger," I said to Cortés and Marina.

"There is danger," Marina said to all of us.

That night, after a shotgun was fired, the Spanish massacre fell on the City of the Gods, and those who did not die pierced by our swords or blasted to pieces by our harquebuses were burned alive. When the Tlaxcaltecs entered, they poured through the city like a savage pestilence, stealing and raping without our being able to stop them.

In Cholula, not one idol was left standing, not one altar unscathed. The 365 Indian temples were whitewashed to banish the demons and dedicated to 365 saints, virgins, and martyrs from our book of saints' lives, passing forever into the service of God Our Lord.

Cholula's punishment was soon known in all the provinces of Mexico. In doubt, the Spaniards opted for force.

My defeat, less known, I declare here today.

Because I understood then that, in doubt, Cortés would believe La Malinche, his woman, and not me, a fellow Spaniard.

[3]

It wasn't always that way. On the coasts of Tabasco, I was his only interpreter. I remember with joy our landing at Champotón, when Cortés depended totally on me, and our rafts plied the river opposite the Indian squadrons lined up on the shores. Cortés proclaimed in Spanish that we had come in peace, as brothers, while I translated into Maya, but also in the language of shadows:

"He's lying! He's come to conquer us, defend yourselves, don't believe him."

What impunity I had, how I delight in remembering it from the bed of an eternity even more ominous than my betrayal!

"We are brothers!"

"We are enemies!"

"We come in peace!"

"We come in war!"

No one, no one in the thick forest of Tabasco, its river, its jungle, its roots sunk forever in the darkness where only the macaws seemed touched by the sun, Tabasco of the first day of creation, cradle of silence broken by the screech of the bird, Tabasco, echo of the initial dawn: no one there, I say, could know that by translating the conquistador I lied. And yet, I spoke the truth.

Hernán Cortés' words of peace, translated by me into the vocabulary of war, provoked a rain of Indian arrows. Taken aback, the captain saw the sky wounded by the arrows and reacted by engaging in battle on the very banks of the river . . . As he disembarked, he lost a sandal in the mud, and because I recovered it for him, I was hit by an arrow in the thigh; fourteen Spaniards were wounded, thanks to me in great measure, but eighteen Indians fell dead . . . We slept there that night, after the victory I didn't want, with large torches and sentinels, on the wet ground and if my dreams were unquiet—the Indians I had induced to fight had been defeated—they were also pleasant, because I proved my power to decide peace or war thanks to my ownership of words.

Poor fool: I lived in a false paradise where, for an instant, language and power coincided with my luck, because when I joined the Spaniards in Yucatán, the former interpreter, a cross-eyed Indian named Melchorejo, whispered into my ear, as if he guessed my intentions: "They're invincible. They speak with the animals."

The next morning, Melchorejo disappeared, leaving his Spanish clothing hung from a silk-cotton tree which Cortés, to indicate Spanish possession, had slashed three times with his knife.

Someone saw the first interpreter flee naked in a canoe. I was left thinking about what he'd said. Everyone would say that the Spaniards were gods and that they spoke with gods. Only Melchorejo divined that their power was to speak with the horses. Was he right?

Days later, the defeated chiefs of this region delivered twenty women as slaves for the Spaniards. One of them caught my eye, not only because of her beauty but because of her arrogance: she overawed not only the other slaves but the chiefs themselves. She had what's called a lot of presence, and her orders brooked no disagreement.

We exchanged looks, and without speaking I said to her, "Be mine, I speak your Maya tongue and love your people, I don't know how to combat the fatality of all that's happening, I can't stop it, but perhaps you and I together, Indian and Spaniard, can save something if we come to an agreement and above all if we love each other a bit . . .

"Do you want me to teach you to speak Castilla?" I asked.

When I came near her, my blood pounded; one of those times when mere seeing provokes pleasure and excitation. It was perhaps augmented because I'd gone back to using Spanish breeches for the first time in a long time, after having worn a loose shirt and nothing underneath it, allowing the heat and the breeze to ventilate my balls freely. Now the cloth caressed me, and the leather squeezed me and my eyes linked me to the woman I saw as my ideal partner for confronting what was to happen. I imagined that together we could change the course of events.

Her name was Malintzin, which means "Penitence."

That same day, the Mercederian Olmedo baptized her Marina, making her the first Christian woman in New Spain.

But her people called her La Malinche, the traitor.

I spoke to her. She didn't answer me. However, she did allow me to admire her.

"Do you want me to teach you to speak . . . ?"

That evening in March of the year 1519, she disrobed before me in the mangrove swamp, while a simultaneous chorus of hummingbirds, dragonflies, rattlesnakes, lizards, and hairless dogs broke loose around her transfigured nakedness. In that instant, the captive Indian woman was svelte and massive, heavy and ethereal, animal and human, sane and insane. She was all that, as if she were not only inseparable from the earth that surrounded her but also its summary and symbol. And also as if she told me that what I was seeing that night I would never see again. She disrobed to deny herself to me.

I dreamed all night about her name, Marina, Malintzin, I dreamed about a son of ours, I dreamed that together she and

I, Marina and Jerónimo, owners of the languages, would also be owners of the lands, an invincible couple because we understood the two voices of Mexico, the voice of men and the voice of the gods.

I imagined her rolling around in my sheets.

The next day, Cortés chose her as his concubine and his interpreter.

I was already the latter for the Spanish captain. I could not be the former.

"You speak Spanish and Maya," she said to me in the language of Yucatán. "I speak Maya and Mexican. Teach me Spanish."

"Let your owner teach you," I answered in rancor.

From my tomb, I assure you, we see our rancor as the most sterile part of our lives. Rancor (and envy, which is sorrow over someone else's well-being) closely follows resentment as a sorrow that wounds the person suffering it more deeply than it does the person who provokes it. Jealousy doesn't do that: jealousy may be the source of exquisite agonies and incomparable excitations. Vanity doesn't do that either: vanity is a human trait that links us to everyone else, the great equalizer of poor and rich, strong and weak. In that, it resembles cruelty, which is the best-distributed thing in the world. But rancor and envy: how was I going to triumph over those who provoked them in me, he and she, the couple of the conquest, Cortés and La Malinche, the couple she and I might have been? Poor Marina, ultimately abandoned by her conquistador, burdened with a fatherless child, stigmatized by her people with the mark of betrayal, and, nevertheless, because of all that, mother and origin of a new nation, which perhaps could only be born and grow against the charges of abandonment, illegitimacy, and betrayal . . .

Poor Malinche, poor rich Malinche as well, who with her man shaped history, but who with me, the poor soldier killed by buboes and not by Indians, would not have passed from the anonymity that surrounded the Indian concubines of Francisco de Barco, native of Ávila, or Juan Álvarez Chico, born in Fregenal . . .

Am I humiliating myself too much? Death authorizes me to say that it seems little compared to the humiliation and failure I felt then. Deprived of the desired female, I substituted the power of the tongue for her. But you've already seen how La Malinche took even that away from me even before the worms dined on it forever.

Cortés' cruelty was refined. He ordered me, since she and I spoke the Indian languages, to take it upon myself to communicate to her the truths and mysteries of our holy religion. The devil has never had a more unfortunate catechist.

[2]

I mean to say that I speak Spanish. It's time to confess that I had to relearn it, because after eight years among the Indians I almost lost it. Now with Cortés' troops, I rediscover my own language, the one that flowed toward my lips from my Castilian mother's breasts. And I quickly learned Mexican, so I could speak to the Aztecs. La Malinche was always one step ahead of me.

The persistent question, nevertheless, is a different one: Did I rediscover myself when I returned to the company and language of the Spaniards?

When they found me among the Indians of Yucatán they thought I was an Indian.

This is how they saw me: dark, hair cropped short, an oar on my shoulder, wearing ancient sandals long beyond repair, an old, ruinous shirt, and a loincloth to cover my shame.

Thus they saw me then: sunburned, my long hair a tangle, my beard shaved off with arrows, my sex old and uncertain under my loincloth, my old shoes, and my lost tongue.

Cortés, as was his custom, gave precise orders to overcome any doubt or obstacle. He ordered me dressed in shirt and doublet, breeches, pointed cap, and hemp sandals, and ordered me to tell how I came to that place. I told him as simply as I could:

"I was born in Écija. Eight years ago, fifteen men and two women, making our way from Darien to the island of Santo Domingo, got lost. Our captains fought each other over money matters, since we were carrying ten thousand gold pesos from Panama to La Española, and the ship, with no one at the helm, smashed against some reefs in Los Alacranes. My comrades and I abandoned our incompetent, unfaithful leaders, taking the lifeboat from the wrecked ship. We thought we were heading toward Cuba, but the heavy currents pushed us far from there toward this land called Yucatán."

At that instant, I could not keep from looking toward a man whose face was tattooed, and whose ears and lower lip were pierced with plugs, surrounded by his wife and three children, whose eyes were begging me for what I already knew. I went on, turning my eyes back to Cortés and seeing that he saw everything.

"Ten men reached this place. Nine were killed, and only I survived. Why did they leave me alive? I'll go to my grave not knowing. There are mysteries it's better not to inquire into. This is one of them . . . Imagine a shipwrecked man, almost drowned, naked, and washed up on a beach as hard as mortar, with a single hut and in it a dog that did not bark when it saw me. Perhaps that saved me, because I sought protection in that shelter while the dog went out to bark at my shipmates, provoking the alarm and attack of the Indians. When they found me hidden in the hut, with the dog licking my hand, they laughed and joked. The dog wagged his tail with joy, and I was taken, not with honors but with camaraderie, to the cluster of primitive huts erected next to the great pyramidal constructions now covered with vegetation . . .

"Ever since, I've been useful. I've helped to build. I've helped them plant their poor crops. But I also planted the seeds of an orange tree that came, along with a sack of wheat and a cask of red wine, in the lifeboat that tossed us up on these shores."

Cortés asked me about my other comrades, staring fixedly at the Indian with the tattooed face accompanied by a woman and three children.

"You haven't told me what happened to your comrades."

In an attempt to distract Cortés' insistent gaze, I went on with my story, which I didn't want to do, finding myself obliged to say what I then told.

"The chiefs in the area divided us among them."

"There were ten. I see only you."

Again I fell into the trap: "Most were sacrificed to the idols."

"And what about the women?"

"They died. The Indians made them grind corn, and they weren't used to spending that much time on their knees in the sun."

"And what about you?"

"They kept me as a slave. All I do is bring in firewood and weed the cornfields."

"Want to come with us . . . ?"

Cortés asked me that, again staring at the Indian with the tattooed face.

"Jerónimo de Aguilar, born in Écija," I blurted out hastily to distract the captain's attention.

Cortés walked over to the Indian with the tattooed face, smiled at him, and patted the head of one of the children, who had curly blond hair despite his dark skin and black eyes. "Cannibalism, slavery, and barbarous customs," said Cortés, staring directly at my unrecognizable companion. "Do you want to stay in this life?"

My only concern was to distract him, capture his attention. As luck would have it, in my old mantle I'd kept one of the oranges, the fruit of the tree Guerrero and I planted here. I showed it to him as if for a moment I was the King of Coins in our Spanish playing cards: I had the sun in my hands. Could any image verify a Spaniard's identity better than the sight of a man eating an orange? I sank my teeth avidly into the skin until they found the hidden flesh of the orange, her flesh, the woman-fruit, the feminine fruit. The juice ran down my chin. I laughed, as if saying to Cortés, What better proof could you want that I'm a Spaniard?

The captain didn't answer me, merely expressing his pleasure that oranges could grow here. He asked me if *we* had brought it, and I, to distract his attention, which was fixed on the unrecognizable Guerrero, said we had, but that in these lands the oranges were larger, not as highly colored, and more bitter, almost like grapefruit. I told the Mayas to gather a sack of orange seeds for the Spanish captain, but he insisted on asking that same question again, staring fixedly at the imperturbable Guerrero: "Do you want to stay in this life?"

He said it to the man with the tattooed face, but I quickly answered that I didn't, that I renounced living among these pagans and would be delighted to join the Spanish troops to wipe out all abominable customs or beliefs and to implant our Holy Religion here . . . Cortés laughed and stopped patting the child's head. He told me then that since I spoke the language of the natives and a bad but comprehensible Spanish, I would join him as his interpreter to translate from Spanish to Maya and from Maya to Castilian. He turned his back on the Indian with the tattooed face.

I had promised my friend Gonzalo Guerrero, the other survivor of the shipwreck, that I wouldn't reveal his identity. It was, in any case, difficult to discern. His tattooed face and pierced ears. His Indian wife. And the three mestizo children Cortés patted on the head and stared at with such prolonged curiosity.

"Brother Aguilar," Guerrero said when the Spaniards arrived. "I'm married, I have three children, and among these people I'm a chief and captain in war. You go your way, but my face is tattooed and my ears pierced. What would the Spaniards say if they saw me this way? And you can see how adorable my children are, and how sweet my woman is . . ."

She scolded me angrily, telling me to go away with the Spaniards and to leave her husband in peace . . .

I had no other intention. It was indispensable that Gonzalo Guerrero remain here so that my own grand enterprise of discovery and conquest be carried out. Ever since we'd arrived here eight years before, Guerrero and I had taken great pleasure in seeing the great Mayan towers at night, when they seemed to come back to life and reveal in the moonlight the exquisite carved script that Guerrero, who came from Palos, said he'd seen in Arab mosques and even in the recently reconquered Granada. But during the day, the sun whitened the great structures to a blinding degree, and life concentrated in the minutia of fires, resin, dyes, and washing, the crying of children, the savory taste of raw deer meat: the life of the village that lived right next to the dead temples.

We entered into that life in a natural way. It's true, of course, that we had no other prospects, but most of all it was the sweetness and dignity of these people that conquered us. They had so little and yet wanted no more. They never told us what had happened to the inhabitants of the splendid cities that resembled biblical descriptions of Babylon and watched over the details of everyday life in the village; we felt it was a kind of respect reserved for the dead.

Only little by little did we learn, connecting bits and pieces of stories here and there as we acquired the language of our captors, that once there were great powers here, which, like all great powers, depended on the weakness of the people and needed to fight other strong nations to convince themselves of their power. We were able to deduce that the Indian nations destroyed each other while the weak people survived, stronger than the strong. The greatness of power fell; the small lives of the people survived. Why? We'll have time to understand why.

Guerrero, as I said, married an Indian and had three children. He was a seaman and had worked in the Palos shipyards. So when the expedition led by Francisco Hernández de Córdoba came to this land a year before Cortés, Guerrero organized the Indian counterattack that caused the calamitous defeat of the expedition right on the coast. Thanks to that, he was raised to the rank of chief and captain, becoming part of the defensive organization of these Indians. Thanks to that as well, he decided to stay among them when I left with Cortés.

Why did Cortés leave him when he'd guessed—his facial expressions all revealed it—who Guerrero was? Perhaps, I later thought, because he didn't want to bring a traitor along. He could have killed him right then and there: but then he couldn't have counted on peace and the good will of the Catoche Mayas. Perhaps he thought it was better to abandon Guerrero to a destiny devoid of destiny: the barbarous wars of sacrifice. But it's also true that Cortés liked to postpone revenge, just to enjoy it more.

In any case, he brought me with him without suspecting that I was the real traitor. Because if I went with Cortés and Guerrero stayed behind in Yucatán, it was by mutual agreement. We wanted to ensure, I with the foreigners and Guerrero among the Indians, that the Indian world would triumph over the European world. I will tell you briefly, with the little breath left to me, why.

While I lived among the Maya, I remained celibate, as if I were waiting for a woman who would be perfectly mine, who would complement my character, passion, and tenderness. I fell in love with my new people, with their simple way of dealing with the matters of life, letting the daily necessities of life take care of themselves naturally but without diminishing the importance of serious things. Above all, they took care of their land, their air, their precious, scarce water hidden in deep wells: this plain of Yucatán has no visible rivers but is crisscrossed by underground streams.

Taking care of the land was their fundamental mission; they were the servants of the land—that's why they'd been born. Their magic stories, their ceremonies, their prayers, I realized, had no other purpose than to keep the land alive and fertile, to honor the ancestors who had in their turn kept it alive, inherited it, and had passed it quickly on, abundant or scanty, but alive, to their descendants.

Endless obligation, long succession, which at first could have seemed to us an eternally repetitive labor of ants, until we realized that doing what they did was its own reward. It was the

Indians' daily offering: in serving nature, they created themselves. It's true: they lived in order to survive; but they also lived so the world would go on feeding their descendants when they died. Death for them was the price for the life of their descendants.

Birth and death therefore were equal celebrations for these natives, events equally worthy of joy and honor. I shall always remember the first funeral ceremony we attended, because in it we discerned a celebration of origins and the continuity of all things, identical to what we celebrate when born. Death, proclaimed the faces, gestures, musical rhythms, is the source of life, death is the first birth. We come from death. We cannot be born unless someone dies for our sake, for us.

They owned nothing, but held everything in common. But there were wars, rivalries incomprehensible for us, as if our innocence deserved only the bounty of peace and not the cruelty of war. Guerrero, spurred on by his wife, decided to take part in the wars among the nations, admitting he did not understand them. But once he'd shown his ability as a shipwright in repelling Hernández de Córdoba's expedition, his desire and mine—the art of making boats and the art of ordering words—joined forces and silently swore an oath, with a shared intelligence and a definite goal . . .

[1]

Little by little—it took us eight years to discover it—Gonzalo Guerrero and I, Jerónimo de Aguilar, gathered enough information to divine (we'd never know it for certain) the destiny of the Mayan peoples, the proximity of fallen grandeur and surviving misery. Why did greatness collapse, why did misery survive?

During those eight years, we saw the fragility of the land and wondered, both of us after all sons of Castilian or Andalusian farmers, how the life of the great abandoned cities could be sustained by such meager soil and such impenetrable forests. We had the answers of our own ancestors: Exploit the riches of the forest lightly, exploit the riches of the plains well, and take care of both. This had been the behavior of the peasants since time immemorial. When it coincided with the behavior of the dynasties, Yucatán lived. When the dynasties put the greatness of power above the greatness of life, the thin soil and the thick forest could not produce enough to meet the demands of kings, priests, warriors, and bureaucrats. Then came wars, the abandonment of the land, the flight to the cities at first and then from the cities later. The land could no longer sustain power. Power fell. The land remained. Those who remained had no power other than the land.

Words remained.

In their public ceremonies, but also in their private prayers, they incessantly repeated the following story:

The world was created by two gods, one named Heart of Heaven and the other named Heart of Earth. When they met, between them they made all things fertile by naming them. They named the earth, and the earth was made. Creation, as it was named, dissolved and multiplied, calling itself by turns fog, cloud, or whirlwind of dust. Named, the mountains shot from the depths of the sea, magic valleys formed, and in them grew pines and cypresses.

The gods filled with joy when they divided the waters and caused the animals to be born. But none of this possessed the same thing which had created it: language. Mist, ocelot, pine, and water: silent. Then the gods decided to create the only beings capable of speaking and of naming all things created by the word of the gods.

And so people were born, with the purpose of sustaining divine creation day by day by means of the same thing that brought forth the earth, the sky, and all things in them: language. When we understood these things, Guerrero and I understood that the real greatness of these people was not in their magnificent temples or their deeds in war but in the most humble vocation of repeating in every minute, in every activity in life, the greatest and most heroic thing of all, which was the creation of the world by the gods.

From then on, we strove to strengthen that mission and to restore to our native Spanish earth the time, beauty, candor, and humanity we found among these Indians . . . Language was the double power shared by gods and men. We found out that the fall of the empires liberated language and men from a falsified servitude. Poor, clean, owners of their words, the Maya could renew their lives and those of the entire world beyond the sea . . .

In the place called Bay of the Bad Fight, the very place where Gonzalo Guerrero's knowledge allowed the Indians to defeat the Spaniards, forests were leveled, planks sawed, hardware manufactured, and the frameworks raised for our Indian fleet . . .

From my Mexican tomb, I encouraged my comrade, the other surviving Spaniard, to answer conquest with conquest. I failed in my attempt to make Cortés fail; you, Gonzalo, must not fail. Do what you swore to me you would do. Look: I'm watching you from my bed in the ancient lake of Tenochtitlán, the fifty-eight times named Jerónimo de Aguilar, the man who was the transitory master of words who lost them in an unequal fight with a woman . . .

[0]

All this I saw. The fall of the great Andalusian city in the moan of the conch shells, the clash of steel against flint, and the fire of Mayan flamethrowers. I saw the burnt water of the Guadalquivir and the burning of the Tower of Gold.

The temples fell, from Cádiz to Seville; the standards, the towers, the trophies. And the day after the defeat, using the stones of the Giralda, we began to build the temple of the four religions, inscribed with the word of Christ, Mohammed, Abraham, and Quetzalcoatl, where all the powers of imagination and language would have their place, without exception, lasting perhaps as long as the names of the thousand gods of a world suddenly animated by the encounter of everything forgotten, prohibited, mutilated . . .

We committed a few crimes, it's true. We gave the members of the Holy Inquisition a taste of their own medicine, burning them in the public plazas, from Logroño to Barcelona and from Oviedo to Córdoba . . . We also burned their archives, along with the laws about purity of blood and being "old Christians," and if some convents (and their tenants) were violated, the ultimate result was an increased mixing of bloods—Indian and Spanish but also Arab and Jew—that in a few years crossed the Pyrenees and spread over all of Europe . . . The complexion of the old continent quickly became darker, as that of southern, Arabian Spain already was.

We revoked the edicts of expulsion for Jews and Moors. They returned with the frozen keys of the houses they'd abandoned in Toledo and Seville in order to unlock once again the wooden doors and to put back into their clothespresses, with burning hands, the old prayer of their love for Spain, the cruel mother who expelled them and whom they, the children of Israel, never stopped loving despite all her cruelties . . . And the return of the Moors filled the air with songs sometimes deep, like a sexual moan, sometimes high, like the voice of the muezzin punctually calling the faithful to prayer. Sweet Mayan songs joined those of the Provençal troubadours, the flute joined the cittern, the flageolet joined the mandolin, and from the sea near the Port of Santa María emerged sirens of all colors who had accompanied us from the islands of the Caribbean . . . All those of us who contributed to the Indian conquest of Spain immediately felt that a universe simultaneously new and recovered, permeable, complex, and fertile, had been born from the contact among the cultures, frustrating the fatal, purifying plan of the Catholic Kings, Ferdinand and Isabella.

But don't think the discovery of Spain by the Maya was an idyll. We could not restrain the religious atavism of some of our captains. The fact is, however, that the Spaniards sacrificed at the altars of Valladolid and Burgos, in the plazas of Cáceres and Jaén, had the honor of dying in a cosmic rite and not in one of those street fights so common in Spain. Or, to use a more gastronomic image: they might have died of indigestion just as well. It's true that this rationale was badly understood by all the humanists, poets, philosophers, and Spanish Erasmists, who at the beginning celebrated our arrival, considering it a liberation, but who are now wondering if they haven't simply exchanged the oppression of the Catholic Kings for that of some bloody popes and Indian chiefs . . .

But you will ask me, Jerónimo de Aguilar, born in Écija, dead of buboes when the Great Tenochtitlán fell, and who now accompanies, like a distant star, my friend and comrade Gonzalo Guerrero, native of Palos, in the conquest of Spain: What was our main weapon?

And while we'd have to mention an army of two thousand Maya which sailed from the Bay of the Bad Fight in Yucatán, joined by squadrons of Carib sailors recruited and trained by Guerrero in Cuba, Borinquén, Caicos, and Great Abaco, we would immediately have to add another reason.

Disembarked in Cádiz, amid the most absolute astonishment, we gave the same answer (you've already guessed) as that of the Indians in Mexico: surprise.

Except that in Mexico, the Spaniards—that is, the white, bearded, and blond gods—were expected. Here, on the other hand, no one expected anyone. The surprise was total, because all the gods were already in Spain. The fact is they'd been forgotten. The Indians managed to reanimate the Spanish gods, and the greatest surprise, which I share with you today, readers of this manuscript which we two shipwrecked Spaniards abandoned for eight years on the Yucatán coast have stitched together, is that you are reading these memoirs in the Spanish language of Cortés, which Marina, La Malinche, had to learn, and not in the Maya language that Marina had to forget or in the Mexican language which I had to learn to communicate in secret with the great but apathetic king Moctezuma.

The reason is obvious. The Spanish language had already learned to speak in Phoenician, Greek, Latin, Arabic, and Hebrew; it was ready now to receive Mayan and Aztec contributions, to enrich itself with them, to enrich them, give them flexibility, imagination, communicability, and writing, turning them into living languages, not the languages of empires but the languages of people and their encounters, infections, dreams, and nightmares as well.

Perhaps Hernán Cortés himself suspected it, and for that reason dissimulated his feelings the day he discovered Guerrero and me living among the Maya, dark, hair cropped short, an oar on my shoulder, wearing one ancient sandal with the other tied around my waist, an old, ruinous shirt, and a loincloth in even worse condition; Guerrero with his tattooed face and pierced ears . . . Perhaps, as if he'd guessed our destiny, the Spanish captain left Guerrero among the Indians so that one day he'd attempt his enterprise, a copy of his own, and conquer Spain with the same spirit Cortés conquered Mexico, which was that of bringing another civilization to one he considered admirable but stained here and there with excesses: sacrifice and fire, oppression and repression, humanity sacrificed to the power of the strong under the pretext of the gods . . . Once Hernán Cortés himself had been sacrificed to the game of political ambition, necessarily reduced to impotence so that no conquistador would ever dream of placing himself above the power of the Crown, and humiliated by the mediocre, suffocated by the bureaucracy, rewarded with money and titles when his ambition had been exterminated, did Hernán Cortés have the brilliant intuition that if he pardoned Gonzalo Guerrero, Gonzalo would return with a Mayan and Carib armada to get revenge for him in his native land?

I don't know. Because Hernán Cortés, for all his malicious intelligence, always lacked that magic imagination which, on the one hand, was the weakness of the Indian world, but, on the other, might someday be its strength: its contribution to the future, its resurrection . . .

I say this because while accompanying Gonzalo Guerrero with my soul from the Bahamas to Cádiz, I myself became a star so I could make the voyage. My ancient light (all luminous stars, I now know, are dead stars) is only that of my questions.

What would have happened if what did happen didn't?

What would have happened if what did not happen did?

I speak and ask questions from death because I suspect that my friend, the other shipwrecked Spaniard, Gonzalo Guerrero, was too busy fighting and conquering. He doesn't have time to tell stories. More to the point: he refuses to tell stories. He has to act, decide, order, punish . . . On the other hand, from death, I have all the time in the world to tell stories. Even (especially) stories about the deeds of my friend Guerrero in this affair of the conquest of Spain.

I fear for him and for the action he has undertaken with such success. I wonder if an event that isn't narrated takes place in reality. Because what isn't invented is only chronicled. Moreover, a catastrophe (all wars are catastrophes) is disputed only if it's told. The telling outlasts the war. The telling disputes the order of things. Silence only confirms that order.

Which is why, in telling, I necessarily wonder where the order is, the moral, the law in all this.

I don't know. Nor does my brother Guerrero, because I've infected him with a painful dream. He goes to bed in his new headquarters, the Alcazar in Seville, and his nights are unquiet because the painful gaze of the last Aztec king, Guatemuz, pierces them like a ghost. A cloud of blood covers his eyes. Whenever he feels his vision blur, he lowers his eyelids. One is made of gold, the other silver.

When he wakes up, weeping over the fate of the Aztec nation, he realizes that instead of tears, down one cheek ran gold and down the other silver, cutting a furrow in them as a knife would, leaving a permanent wound in them which, may it please God, death has healed.

This, I realize, is a doubtful thing. On the other hand, my only certitude, you see, is that language and words triumphed on the two shores. I know because the form of this tale is like a countdown, which has been associated too often with mortal explosions, overcoming a rival in the ring, or apocalyptic events. I'd like to use it today, beginning with ten and ending with zero, to indicate instead a perpetual rebeginning of stories perpetually unfinished, but only on condition that they are presided over, as in the Mayan story of the gods of Heaven and Earth, by language.

That is perhaps the true star that crosses the sea and links the two shores. The Spaniards—I must clarify this point while I still have time—did not understand it at first. When I reached Seville mounted on my verbal star, they confused its fleetingness and its light with that of a terrible bird, the combination of all the birds of prey that fly in the deepest obscurity, but less frightening in their flight than in their *landing,* their ability to drag themselves along the earth with the mercurial destruction of a poison: a vulture in the skies, a serpent on the ground, this mythological being that flew over Seville and dragged itself over Estremadura, blinded the saints, and seduced the demons of Spain, frightening all with its newness, was, like the Spanish horses in Mexico, invincible.

Transformed into a monster, this beast was, nevertheless, only a word. And the word unfolds, made of scales in the air, made of feathers on earth, like a single question: How long before the present arrives?

Twin sister of God, twin sister of man: over the lake of Mexico, along the river of Seville, the eyelids of the sun and the moon open at the same time. Our faces are streaked by fire, but at the same time our tongues are furrowed by memory and desire. The words live on the two shores. And they do not heal. ᴄᴖ

Interpretive Questions
for Discussion

Why does Jerónimo de Aguilar attempt to use "the power of words" to ensure that the Indian world will triumph over the European world?

1. Why does Aguilar say that, in defeating Moctezuma, the Spaniards killed not only the power of the Indians, but also the magic surrounding it? (66) Why does Aguilar regard "magic imagination" as both the weakness of the Indian world and its potential strength? (99)

2. Why are both Aguilar and Guerrero troubled by the memory of Guatemuz, the last emperor of the Aztecs, who, unlike his uncle Moctezuma, "fought like a hero"? (66, 100)

3. Why does Aguilar translate Cortés' peace offering to make Guatemuz the governor of Mexico and its provinces as a threat? Why, in response to the threat, do Guatemuz' tears change into streams of gold and silver that wound his cheeks permanently? (66–67)

4. Why does Aguilar say that, in mistranslating Cortés, he "merely confirmed the power of words"? Why is Aguilar not sure whether he has merely told the truth with his lies or made it inevitable? (67–68)

5. Why does Aguilar hate himself for betraying Cortés? Why does he hate himself even more for his "inferiority in the arts of dissimulation, trickery, and dramatic pauses"? (74)

6. Why does Aguilar doubt that the Spaniards understood of Moctezuma "how alien to him treacherous political machinations were, and how natural, by contrast, was the proximity of a religious world impenetrable to Europeans"? Why does Aguilar think of Moctezuma as "the first man"? (76)

7. Why does Aguilar say that language "was power; and more than power, it was the very life that animated my plans, my own program of discovery, unique, surprising, unrepeatable"? (81)

8. Why is Aguilar horrified to think that the Indians would exchange a religion that demanded human sacrifice for one that allowed divine sacrifice? (83)

9. Why does Aguilar dream that together he and Marina, "owners of the languages, would also be owners of the lands, an invincible couple because we understood the two voices of Mexico, the voice of men and the voice of the gods"? (86–87)

10. Why does Aguilar fall in love with his "new people" because "they took care of their land"? Why does he say that, "in serving nature, they created themselves"? (93–94)

11. Why does Aguilar see the destiny of the Mayan peoples as "the proximity of fallen grandeur and surviving misery"? Why does he contrast the simple folk of Mexico favorably with the greater civilizations of both the New World and Europe? (94–96)

12. Why does Aguilar say that "the real greatness" of the Indians "was not in their magnificent temples or their deeds in war but in the most humble vocation of repeating in every minute, in every activity in life, the greatest and most heroic thing of all, which was the creation of the world by the gods"? (95)

Suggested textual analyses

Pages 66–68: beginning, "From my grave, I try to judge things calmly;" and ending, "A woman was to blame."

Pages 93–96: beginning, "While I lived among the Maya," and ending, "and those of the entire world beyond the sea . . ."

Why are Moctezuma and Aguilar both defeated by Marina, "La Malinche"?

1. Why does Marina side with Cortés against her own people? Why does she, on her own initiative, flatteringly advise Moctezuma to cooperate with the Spanish? (73)

2. Why do the translators have more power than the principals in the encounters between the Spanish and the Indians? (67, 73, 84–85, 86–87)

3. Why does Aguilar conclude that Moctezuma's weakness was caused by losing control over words rather than men? Why does the realization that Marina owns a vocabulary forbidden to him convince Moctezuma that he is no longer sovereign? (73)

4. Why is Moctezuma unable to use the words given to him by Aguilar, words that could give him "more power than all the horses and harquebuses the Spaniards possessed, if the Aztec king would only decide to speak to his men, his people, instead of speaking to the gods"? (74)

5. When Aguilar attempts to use words, imagination, and lies to "frustrate the fatal plan" that will lead to Moctezuma's demise, why does he find that "when words, imagination, and lies jumble together, the result is the truth"? (75)

6. Why does Aguilar portray the triumph of Cortés over Moctezuma as the triumph of La Malinche over himself? Why does he say that he and Doña Marina "fought, truly fought, in the drama of Cholula"? (78)

7. Why does Aguilar regard La Malinche's learning to speak Spanish as a betrayal of both himself and Cortés? (79–80)

8. Why is Marina more successful than Aguilar in using words to manipulate both Cortés and Moctezuma?

9. Why is Marina willing to lie to Cortés to get what she wants? Why does she want "to make an example of Cholula to preclude future betrayals"? (82–84)

10. Why does Aguilar propose without speaking that he and Marina work together "to combat the fatality" of the Spanish invasion? (86)

11. Why does Marina disrobe before Aguilar? Why does she appear to him in her nakedness as "svelte and massive, heavy and ethereal, animal and human, sane and insane . . . as if she were not only inseparable from the earth that surrounded her but also its summary and symbol"? (86)

12. Why does Aguilar see Marina, abandoned by Cortés and stigmatized by her people with the mark of betrayal, as "mother and origin of a new nation, which perhaps could only be born and grow against the charges of abandonment, illegitimacy, and betrayal"? (87) Are we meant to think of Marina as a heroic figure or as a traitor to her people?

Suggested textual analyses

Pages 73–78: beginning, "Once again, it was the interpreter Doña Marina who decided the struggle," and ending, "Then came the defeat I've already told of."

Pages 82–87: beginning, "Marina told Cortés:" and ending, "against the charges of abandonment, illegitimacy, and betrayal. . . ."

Why does the author conclude his history-based story of the Spanish conquest of Mexico with the fantasy of the Mayan conquest of Spain?

1. Why does the author make his narrator the ghost of Jerónimo de Aguilar, a minor member of Cortés' entourage? Why does Aguilar say that from the Olympian vantage point of death he sees "everything that's happened as the meeting of two old worlds"? (62)

2. Why does Aguilar say that neither the conquered nor the conquerors escaped unscathed from "this venture of discovery and conquest," and that both "should have built a new world after their shared defeat"? (62)

3. Why does Aguilar wonder whether, in mistranslating Cortés, he has rightly revealed the truth or inadvertently served as the intermediary of a fatal destiny? (67–68)

4. Why is Aguilar hopeful that Gonzalo Guerrero might succeed where he has failed? (96)

5. Why does the last section of the story begin with the same claim of eyewitness accuracy as the first, even though the first is historical and the last isn't? (96)

6. Why does the Indian conquest of Spain result in "a universe simultaneously new and recovered, permeable, complex, and fertile" that is "born from the contact among the cultures"? Why are we told nonetheless that the Indians commit their own crimes of cultural imperialism? (97–98)

7. Why is Aguilar against the triumph of the Spanish, but for the triumph of the Spanish language? (98–99)

8. Why does Aguilar say, "Things could always have happened exactly opposite to the way the chronicle records them. Always"? (63) Why is he troubled by wondering what would have happened if what did happen didn't and if what didn't happen did? (100)

9. Why does Aguilar point out that his friend Gonzalo Guerrero is too busy fighting and conquering to tell stories, whereas he himself, from death, has all the time in the world? (100)

10. Why does Aguilar say that "the telling disputes the order of things" but "silence only confirms that order"? Why does recognizing this make him wonder "where the order is, the moral, the law" in the story he has told? (100)

11. Why does Aguilar give his tale the form of a "countdown" that indicates "a perpetual rebeginning of stories perpetually unfinished" and "presided over . . . by language"? Why is this "perhaps the true star that crosses the sea and links the two shores"? (100–101)

12. Why does Aguilar say that "language and words triumphed on the two shores," yet they "do not heal"? (100–101)

Suggested textual analysis
Pages 96–101: from "All this I saw," to the end of the story.

For Further Reflection

1. Do you see the Spanish conquest of Mexico as a tragedy or as a painful but necessary step in the blending of two cultures?

2. Do you agree with the author's suggestion that imagination is as important as memory in the writing of history? Is history a kind of literature?

3. Is true power in the hands of those who control language and communication?

4. Is Aguilar right when he observes that power tends to decay and weakness survive in human culture?

5. Do you agree with Aguilar's suggestion that the highest calling of human beings is "repeating in every minute, in every activity of life, the greatest and most heroic thing of all . . . the creation of the world by the gods"?

6. Must one be removed from active life, like Solís and the deceased Aguilar, in order to contemplate stories about it and illuminate it with questions?

7. Do you agree with the author's suggestion that it was a good thing for the languages of Europe to become the languages of the New World?

The Souls of

Black Folk

(selection)

W. E. B. Du Bois

W. E. B. Du Bois (1868–1963),
historian, editor, writer, educator, civil rights
activist, and sociologist, was born in Great
Barrington, Massachusetts. Generally,
Du Bois had an idyllic childhood. He recalled
that in his small New England community
the color line was not sharply drawn—social
class and town roots seemed to be more
important than skin color. Du Bois was
educated at Fisk, Harvard, and the University
of Berlin and, in 1896, was the first African
American to receive a Ph.D. from Harvard.
Du Bois led the opposition to what he saw
as Booker T. Washington's philosophy of
accommodation to white supremacy and in
1909 cofounded the National Association
for the Advancement of Colored People.
During the McCarthy era, Du Bois was
charged with subversion, and, in 1961, he
renounced his United States citizenship.
Du Bois died two years later in Accra,
Ghana, where he is buried.

THE FORETHOUGHT

HEREIN LIE BURIED many things which if read with patience may show the strange meaning of being black here at the dawning of the twentieth century. This meaning is not without interest to you, gentle reader; for the problem of the twentieth century is the problem of the color line. I pray you, then, receive my little book in all charity, studying my words with me, forgiving mistake and foible for sake of the faith and passion that is in me, and seeking the grain of truth hidden there.

I have sought here to sketch, in vague, uncertain outline, the spiritual world in which ten thousand thousand Americans live and strive. [. . .] Before each chapter, as now printed, stands a bar of the Sorrow Songs—some echo of haunting melody from the only American music which welled up from black souls in the dark past. And, finally, need I add that I who speak here am bone of the bone and flesh of the flesh of them that live within the Veil?

Atlanta, Georgia, February 1, 1903   W. E. B. Du Bois

OF OUR SPIRITUAL STRIVINGS

O water, voice of my heart, crying in the sand,
   All night long crying with a mournful cry,
As I lie and listen, and cannot understand
     The voice of my heart in my side or the voice
       of the sea,
   O water, crying for rest, is it I, is it I?
   All night long the water is crying to me.

Unresting water, there shall never be rest
   Till the last moon droop and the last tide fail,
And the fire of the end begin to burn in the west;
     And the heart shall be weary and wonder and cry
      like the sea,
   All life long crying without avail,
   As the water all night long is crying to me.

ARTHUR SYMONS

Between me and the other world there is ever an unasked question: unasked by some through feelings of delicacy; by others through the difficulty of rightly framing it. All, nevertheless, flutter round it. They approach me in a half-hesitant sort of way, eye me curiously or compassionately, and then, instead of saying directly, How does it feel to be a problem? they say, I know an excellent colored man in my town; or, I fought at Mechanicsville; or, Do not these Southern outrages make your blood boil? At these I smile, or am interested, or reduce the boiling to a simmer, as the occasion may require. To the real question, How does it feel to be a problem? I answer seldom a word.

And yet, being a problem is a strange experience—peculiar even for one who has never been anything else, save perhaps in babyhood and in Europe. It is in the early days of rollicking boyhood that the revelation first bursts upon one, all in a day, as it were. I remember well when the shadow swept across me. I was a little thing, away up in the hills of New England, where the dark Housatonic winds between Hoosac and Taghkanic to the sea. In a wee wooden schoolhouse, something put it into the boys' and girls' heads to buy gorgeous visiting cards—ten cents a package—and exchange. The exchange was merry, till one girl, a tall newcomer, refused my card—refused it peremptorily, with a glance. Then it dawned upon me with a certain suddenness that I was different from the others; or like, mayhap, in heart and life and longing, but shut out from their world by a vast veil. I had thereafter no desire to tear down that veil, to creep through; I held all beyond it in common contempt, and lived above it in a region of blue sky and great wandering shadows. That sky was bluest when I could beat my mates at examination time, or beat them at a foot race, or even beat their stringy heads. Alas, with the years all this fine contempt began to fade; for the worlds I longed for, and all their dazzling opportunities, were theirs, not mine. But they should not keep these prizes, I said; some, all, I would wrest from them. Just how I would do it I could never decide: by reading law, by healing the sick, by telling the wonderful tales that swam in my head—some way. With other black boys the strife was not so fiercely sunny: their youth shrunk into tasteless sycophancy, or into silent hatred of the pale world about them and mocking distrust of everything white; or wasted itself in a bitter cry, Why did God make me an outcast and a stranger in mine own house? The shades of the prison house closed round about us all: walls strait and stubborn to the whitest, but relentlessly narrow, tall, and unscalable to sons of night who must plod darkly on in resignation, or beat unavailing palms against the stone, or steadily, half hopelessly, watch the streak of blue above.

After the Egyptian and Indian, the Greek and Roman, the Teuton and Mongolian, the Negro is a sort of seventh son, born with a veil, and gifted with second sight in this American world—a world which yields him no true self-consciousness, but only lets him see himself through the revelation of the other world. It is a peculiar sensation, this double-consciousness, this sense of always looking at one's self through the eyes of others, of measuring one's soul by the tape of a world that looks on in amused contempt and pity. One ever feels his twoness—an American, a Negro; two souls, two thoughts, two unreconciled strivings; two warring ideals in one dark body, whose dogged strength alone keeps it from being torn asunder.

The history of the American Negro is the history of this strife—this longing to attain self-conscious manhood, to merge his double self into a better and truer self. In this merging he wishes neither of the older selves to be lost. He would not Africanize America, for America has too much to teach the world and Africa. He would not bleach his Negro soul in a flood of white Americanism, for he knows that Negro blood has a message for the world. He simply wishes to make it possible for a man to be both a Negro and an American, without being cursed and spit upon by his fellows, without having the doors of Opportunity closed roughly in his face.

This, then, is the end of his striving; to be a coworker in the kingdom of culture, to escape both death and isolation, to husband and use his best powers and his latent genius. These powers of body and mind have in the past been strangely wasted, dispersed, or forgotten. The shadow of a mighty Negro past flits through the tale of Ethiopia the Shadowy and of Egypt the Sphinx. Throughout history, the powers of single black men flash here and there like falling stars, and die sometimes before the world has rightly gauged their brightness. Here in America, in the few days since Emancipation, the black man's turning hither and thither in hesitant and doubtful striving has often made his very strength to lose effectiveness, to seem like absence of power, like weakness. And yet it is not weakness—it is the contradiction of double aims. The double-aimed struggle of the black artisan—on the one hand to escape white contempt for a nation of mere hewers of wood and drawers of water, and on the other hand to plough and nail and dig for a poverty-stricken horde—could only result in making him a poor craftsman, for he had but half a heart in either cause. By the poverty and ignorance of his people, the Negro minister or doctor was tempted toward quackery and demagogy; and by the criticism of the other world, toward ideals that made him ashamed of his lowly tasks. The would-be black savant was confronted by the paradox that the knowledge his people needed was a twice-told tale to his white neighbors, while the knowledge which would teach the white world was Greek to his own flesh and blood. The innate love of harmony and beauty that set the ruder souls of his people a-dancing and a-singing raised but confusion and doubt in the soul of the black artist; for the beauty revealed to him was the soul-beauty of a race which his larger audience despised, and he could not articulate the message of another people. This waste of double aims, this seeking to satisfy two unreconciled ideals, has wrought sad havoc with the courage and faith and deeds of ten thousand thousand people—has sent them often wooing false gods and invoking false means of salvation, and at times has even seemed about to make them ashamed of themselves.

Away back in the days of bondage they thought to see in one divine event the end of all doubt and disappointment; few men ever worshipped Freedom with half such unquestioning faith as did the American Negro for two centuries. To him, so far as he thought and dreamed, slavery was indeed the sum of all villainies, the cause of all sorrow, the root of all prejudice; Emancipation was the key to a promised land of sweeter beauty than ever stretched before the eyes of wearied Israelites. In song and exhortation swelled one refrain—Liberty; in his tears and curses the God he implored had Freedom in his right hand. At last it came—suddenly, fearfully, like a dream. With one wild carnival of blood and passion came the message in his own plaintive cadences:

Shout, O children!
Shout, you're free!
For God has bought your liberty!

Years have passed away since then—ten, twenty, forty; forty years of national life, forty years of renewal and development, and yet the swarthy specter sits in its accustomed seat at the Nation's feast. In vain do we cry to this our vastest social problem:

Take any shape but that, and my firm nerves
Shall never tremble!

The Nation has not yet found peace from its sins; the freedman has not yet found in freedom his promised land. Whatever of good may have come in these years of change, the shadow of a deep disappointment rests upon the Negro people—a disappointment all the more bitter because the unattained ideal was unbounded save by the simple ignorance of a lowly people.

The first decade was merely a prolongation of the vain search for freedom, the boon that seemed ever barely to elude their grasp—like a tantalizing will-o'-the-wisp, maddening and misleading the headless host. The holocaust of war, the terrors of the Ku Klux Klan, the lies of carpetbaggers, the disorganization of industry, and the contradictory advice of friends and foes, left the bewildered serf with no new watchword beyond the old cry for freedom. As the time flew, however, he began to grasp a new idea. The ideal of liberty demanded for its attainment powerful means, and these the Fifteenth Amendment gave him. The ballot, which before he had looked upon as a visible sign of freedom, he now regarded as the chief means of gaining and perfecting the liberty with which war had partially endowed him. And why not? Had not votes made war and emancipated millions? Had not votes enfranchised the freedmen? Was anything impossible to a power that had done all this? A million black men started with renewed zeal to vote themselves into the kingdom. So the decade flew away, the revolution of 1876 came, and left the half-free serf weary, wondering, but still inspired. Slowly but steadily, in the following years, a new vision began gradually to replace the dream of political power—a powerful movement, the rise of another ideal to guide the unguided, another pillar of fire by night after a clouded day. It was the ideal of "book learning"; the curiosity, born of compulsory ignorance, to know and test the power of the cabalistic letters of the white man, the longing to know. Here at last seemed to have been discovered the mountain path to Canaan; longer than the highway of Emancipation and law, steep and rugged, but straight, leading to heights high enough to overlook life.

Up the new path the advance guard toiled, slowly, heavily, doggedly; only those who have watched and guided the faltering feet, the misty minds, the dull understandings of the dark pupils of these schools know how faithfully, how piteously, this people strove to learn. It was weary work. The cold statistician wrote down the inches of progress here and there, noted also where here and there a foot had slipped or someone had fallen. To the tired climbers, the horizon was ever dark, the mists were often cold, the Canaan was always dim and far away. If, however, the vistas disclosed as yet no goal, no resting place, little but flattery and criticism, the journey at least gave leisure for reflection and self-examination; it changed the child of Emancipation to the youth with dawning self-consciousness, self-realization, self-respect. In those somber forests of his striving his own soul rose before him, and he saw himself—darkly as through a veil; and yet he saw in himself some faint revelation of his power, of his mission. He began to have a dim feeling that, to attain his place in the world, he must be himself, and not another. For the first time he sought to analyze the burden he bore upon his back, that deadweight of social degradation partially masked behind a half-named Negro problem. He felt his poverty; without a cent, without a home, without land, tools, or savings, he had entered into competition with rich, landed, skilled neighbors. To be a poor man is hard, but to be a poor race in a land of dollars is the very bottom of hardships. He felt the weight of his ignorance—not simply of letters, but of life, of business, of the humanities; the accumulated sloth and shirking and awkwardness of decades and centuries shackled his hands and feet. Nor was his burden all poverty and ignorance. The red stain of bastardy, which two centuries of systemic legal defilement of Negro women had stamped upon his race, meant not only the loss of ancient African chastity, but also the hereditary weight of a mass of corruption from white adulterers, threatening almost the obliteration of the Negro home.

A people thus handicapped ought not to be asked to race with the world, but rather allowed to give all its time and thought to its own social problems. But alas! while sociologists gleefully count his bastards and his prostitutes, the very soul of the toiling, sweating black man is darkened by the shadow of a vast despair. Men call the shadow prejudice, and learnedly explain it as the natural defense of culture against barbarism, learning against ignorance, purity against crime, the "higher" against the "lower" races. To which the Negro cries Amen! and swears that to so much of this strange prejudice as is founded on just homage to civilization, culture, righteousness, and progress, he humbly bows and meekly does obeisance. But before that nameless prejudice that leaps beyond all this he stands helpless, dismayed, and well-nigh speechless; before that personal disrespect and mockery, the ridicule and systematic humiliation, the distortion of fact and wanton license of fancy, the cynical ignoring of the better and the boisterous welcoming of the worse, the all-pervading desire to inculcate disdain for everything black, from Toussaint to the devil—before this there rises a sickening despair that would disarm and discourage any nation save that black host to whom "discouragement" is an unwritten word.

But the facing of so vast a prejudice could not but bring the inevitable self-questioning, self-disparagement, and lowering of ideals which ever accompany repression and breed in an atmosphere of contempt and hate. Whispering and portents came borne upon the four winds: Lo! we are diseased and dying, cried the dark hosts; we cannot write, our voting is vain; what need of education, since we must always cook and serve? And the Nation echoed and enforced this self-criticism, saying: Be content to be servants, and nothing more; what need of higher culture for half-men? Away with the black man's ballot, by force or fraud—and behold the suicide of a race! Nevertheless, out of the evil came something of good—the more careful adjustment of education to real life, the clearer perception of the Negroes' social responsibilities, and the sobering realization of the meaning of progress.

So dawned the time of Sturm und Drang: storm and stress today rocks our little boat on the mad waters of the world sea; there is within and without the sound of conflict, the burning of body and rending of soul; inspiration strives with doubt, and faith with vain questionings. The bright ideals of the past— physical freedom, political power, the training of brains and the training of hands—all these in turn have waxed and waned, until even the last grows dim and overcast. Are they all wrong— all false? No, not that, but each alone was oversimple and incomplete—the dreams of a credulous race-childhood, or the fond imaginings of the other world which does not know and does not want to know our power. To be really true, all these ideals must be melted and welded into one. The training of the schools we need today more than ever—the training of deft hands, quick eyes and ears, and above all the broader, deeper, higher culture of gifted minds and pure hearts. The power of the ballot we need in sheer self-defense—else what shall save us from a second slavery? Freedom, too, the long-sought, we still seek—the freedom of life and limb, the freedom to work and think, the freedom to love and aspire. Work, culture, liberty— all these we need, not singly but together, not successively but together, each growing and aiding each, and all striving toward that vaster ideal that swims before the Negro people, the ideal of human brotherhood, gained through the unifying ideal of Race; the ideal of fostering and developing the traits and talents of the Negro, not in opposition to or contempt for other races, but rather in large conformity to the greater ideals of the American Republic, in order that some day on American soil two world-races may give each to each those characteristics both so sadly lack. We the darker ones come even now not altogether empty-handed: there are today no truer exponents of the pure human spirit of the Declaration of Independence than the American Negroes; there is no true American music but the wild sweet melodies of the Negro slave; the American fairy tales and folklore are Indian and African; and, all in all, we black men seem the sole oasis of simple faith and reverence in a dusty desert of dollars and smartness. Will America be poorer if she replace her brutal dyspeptic blundering with light-hearted but determined Negro humility? or her coarse and cruel wit with loving jovial good humor? or her vulgar music with the soul of the Sorrow Songs?

Merely a concrete test of the underlying principles of the great republic is the Negro Problem, and the spiritual striving of the freedmen's sons is the travail of souls whose burden is almost beyond the measure of their strength, but who bear it in the name of an historic race, in the name of this the land of their fathers' fathers, and in the name of human opportunity.

And now what I have briefly sketched in large outline let me on coming pages tell again in many ways, with loving emphasis and deeper detail, that men may listen to the striving in the souls of black folk.

Of the Sons of Master and Man

Life treads on life, and heart on heart;
We press too close in church and mart
To keep a dream or grave apart.

MRS. BROWNING

The world-old phenomenon of the contact of diverse races of men is to have new exemplification during the new century. Indeed, the characteristic of our age is the contact of European civilization with the world's undeveloped peoples. Whatever we may say of the results of such contact in the past, it certainly forms a chapter in human action not pleasant to look back upon. War, murder, slavery, extermination, and debauchery— this has again and again been the result of carrying civilization and the blessed gospel to the isles of the sea and the heathen without the law. Nor does it altogether satisfy the conscience of the modern world to be told complacently that all this has been right and proper, the fated triumph of strength over weakness, of righteousness over evil, of superiors over inferiors. It would certainly be soothing if one could readily believe all this; and yet there are too many ugly facts for everything to be thus easily explained away. We feel and know that there are many delicate differences in race psychology, numberless changes that our crude social measurements are not yet able to follow minutely, which explain much of history and social development. At the same time, too, we know that these considerations have never adequately explained or excused the triumph of brute force and cunning over weakness and innocence.

It is, then, the strife of all honorable men of the twentieth century to see that in the future competition of races the survival of the fittest shall mean the triumph of the good, the beautiful, and the true; that we may be able to preserve for future civilization all that is really fine and noble and strong, and not continue to put a premium on greed and impudence and cruelty. To bring this hope to fruition, we are compelled daily to turn more and more to a conscientious study of the phenomena of race contact—to a study frank and fair, and not falsified and colored by our wishes or our fears. And we have in the South as fine a field for such a study as the world affords—a field, to be sure, which the average American scientist deems somewhat beneath his dignity, and which the average man who is not a scientist knows all about, but nevertheless a line of study which by reason of the enormous race complications with which God seems about to punish this nation must increasingly claim our sober attention, study, and thought, we must ask, what are the actual relations of whites and blacks in the South? and we must be answered, not by apology or fault-finding, but by a plain, unvarnished tale.

In the civilized life of today the contact of men and their relations to each other falls in a few main lines of action and communication: there is, first, the physical proximity of homes and dwelling places, the way in which neighborhoods group themselves, and the contiguity of neighborhoods. Secondly, and in our age chiefest, there are the economic relations—the methods by which individuals cooperate for earning a living, for the mutual satisfaction of wants, for the production of wealth. Next, there are the political relations, the cooperation in social control, in group government, in laying and paying the burden of taxation. In the fourth place there are the less tangible but highly important forms of intellectual contact and commerce, the interchange of ideas through conversation and conference, through periodicals and libraries; and, above all, the gradual formation for each community of that curious tertium quid which we call public opinion. Closely allied with this come the various forms of social contact in everyday life, in travel, in theatres, in house gatherings, in marrying and giving in marriage. Finally, there are the varying forms of religious enterprise, of moral teaching and benevolent endeavor. These are the principle ways in which men living in the same communities are brought into contact with each other. It is my present task, therefore, to indicate, from my point of view, how the black race in the South meet and mingle with the whites in these matters of everyday life.

First, as to physical dwelling. It is usually possible to draw in nearly every Southern community a physical color line on the map, on the one side of which whites dwell and on the other Negroes. The winding and intricacy of the geographical color line varies, of course, in different communities. I know some towns where a straight line drawn through the middle of the main street separates nine-tenths of the whites from nine-tenths of the blacks. In other towns the older settlement of whites has been encircled by a broad band of blacks; in still other cases little settlements or nuclei of blacks have sprung up amid surrounding whites. Usually in cities each street has its distinctive color, and only now and then do the colors meet in close proximity. Even in the country something of this segregation is manifest in the smaller areas, and of course in the larger phenomena of the Black Belt.

All this segregation by color is largely independent of that natural clustering of social grades common to all communities. A Negro slum may be in dangerous proximity to a white residence quarter, while it is quite common to find a white slum planted in the heart of a respectable Negro district. One thing, however, seldom occurs: the best of the whites and the best of the Negroes almost never live in anything like close proximity. It thus happens that in nearly every Southern town and city, both whites and blacks see commonly the worst of each other. This is a vast change from the situation in the past, when, through the close contact of master and house servant in the patriarchal big house, one found the best of both races in close contact and sympathy, while at the same time the squalor and dull round of toil among the field hands was removed from the sight and hearing of the family. One can easily see how a person who saw slavery thus from his father's parlors, and sees freedom on the streets of a great city, fails to grasp or comprehend the whole of the new picture. On the other hand, the settled belief of the mass of the Negroes that the Southern white people do not have the black man's best interests at heart has been intensified in later years by this continual daily contact of the better class of blacks with the worst representatives of the white race.

Coming now to the economic relations of the races, we are on ground made familiar by study, much discussion, and no little philanthropic effort. And yet with all this there are many essential elements in the cooperation of Negroes and whites for work and wealth that are too readily overlooked or not thoroughly understood. The average American can easily conceive of a rich land awaiting development and filled with black laborers. To him the Southern problem is simply that of making efficient workingmen out of this material, by giving them the requisite technical skill and the help of invested capital. The problem, however, is by no means as simple as this, from the obvious fact that these workingmen have been trained for centuries as slaves. They exhibit, therefore, all the advantages and defects of such training; they are willing and good-natured, but not self-reliant, provident, or careful. If now the economic development of the South is to be pushed to the verge of exploitation, as seems probable, then we have a mass of workingmen thrown into relentless competition with the workingmen of the world, but handicapped by a training the very opposite to that of the modern self-reliant democratic laborer. What the black laborer needs is careful personal guidance, group leadership of men with hearts in their bosoms, to train them to foresight, carefulness, and honesty. Nor does it require any fine-spun theories of racial differences to prove the necessity of such group training after the brains of the race have been knocked out by two hundred and fifty years of assiduous education in submission, carelessness, and stealing. After Emancipation, it was the plain duty of someone to assume this group leadership and training of the Negro laborer. I will not stop here to inquire whose duty it was, whether that of the white ex-master who had profited by unpaid toil, or the Northern philanthropist whose persistence brought on the crisis, or the National Government whose edict freed the bondsmen; I will not stop to ask whose duty it was, but I insist it was the duty of someone to see that these workingmen were not left alone and unguided, without capital, without land, without skill, without economic organization, without even the bald protection of law, order, and decency—left in a great land, not to settle down to slow and careful internal development, but destined to be thrown almost immediately into relentless and sharp competition with the best of modern workingmen under an economic system where every participant is fighting for himself, and too often utterly regardless of the rights or welfare of his neighbor.

For we must never forget that the economic system of the South today which has succeeded the old regime is not the same system as that of the old industrial North, of England, or of France, with their trade unions, their restrictive laws, their written and unwritten commercial customs, and their long experience. It is, rather, a copy of that England of the early nineteenth century, before the factory acts—the England that wrung pity from thinkers and fired the wrath of Carlyle. The rod of empire that passed from the hands of Southern gentlemen in 1865, partly by force, partly by their own petulance, has never returned to them. Rather it has passed to those men who have come to take charge of the industrial exploitation of the New South— the sons of poor whites fired with a new thirst for wealth and power, thrifty and avaricious Yankees, and unscrupulous immigrants. Into the hands of these men the Southern laborers, white and black, have fallen; and this to their sorrow. For the laborers as such, there is in these new captains of industry neither love nor hate, neither sympathy nor romance; it is a cold question of dollars and dividends. Under such a system all labor is bound to suffer. Even the white laborers are not yet intelligent, thrifty, and well trained enough to maintain themselves against the powerful inroads of organized capital. The results among them, even, are long hours of toil, low wages, child labor, and lack of protection against usury and cheating. But among the black laborers all this is aggravated, first, by a race prejudice which varies from a doubt and distrust among the best element of whites to a frenzied hatred among the worst; and, secondly, it is aggravated, as I have said before, by the wretched economic heritage of the freedmen from slavery. With this training it is difficult for the freedman to learn to grasp the opportunities already opened to him, and the new opportunities are seldom given him, but go by favor to the whites.

Left by the best elements of the South with little protection or oversight, he has been made in law and custom the victim of the worst and most unscrupulous men in each community. The crop-lien system which is depopulating the fields of the South is not simply the result of shiftlessness on the part of Negroes, but is also the result of cunningly devised laws as to mortgages, liens, and misdemeanors, which can be made by conscienceless men to entrap and snare the unwary until escape is impossible, further toil a farce, and protest a crime. I have seen, in the Black Belt of Georgia, an ignorant, honest Negro buy and pay for a farm in installments three separate times, and then in the face of law and decency the enterprising American who sold it to him pocketed money and deed and left the black man landless, to labor on his own land at thirty cents a day. I have seen a black farmer fall in debt to a white storekeeper, and that storekeeper go to his farm and strip it of every single marketable article—mules, ploughs, stored crops, tools, furniture, bedding, clocks, looking glass—and all this without a sheriff or officer, in the face of the law for homestead exemptions, and without rendering to a single responsible person any account or reckoning. And such proceedings can happen, and will happen, in any community where a class of ignorant toilers are placed by custom and race prejudice beyond the pale of sympathy and race brotherhood. So long as the best elements of a community do not feel in duty bound to protect and train and care for the weaker members of their group, they leave them to be preyed upon by these swindlers and rascals.

This unfortunate economic situation does not mean the hindrance of all advance in the black South, or the absence of a class of black landlords and mechanics who, in spite of disadvantages, are accumulating property and making good citizens. But it does mean that this class is not nearly so large as a fairer economic system might easily make it, that those who survive in the competition are handicapped so as to accomplish much less than they deserve to, and that, above all, the *personnel* of the successful class is left to chance and accident, and not to any intelligent culling or reasonable methods of selection. As a remedy for this, there is but one possible procedure. We must accept some of the race prejudice in the South as a fact—deplorable in its intensity, unfortunate in results, and dangerous for the future, but nevertheless a hard fact which only time can efface. We cannot hope, then, in this generation, or for several generations, that the mass of the whites can be brought to assume that close sympathetic and self-sacrificing leadership of the blacks which their present situation so eloquently demands. Such leadership, such social teaching and example, must come from the blacks themselves. For some time men doubted as to whether the Negro could develop such leaders; but today no one seriously disputes the capability of individual Negroes to assimilate the culture and common sense of modern civilization, and to pass it on, to some extent at least, to their fellows. If this is true, then here is the path out of the economic situation, and here is the imperative demand for trained Negro leaders of character and intelligence—men of skill, men of light and leading, college-bred men, black captains of industry, and missionaries of culture; men who thoroughly comprehend and know modern civilization, and can take hold of Negro communities and raise and train them by force of precept and example, deep sympathy, and the inspiration of common blood and ideals. But if such men are to be effective they must have some power—they must be backed by the best public opinion of these communities and able to wield for their objects and aims such weapons as the experience of the world has taught are indispensable to human progress.

Of such weapons, the greatest, perhaps, in the modern world is the power of the ballot; and this brings me to a consideration of the third form of contact between whites and blacks in the South—political activity.

In the attitude of the American mind toward Negro suffrage can be traced with unusual accuracy the prevalent conceptions of government. In the fifties we were near enough to the echoes of the French Revolution to believe pretty thoroughly in universal suffrage. We argued, as we thought then rather logically, that no social class was so good, so true, and so disinterested as to be trusted wholly with the political destiny of its neighbors; that in every state the best arbiters of their own welfare are the persons directly affected; consequently that it is only by arming every hand with a ballot—with the right to have a voice in the policy of the state—that the greatest good to the greatest number could be attained. To be sure, there were objections to these arguments, but we thought we had answered them tersely and convincingly; if someone complained of the ignorance of voters, we answered, "Educate them." If another complained of their venality, we replied, "Disfranchise them or put them in jail." And, finally, to the men who feared demagogues and the natural perversity of some human beings we insisted that time and bitter experience would teach the most hardheaded. It was at this time that the question of Negro suffrage in the South was raised. Here was a defenseless people suddenly made free. How were they to be protected from those who did not believe in their freedom and were determined to thwart it? Not by force, said the North; not by government guardianship, said the South; then by the ballot, the sole and legitimate defense of a free people, said the Common Sense of the Nation. No one thought, at the time, that the ex-slaves could use the ballot intelligently or very effectively; but they did think that the possession of so great power by a great class in the nation would compel their fellows to educate this class to its intelligent use.

Meantime, new thoughts came to the nation: the inevitable period of moral retrogression and political trickery that ever follows in the wake of war overtook us. So flagrant became the political scandals that reputable men began to leave politics alone, and politics consequently became disreputable. Men began to pride themselves on having nothing to do with their own government, and to agree tacitly with those who regarded public office as a private perquisite. In this state of mind it became easy to wink at the suppression of the Negro vote in the South, and to advise self-respecting Negroes to leave politics entirely alone. The decent and reputable citizens of the North who neglected their own civic duties grew hilarious over the exaggerated importance with which the Negro regarded the franchise. Thus it easily happened that more and more the better class of Negroes followed the advice from abroad and the pressure from home, and took no further interest in politics, leaving to the careless and the venal of their race the exercise of their rights as voters. The black vote that still remained was not trained and educated, but further debauched by open and unblushing bribery, or force and fraud; until the Negro voter was thoroughly inoculated with the idea that politics was a method of private gain by disreputable means.

And finally, now, today, when we are awakening to the fact that the perpetuity of republican institutions on this continent depends on the purification of the ballot, the civic training of voters, and the raising of voting to the plane of a solemn duty which a patriotic citizen neglects to his peril and to the peril of his children's children—in this day, when we are striving for a renaissance of civic virtue, what are we going to say to the black voter of the South? Are we going to tell him still that politics is a disreputable and useless form of human activity? Are we going to induce the best class of Negroes to take less and less interest in government, and to give up their right to take

such an interest, without a protest? I am not saying a word
against all legitimate efforts to purge the ballot of ignorance,
pauperism, and crime. But few have pretended that the present
movement for disfranchisement in the South is for such a purpose; it has been plainly and frankly declared in nearly every
case that the object of the disfranchising laws is the elimination
of the black man from politics.

Now, is this a minor matter which has no influence on the
main question of the industrial and intellectual development of
the Negro? Can we establish a mass of black laborers and arti-
sans and landholders in the South who, by law and public opinion, have absolutely no voice in shaping the laws under which
they live and work? Can the modern organization of industry,
assuming as it does free democratic government and the power
and ability of the laboring classes to compel respect for their
welfare—can this system be carried out in the South when half
its laboring force is voiceless in the public councils and power-
less in its own defense? Today the black man of the South has
almost nothing to say as to how much he shall be taxed, or how
those taxes shall be expended; as to who shall execute the laws,
and how they shall do it; as to who shall make the laws, and
how they shall be made. It is pitiable that frantic efforts must be
made at critical times to get lawmakers in some states even to
listen to the respectful presentation of the black man's side of a
current controversy. Daily the Negro is coming more and more
to look upon law and justice, not as protecting safeguards, but
as sources of humiliation and oppression. The laws are made by
men who have little interest in him; they are executed by men
who have absolutely no motive for treating the black people
with courtesy or consideration; and, finally, the accused law-
breaker is tried, not by his peers, but too often by men who
would rather punish ten innocent Negroes than let one guilty
one escape.

I should be the last one to deny the patent weaknesses and
shortcomings of the Negro people; I should be the last to with-
hold sympathy from the white South in its efforts to solve its

intricate social problems. I freely acknowledged that it is possible, and sometimes best, that a partially undeveloped people should be ruled by the best of their stronger and better neighbors for their own good, until such time as they can start and fight the world's battles alone. I have already pointed out how sorely in need of such economic and spiritual guidance the emancipated Negro was, and I am quite willing to admit that if the representatives of the best white Southern public opinion were the ruling and guiding powers in the South today the conditions indicated would be fairly well fulfilled. But the point I have insisted upon, and now emphasize again, is that the best opinion of the South today is not the ruling opinion. That to leave the Negro helpless and without a ballot today is to leave him, not to the guidance of the best, but rather to the exploitation and debauchment of the worst; that this is no truer of the South than of the North—of the North than of Europe: in any land, in any country under modern free competition, to lay any class of weak and despised people, be they white, black, or blue, at the political mercy of their stronger, richer, and more resourceful fellows, is a temptation which human nature seldom has withstood and seldom will withstand.

Moreover, the political status of the Negro in the South is closely connected with the question of Negro crime. There can be no doubt that crime among Negroes has sensibly increased in the last thirty years, and that there has appeared in the slums of great cities a distinct criminal class among the blacks. In explaining this unfortunate development, we must note two things: (1) that the inevitable result of Emancipation was to increase crime and criminals, and (2) that the police system of the South was primarily designed to control slaves. As to the first point, we must not forget that under a strict slave system there can scarcely be such a thing as crime. But when these variously constituted human particles are suddenly thrown broadcast on the sea of life, some swim, some sink, and some hang suspended, to be forced up or down by the chance currents of a busy hurrying world. So great an economic and social revolution as swept the South in '63 meant a weeding out among the Negroes of the incompetents and vicious, the beginning of a differentiation of social grades. Now a rising group of people are not lifted bodily from the ground like an inert solid mass, but rather stretch upward like a living plant with its roots still clinging in the mould. The appearance, therefore, of the Negro criminal was a phenomenon to be awaited; and while it causes anxiety, it should not occasion surprise.

Here again the hope for the future depended peculiarly on careful and delicate dealing with these criminals. Their offenses at first were those of laziness, carelessness, and impulse, rather than of malignity or ungoverned viciousness. Such misdemeanors needed discriminating treatment, firm but reformatory, with no hint of injustice, and full proof of guilt. For such dealing with criminals, white or black, the South had no machinery, no adequate jails or reformatories; its police system was arranged to deal with blacks alone, and tacitly assumed that every white man was ipso facto a member of that police. Thus grew up a double system of justice, which erred on the white side by undue leniency and the practical immunity of red-handed criminals, and erred on the black side by undue severity, injustice, and lack of discrimination. For, as I have said, the police system of the South was originally designed to keep track of all Negroes, not simply of criminals; and when the Negroes were freed and the whole South was convinced of the impossibility of free Negro labor, the first and almost universal device was to use the courts as a means of reenslaving the blacks. It was not then a question of crime, but rather one of color, that settled a man's conviction on almost any charge. Thus Negroes came to look upon courts as instruments of injustice and oppression, and upon those convicted in them as martyrs and victims.

When, now, the real Negro criminal appeared, and instead of petty stealing and vagrancy we began to have highway robbery, burglary, murder, and rape, there was a curious effect on both sides the color line: the Negroes refused to believe the evidence of white witnesses or the fairness of white juries, so that the greatest deterrent to crime, the public opinion of one's own social caste, was lost, and the criminal was looked upon as crucified rather than hanged. On the other hand, the whites, used to being careless as to the guilt or innocence of accused Negroes, were swept in moments of passion beyond law, reason, and decency. Such a situation is bound to increase crime, and has increased it. To natural viciousness and vagrancy are being daily added motives of revolt and revenge which stir up all the latent savagery of both races and make peaceful attention to economic development often impossible.

But the chief problem in any community cursed with crime is not the punishment of the criminals, but the preventing of the young from being trained to crime. And here again the peculiar conditions of the South have prevented proper precautions. I have seen twelve-year-old boys working in chains on the public streets of Atlanta, directly in front of the schools, in company with old and hardened criminals; and this indiscriminate mingling of men and women and children makes the chain gangs perfect schools of crime and debauchery. The struggle for reformatories, which has gone on in Virginia, Georgia, and other states, is the one encouraging sign of the awakening of some communities to the suicidal results of this policy.

It is the public schools, however, which can be made, outside the homes, the greatest means of training decent, self-respecting citizens. We have been so hotly engaged recently in discussing trade schools and the higher education that the pitiable plight of the public-school system in the South has almost dropped from view. Of every five dollars spent for public education in the state of Georgia, the white schools get four dollars and the Negro one dollar; and even then the white public-school system, save in the cities, is bad and cries for reform. If this is true of the whites, what of the blacks? I am becoming more and more convinced, as I look upon the system of common-school training in the South, that the national government must soon step in and aid popular education in some way. Today it has been only by the most strenuous efforts on the part of the thinking men of the

South that the Negro's share of the school fund has not been cut down to a pittance in some half-dozen states; and that movement not only is not dead, but in many communities is gaining strength. What in the name of reason does this nation expect of a people, poorly trained and hard pressed in severe economic competition, without political rights, and with ludicrously inadequate common-school facilities? What can it expect but crime and listlessness, offset here and there by the dogged struggles of the fortunate and more determined who are themselves buoyed by the hope that in due time the country will come to its senses?

I have thus far sought to make clear the physical, economic, and political relations of the Negroes and whites in the South, as I have conceived them, including, for the reasons set forth, crime and education. But after all that has been said on these more tangible matters of human contact, there still remains a part essential to a proper description of the South which it is difficult to describe or fix in terms easily understood by strangers. It is, in fine, the atmosphere of the land, the thought and feeling, the thousand and one little actions which go to make up life. In any community or nation it is these little things which are most elusive to the grasp and yet most essential to any clear conception of the group life taken as a whole. What is thus true of all communities is peculiarly true of the South, where, outside of written history and outside of printed law, there has been going on for a generation as deep a storm and stress of human souls, as intense a ferment of feeling, as intricate a writhing of spirit, as ever a people experienced. Within and without the somber veil of color vast social forces have been at work—efforts for human betterment, movements toward disintegration and despair, tragedies and comedies in social and economic life, and a swaying and lifting and sinking of human hearts which have made this land a land of mingled sorrow and joy, of change and excitement and unrest.

The center of this spiritual turmoil has ever been the millions of black freedmen and their sons, whose destiny is so fatefully bound up with that of the nation. And yet the casual observer

visiting the South sees at first little of this. He notes the growing frequency of dark faces as he rides along, but otherwise the
days slip lazily on, the sun shines, and this little world seems
as happy and contented as other worlds he has visited. Indeed,
on the question of questions—the Negro Problem—he hears
so little that there almost seems to be a conspiracy of silence;
the morning papers seldom mention it, and then usually in a
far-fetched academic way, and indeed almost everyone seems to
forget and ignore the darker half of the land, until the astonished visitor is inclined to ask if after all there *is* any problem
here. But if he lingers long enough there comes the awakening:
perhaps in a sudden whirl of passion which leaves him gasping
at its bitter intensity; more likely in a gradually dawning sense
of things he had not at first noticed. Slowly but surely his eyes
begin to catch the shadows of the color line: here he meets
crowds of Negroes and whites; then he is suddenly aware that
he cannot discover a single dark face; or again at the close of a
day's wandering he may find himself in some strange assembly,
where all faces are tinged brown or black, and where he has the
vague, uncomfortable feeling of the stranger. He realizes at last
that silently, resistlessly, the world about flows by him in two
great streams: they ripple on in the same sunshine, they
approach and mingle their waters in seeming carelessness—
then they divide and flow wide apart. It is done quietly; no mis-
takes are made, or if one occurs, the swift arm of the law and
of public opinion swings down for a moment, as when the other
day a black man and a white woman were arrested for talking
together on Whitehall Street in Atlanta.

Now if one notices carefully one will see that between these
two worlds, despite much physical contact and daily intermin-
gling, there is almost no community of intellectual life or point
of transference where the thoughts and feelings of one race can
come into direct contact and sympathy with the thoughts and
feelings of the other. Before and directly after the war, when all
the best of the Negroes were domestic servants in the best of the
white families, there were bonds of intimacy, affection, and

sometimes blood relationship between the races. They lived in the same home, shared in the family life, often attended the same church, and talked and conversed with each other. But the increasing civilization of the Negro since then has naturally meant the development of higher classes: there are increasing numbers of ministers, teachers, physicians, merchants, mechanics, and independent farmers, who by nature and training are the aristocracy and leaders of the blacks. Between them, however, and the best element of the whites, there is little or no intellectual commerce. They go to separate churches, they live in separate sections, they are strictly separated in all public gatherings, they travel separately, and they are beginning to read different papers and books. To most libraries, lectures, concerts, and museums, Negroes are either not admitted at all, or on terms peculiarly galling to the pride of the very classes who might otherwise be attracted. The daily paper chronicles the doings of the black world from afar with no great regard for accuracy; and so on, throughout the category of means for intellectual communication—schools, conferences, efforts for social betterment, and the like—it is usually true that the very representatives of the two races, who for mutual benefit and the welfare of the land ought to be in complete understanding and sympathy, are so far strangers that one side thinks all whites are narrow and prejudiced, and the other thinks educated Negroes dangerous and insolent. Moreover, in a land where the tyranny of public opinion and the intolerance of criticism is for obvious historical reasons so strong as in the South, such a situation is extremely difficult to correct. The white man, as well as the Negro, is bound and barred by the color line, and many a scheme of friendliness and philanthropy, of broad-minded sympathy and generous fellowship between the two has dropped stillborn because some busybody has forced the color question to the front and brought the tremendous force of unwritten law against the innovators.

It is hardly necessary for me to add very much in regard to the social contact between the races. Nothing has come to replace that finer sympathy and love between some masters and house servants which the radical and more uncompromising drawing of the color line in recent years has caused almost completely to disappear. In a world where it means so much to take a man by the hand and sit beside him, to look frankly into his eyes and feel his heart beating with red blood; in a world where a social cigar or a cup of tea together means more than legislative halls and magazine articles and speeches—one can imagine the consequences of the almost utter absence of such social amenities between estranged races, whose separation extends even to parks and streetcars.

Here there can be none of that social going down to the people—the opening of heart and hand of the best to the worst, in generous acknowledgment of a common humanity and a common destiny. On the other hand, in matters of simple almsgiving, where there can be no question of social contact, and in the succor of the aged and sick, the South, as if stirred by a feeling of its unfortunate limitations, is generous to a fault. The black beggar is never turned away without a good deal more than a crust, and a call for help for the unfortunate meets quick response. I remember one cold winter in Atlanta, when I refrained from contributing to a public relief fund lest Negroes should be discriminated against, I afterward inquired of a friend: "Were any black people receiving aid?" "Why," said he, "they were *all* black."

And yet this does not touch the kernel of the problem. Human advancement is not a mere question of almsgiving, but rather of sympathy and cooperation among classes who would scorn charity. And here is a land where, in the higher walks of life, in all the higher striving for the good and noble and true, the color line comes to separate natural friends and coworkers; while at the bottom of the social group, in the saloon, the gambling hell, and the brothel, that same line wavers and disappears.

I have sought to paint an average picture of real relations between the sons of master and man in the South. I have not glossed over matters for policy's sake, for I fear we have already gone too far in that sort of thing. On the other hand, I have sincerely sought to let no unfair exaggerations creep in. I do not doubt that in some Southern communities conditions are better than those I have indicated; while I am no less certain that in other communities they are far worse.

Nor does the paradox and danger of this situation fail to interest and perplex the best conscience of the South. Deeply religious and intensely democratic as are the mass of the whites, they feel acutely the false position in which the Negro problems place them. Such an essentially honest-hearted and generous people cannot cite the caste-leveling precepts of Christianity, or believe in equality of opportunity for all men, without coming to feel more and more with each generation that the present drawing of the color line is a flat contradiction to their beliefs and professions. But just as often as they come to this point, the present social condition of the Negro stands as a menace and a portent before even the most open-minded: if there were nothing to charge against the Negro but his blackness or other physical peculiarities, they argue, the problem would be comparatively simple; but what can we say to his ignorance, shiftlessness, poverty, and crime? can a self-respecting group hold anything but the least possible fellowship with such persons and survive? and shall we let a mawkish sentiment sweep away the culture of our fathers or the hope of our children? The argument so put is of great strength, but it is not a whit stronger than the argument of thinking Negroes: granted, they reply, that the condition of our masses is bad; there is certainly on the one hand adequate historical cause for this, and unmistakable evidence that no small number have, in spite of tremendous disadvantages, risen to the level of American civilization. And when, by proscription and prejudice, these same Negroes are classed with and treated like the lowest of their people, simply *because* they are Negroes, such a policy not only discourages thrift and intelligence among black men, but puts a direct premium on the very things you complain of—inefficiency and crime. Draw lines of crime, of incompetency, of vice, as tightly and uncompromisingly as you will, for these things must be proscribed; but a color line not only does not accomplish this purpose, but thwarts it.

In the face of two such arguments, the future of the South depends on the ability of the representatives of these opposing views to see and appreciate and sympathize with each other's position—for the Negro to realize more deeply than he does at present the need of uplifting the masses of his people, for the white people to realize more vividly than they have yet done the deadening and disastrous effect of a color prejudice that classes Phillis Wheatley and Sam Hose in the same despised class.

It is not enough for the Negroes to declare that color prejudice is the sole cause of their social condition, nor for the white South to reply that their social condition is the main cause of prejudice. They both act as reciprocal cause and effect, and a change in neither alone will bring the desired effect. Both must change, or neither can improve to any great extent. The Negro cannot stand the present reactionary tendencies and unreasoning drawing of the color line indefinitely without discouragement and retrogression. And the condition of the Negro is ever the excuse for further discrimination. Only by a union of intelligence and sympathy across the color line in this critical period of the Republic shall justice and right triumph,

> *That mind and soul according well,*
> *May make one music as before,*
>   *But vaster.* ∾

Interpretive Questions
for Discussion

According to Du Bois, how can the Negro overcome the feeling of "double-consciousness" and "merge his double self into a better and truer self"?

1. Why does being both an American and a Negro mean having "two souls, two thoughts, two unreconciled strivings; two warring ideals in one dark body"? Why is the history of the American Negro the history of this strife? (114)

2. Why does Du Bois sense that between him and the world there is ever the unasked question, "How does it feel to be a problem?" Why does he refuse to answer the question? (112)

3. Why was Du Bois' struggle with the veil of race more "fiercely sunny" than that of other black boys? Why didn't he succumb to tasteless sycophancy, silent hatred, or bitter despair? (113)

4. Why does "book learning" change "the child of Emancipation to the youth with dawning self-consciousness, self-realization, self-respect"? Why does it help him realize that "to attain his place in the world, he must be himself, and not another"? (117)

5. According to Du Bois, why does the "half-named Negro problem" mask the "deadweight of social degradation" the black man bears on his back? (117)

6. Why does Du Bois say that "the Negro cries Amen!" to prejudice that is "founded on just homage to civilization, culture, righteousness, and progress"? (118)

7. Why are the past ideals of improving the lot of black people only "dreams of a credulous race-childhood" if taken individually, but true if "melted and welded into one"? (119)

8. Why does Du Bois think that the "ideal of human brotherhood" can be "gained through the unifying ideal of Race"? Why does he think that the black and white races may one day "give each to each those characteristics both so sadly lack"? (119–120)

9. Why does Du Bois call the Negro Problem "merely a concrete test of the underlying principles of the great republic"? (120)

10. Is Du Bois suggesting that the problem of double-consciousness arose only after Emancipation?

Suggested textual analyses
Pages 113–114: beginning, "After the Egyptian and Indian," and ending, "closed roughly in his face."

Pages 119–120: beginning, "So dawned the time of Sturm und Drang:" and ending, "and in the name of human opportunity."

According to Du Bois, why is the problem of the twentieth century the problem of the color line?

1. Why does Du Bois say that "the characteristic of our age is the contact of European civilization with the world's undeveloped peoples"? (121)

2. Why does Du Bois focus his arguments—and his hopes— on contact between races rather than on the actions and responsibilities of either race individually?

3. Why does Du Bois think that "a conscientious study of the phenomena of race contact" can "preserve for future civilization all that is really fine and noble and strong"? (122)

4. Why does Du Bois say, "What the black laborer needs is careful personal guidance, group leadership of men with hearts in their bosoms"? (124)

5. Why does Du Bois focus on contact between the races as the definitive issue, yet conclude that the "close sympathetic and self-sacrificing leadership of the blacks which their present situation so eloquently demands . . . must come from the blacks themselves"? (121–122, 127)

6. In his study of race contact, why does Du Bois stress the intangible aspects of the color line in the South—"the atmosphere of the land"? Why are "these little things . . . most elusive to the grasp and yet most essential to any clear conception of the group life taken as a whole"? (134)

7. Why is the "question of questions—the Negro Problem" hidden from the casual observer visiting the South as if by "a conspiracy of silence"? Why is the visitor inclined to ask "if after all there *is* any problem here"? (135)

8. Why does Du Bois say that "the white man, as well as the Negro, is bound and barred by the color line"? (136)

9. Why does Du Bois suggest that it is as important for black people to "see and appreciate and sympathize" with the position of white people as it is for white people to see, appreciate, and sympathize with the position of black people? (139)

10. Why does Du Bois insist that the "color prejudice" of white people and the "social condition" of black people "both act as reciprocal cause and effect, and a change in neither alone will bring the desired effect"? (139)

Pages 121–122: beginning, "The world-old phenomenon," and ending, "but by a plain, unvarnished tale."

Pages 134–135: beginning, "I have thus far sought to make clear," and ending, "on Whitehall Street in Atlanta."

Does Du Bois think that the best way to deal with the color line is to strengthen the class line?

1. Why does Du Bois point out that segregation by color is less "natural" than the "clustering of social grades common to all communities"? Why does he think that race relations would benefit from more contact between "the best of both races"? (123)

2. Why does Du Bois suggest that in some ways contact between the races was more ennobling for both under slavery than it is after Emancipation? (123–124, 135–137)

3. Why does Du Bois complain that for black Americans, "the *personnel* of the successful class is left to chance and accident, and not to any intelligent culling or reasonable methods of selection"? (127)

4. Why does Du Bois regret especially the lack of "community of intellectual life or point of transference where the thoughts and feelings of one race can come into direct contact and sympathy with the thoughts and feelings of the other"? (135)

5. What does Du Bois mean when he says that "the increasing civilization of the Negro" since Emancipation "has naturally meant the development of higher classes"? Why does he seem to think that an "aristocracy" of blacks is necessary to fulfill the promise of Emancipation? (136)

6. Why does Du Bois lament that in the relationship between white and black people "there can be none of that social going down to the people—the opening of heart and hand of the best to the worst"? (137)

7. Why does Du Bois see social contact between the races as more important than generosity of whites to blacks? Why is human advancement a question of "sympathy and cooperation among classes who would scorn charity"? (137)

8. Why does Du Bois say that there can be no progress in race relations when the Negroes who have "risen to the level of American civilization" are "classed with and treated like the lowest of their people"? (138)

9. Why does Du Bois envision "a union of intelligence and sympathy across the color line" rather than the elimination of the color line altogether? (139)

10. Why does Du Bois place his faith in contact between the races when, despite his personal achievement and respected position in society, he still feels himself to be a problem to every white person he meets?

Suggested textual analyses

Pages 135–137: beginning, "Now if one notices carefully," and ending, "that same line wavers and disappears."

Pages 138–139: beginning, "Nor does the paradox and danger of this situation," and ending, "but a color line not only does not accomplish this purpose, but thwarts it."

FOR FURTHER REFLECTION

1. Have we achieved the "frank and fair" discussion of race relations that Du Bois envisions?

2. Should people have to earn or prove their worthiness for political rights?

3. Would you agree that the solution to racial conflict is for all races to rise "to the level of American civilization"?

4. Does America need to observe some class distinctions in order to promote the good, the beautiful, and the true?

5. Is it important for black people and white people to read the same books?

6. Work, culture, liberty—are these the solutions for racial harmony today?

7. If he were alive today, would Du Bois still perceive that between him and the world is ever the unasked question of how it feels to be a problem?

THE ANTHEAP

Doris Lessing

DORIS LESSING (1919–   ), British novelist
and short story writer, grew up on a farm
in Rhodesia (now Zimbabwe). She joined
the Communist Party and became involved
in anti-racist politics while living in South
Africa. After moving to England in 1949,
Lessing also became active in the peace
movement. Her extensive and varied literary
output reflects her interest in political and
social issues, particularly from a woman's
point of view. Lessing is best known for her
novel *The Golden Notebook*. She has also
written a series of science fiction novels,
Canopus in Argos: Archives, and five novels
featuring an autobiographical character
named Martha Quest, collectively titled
Children of Violence. Lessing's other works
include *The Grass Is Singing, Briefing for
a Descent into Hell, The Good Terrorist,*
and *The Fifth Child*.

B EYOND THE PLAIN rose the mountains, blue and
hazy in a strong blue sky. Coming closer they were brown and
grey and green, ranged heavily one beside the other, but the sky
was still blue. Climbing up through the pass the plain flattened
and diminished behind, and the peaks rose sharp and dark grey
from lower heights of heaped granite boulders, and the sky
overhead was deeply blue and clear and the heat came shim-
mering off in waves from every surface. "Through the range,
down the pass, and into the plain the other side—let's go
quickly, there it will be cooler, the walking easier." So thinks the
traveller. So the traveller has been thinking for many centuries,
walking quickly to leave the stifling mountains, to gain the
cool plain where the wind moves freely. But there is no plain.
Instead, the pass opens into a hollow which is closely surrounded by *kopjes:* the mountains clench themselves into a fist
here, and the palm is a mile-wide reach of thick bush, where the
heat gathers and clings, radiating from boulders, rocking off the
trees, pouring down from a sky which is not blue, but thick and

low and yellow, because of the smoke that rises, and has been rising so long from this mountain-imprisoned hollow. For though it is hot and close and arid half the year, and then warm and steamy and wet in the rains, there is gold here, so there are always people, and everywhere in the bush are pits and slits where the prospectors have been, or shallow holes, or even deep shafts. They say that the Bushmen were here, seeking gold, hundreds of years ago. Perhaps, it is possible. They say that trains of Arabs came from the coast, with slaves and warriors, looking for gold to enrich the courts of the Queen of Sheba. No one has proved they did not.

But it is at least certain that at the turn of the century there was a big mining company which sunk half a dozen fabulously deep shafts, and found gold going ounces to the ton sometimes, but it is a capricious and chancy piece of ground, with the reefs all broken and unpredictable, and so this company loaded its heavy equipment into lorries and off they went to look for gold somewhere else, and in a place where the reefs lay more evenly.

For a few years the hollow in the mountains was left silent, no smoke rose to dim the sky, except perhaps for an occasional prospector, whose fire was a single column of wavering blue smoke, as from the cigarette of a giant, rising into the blue, hot sky.

Then all at once the hollow was filled with violence and noise and activity and hundreds of people. Mr. Macintosh had bought the rights to mine this gold. They told him he was foolish, that no single man, no matter how rich, could afford to take chances in this place.

But they did not reckon with the character of Mr. Macintosh, who had already made a fortune and lost it, in Australia, and then made another in New Zealand, which he still had. He proposed to increase it here. Of course, he had no intention of sinking those expensive shafts which might not reach gold and hold the dipping, chancy reefs and seams. The right course was quite clear to Mr. Macintosh, and this course he followed, though it was against every known rule of proper mining.

He simply hired hundreds of African labourers and set them to shovel up the soil in the centre of that high, enclosed hollow in the mountains, so that there was soon a deeper hollow, then a vast pit, then a gulf like an inverted mountain. Mr. Macintosh was taking great swallows of the earth, like a gold-eating monster, with no fancy ideas about digging shafts or spending money on roofing tunnels. The earth was hauled, at first, up the shelving sides of the gulf in buckets, and these were suspended by ropes made of twisted bark fibre, for why spend money on steel ropes when this fibre was offered free to mankind on every tree? And if it got brittle and broke and the buckets went plunging into the pit, then they were not harmed by the fall, and there was plenty of fibre left on the trees. Later, when the gulf grew too deep, there were trucks on rails, and it was not unknown for these, too, to go sliding and plunging to the bottom, because in all Mr. Macintosh's dealings there was a fine, easy good humour, which meant he was more likely to laugh at such an accident than grow angry. And if someone's head got in the way of the falling buckets or trucks, then there were plenty of black heads and hands for the hiring. And if the loose, sloping bluffs of soil fell in landslides, or if a tunnel, narrow as an ant-bear's hole, that was run off sideways from the main pit like a tentacle exploring for new reefs, caved in suddenly, swallowing half a dozen men—well, one can't make an omelette without breaking eggs. This was Mr. Macintosh's favourite motto.

The Africans who worked this mine called it "the pit of death," and they called Mr. Macintosh "The Gold Stomach." Nevertheless, they came in their hundreds to work for him, thus providing free arguments for those who said: "The native doesn't understand good treatment, he only appreciates the whip, look at Macintosh, he's never short of labour."

Mr. Macintosh's mine, raised high in the mountains, was far from the nearest police station, and he took care that there was always plenty of kaffir beer brewed in the compound, and if the police patrols came searching for criminals, these could count on Mr. Macintosh facing the police for them and assuring them that such and such a native, Registration Number Y2345678, had never worked for him. Yes, of course they could see his books.

Mr. Macintosh's books and records might appear to the simple-minded as casual and ineffective, but these were not the words used of his methods by those who worked for him, and so Mr. Macintosh kept his books himself. He employed no bookkeeper, no clerk. In fact, he employed only one white man, an engineer. For the rest, he had six overseers or boss-boys whom he paid good salaries and treated like important people.

The engineer was Mr. Clarke, and his house and Mr. Macintosh's house were on one side of the big pit, and the compound for the Africans was on the other side. Mr. Clarke earned fifty pounds a month, which was more than he would earn anywhere else. He was a silent, hardworking man, except when he got drunk, which was not often. Three or four times in the year he would be off work for a week, and then Mr. Macintosh did his work for him till he recovered, when he greeted him with the good-humoured words: "Well, laddie, got that off your chest?"

Mr. Macintosh did not drink at all. His not drinking was a passionate business, for like many Scots people he ran to extremes. Never a drop of liquor could be found in his house. Also, he was religious, in a reminiscent sort of way, because of his parents, who had been very religious. He lived in a two-roomed shack, with a bare wooden table in it, three wooden chairs, a bed, and a wardrobe. The cook boiled beef and carrots and potatoes three days a week, roasted beef three days, and cooked a chicken on Sundays.

Mr. Macintosh was one of the richest men in the country, he was more than a millionaire. People used to say of him: But for heaven's sake, he could do anything, go anywhere, what's the point of having so much money if you live in the back of beyond with a parcel of blacks on top of a big hole in the ground?

But to Mr. Macintosh it seemed quite natural to live so, and when he went for a holiday to Cape Town, where he lived in the most expensive hotel, he always came back again long before he was expected. He did not like holidays. He liked working.

He wore old, oily khaki trousers, tied at the waist with an old red tie, and he wore a red handkerchief loose around his neck over a white cotton singlet. He was short and broad and strong, with a big square head tilted back on a thick neck. His heavy brown arms and neck sprouted thick black hair around the edges of the singlet. His eyes were small and grey and shrewd. His mouth was thin, pressed tight in the middle. He wore an old felt hat on the back of his head, and carried a stick cut from the bush, and he went strolling around the edge of the pit, slashing the stick at bushes and grass or sometimes at lazy Africans, and he shouted orders to his boss-boys, and watched the swarms of workers far below him in the bottom of the pit, and then he would go to his little office and make up his books, and so he spent his day. In the evenings he sometimes asked Mr. Clarke to come over and play cards.

Then Mr. Clarke would say to his wife: "Annie, he wants me," and she nodded and told her cook to make supper early.

Mrs. Clarke was the only white woman on the mine. She did not mind this, being a naturally solitary person. Also, she had been profoundly grateful to reach this haven of fifty pounds a month with a man who did not mind her husband's bouts of drinking. She was a woman of early middle age, with a thin, flat body, a thin, colourless face, and quiet blue eyes. Living here, in this destroying heat, year after year, did not make her ill, it sapped her slowly, leaving her rather numbed and silent. She spoke very little, but then she roused herself and said what was necessary.

For instance, when they first arrived at the mine it was to a two-roomed house. She walked over to Mr. Macintosh and said: "You are alone, but you have four rooms. There are two of us and the baby, and we have two rooms. There's no sense in it." Mr. Macintosh gave her a quick, hard look, his mouth tightened, and then he began to laugh. "Well, yes, that is so," he said, laughing, and he made the change at once, chuckling every time he remembered how the quiet Annie Clarke had put him in his place.

Similarly, about once a month Annie Clarke went to his house and said: "Now get out of my way, I'll get things straight for you." And when she'd finished tidying up she said: "You're nothing but a pig, and that's the truth." She was referring to his habit of throwing his clothes everywhere, or wearing them for weeks unwashed, and also to other matters which no one else dared to refer to, even as indirectly as this. To this he might reply, chuckling with the pleasure of teasing her: "You're a married woman, Mrs. Clarke," and she said: "Nothing stops you getting married that I can see." And she walked away very straight, her cheeks burning with indignation.

She was very fond of him, and he of her. And Mr. Clarke liked and admired him, and he liked Mr. Clarke. And since Mr. Clarke and Mrs. Clarke lived amiably together in their four-roomed house, sharing bed and board without ever quarrelling, it was to be presumed they liked each other too. But they seldom spoke. What was there to say?

It was to this silence, to these understood truths, that little Tommy had to grow up and adjust himself.

Tommy Clarke was three months old when he came to the mine, and day and night his ears were filled with noise, every day and every night for years, so that he did not think of it as noise, rather, it was a different sort of silence. The mine-stamps thudded gold, gold, gold, gold, gold, gold, on and on, never changing, never stopping. So he did not hear them. But there came a day when the machinery broke, and it was when Tommy was three years old, and the silence was so terrible and so empty that he went screeching to his mother: "It's stopped, it's stopped," and he wept, shivering, in a corner until the thudding began again. It was as if the heart of the world had gone silent. But when it started to beat, Tommy heard it, and he knew the difference between silence and sound, and his ears acquired a new sensitivity, like a conscience. He heard the shouting and the singing from the swarms of working Africans, reckless, noisy people because of the danger they always must live with. He heard the picks ringing on stone, the softer, deeper thud of picks on thick earth. He heard the clang of the trucks, and the roar of falling earth, and the rumbling of trolleys on rails. And at night the owls hooted and the nightjars screamed, and the crickets chirped. And when it stormed it seemed the sky itself was flinging down bolts of noise against the mountains, for the thunder rolled and crashed, and the lightning darted from peak to peak around him. It was never silent, never, save for that awful moment when the big heart stopped beating. Yet later he longed for it to stop again, just for an hour, so that he might hear a true silence. That was when he was a little older, and the quietness of his parents was beginning to trouble him. There they were, always so gentle, saying so little, only: That's how things are; or: You ask so many questions; or: You'll understand when you grow up.

It was a false silence, much worse than that real silence had been.

He would play beside his mother in the kitchen, who never said anything but Yes, and No, and—with a patient, sighing voice, as if even his voice tired her: You talk so much, Tommy!

And he was carried on his father's shoulders around the big, black working machines, and they couldn't speak because of the din the machines made. And Mr. Macintosh would say: Well, laddie? and give him sweets from his pocket, which he always kept there, especially for Tommy. And once he saw Mr. Macintosh and his father playing cards in the evening, and they didn't talk at all, except for the words that the game needed.

So Tommy escaped to the friendly din of the compound across the great gulf, and played all day with the black children, dancing in their dances, running through the bush after rabbits, or working wet clay into shapes of bird or beast. No silence there, everything noisy and cheerful, and at evening he returned to his equable, silent parents, and after the meal he lay in bed listening to the thud, thud, thud, thud, thud, thud, of the stamps. In the compound across the gulf they were drinking and dancing, the drums made a quick beating against the slow thud of the stamps, and the dancers around the fires yelled, a high, undulating sound like a big wind coming fast and crooked through a cap in the mountains. That was a different world, to which he belonged as much as to this one, where people said: Finish your pudding; or: It's time for bed; and very little else.

When he was five years old he got malaria and was very sick. He recovered, but in the rainy season of the next year he got it again. Both times Mr. Macintosh got into his big American car and went streaking across the thirty miles of bush to the nearest hospital for the doctor. The doctor said quinine, and be careful to screen for mosquitoes. It was easy to give quinine, but Mrs. Clarke, that tired, easy-going woman, found it hard to say: Don't, and Be in by six; and Don't go near the water; and so, when Tommy was seven, he got malaria again. And now Mrs. Clarke was worried, because the doctor spoke severely, mentioning blackwater.

Mr. Macintosh drove the doctor back to his hospital and then came home, and at once went to see Tommy, for he loved Tommy very deeply.

Mrs. Clarke said: "What do you expect, with all these holes everywhere, they're full of water all the wet season."

"Well, lassie, I can't fill in all the holes and shafts, people have been digging up here since the Queen of Sheba."

"Never mind about the Queen of Sheba. At least you could screen our house properly."

"I pay your husband fifty pounds a month," said Mr. Macintosh, conscious of being in the right.

"Fifty pounds and a proper house," said Annie Clarke.

Mr. Macintosh gave her that quick, narrow look, and then laughed loudly. A week later the house was encased in fine wire mesh all round from roof edge to verandah edge, so that it looked like a new meat safe, and Mrs. Clarke went over to Mr. Macintosh's house and gave it a grand cleaning, and when she left she said: "You're nothing but a pig, you're as rich as the Oppenheimers, why don't you buy yourself some new vests at least. And you'll be getting malaria, too, the way you go traipsing about at nights."

She returned to Tommy, who was seated on the verandah behind the grey-glistening wire netting, in a big deck chair. He was very thin and white after the fever. He was a long child, bony, and his eyes were big and black, and his mouth full and pouting from the petulances of the illness. He had a mass of richly brown hair, like caramels, on his head. His mother looked at this pale child of hers, who was yet so brightly coloured and full of vitality, and her tired willpower revived enough to determine a new régime for him. He was never to be out after six at night, when the mosquitoes were abroad. He was never to be out before the sun rose.

"You can get up," she said, and he got up, thankfully throwing aside his covers.

"I'll go over to the compound," he said at once.

She hesitated, and then said: "You mustn't play there anymore."

"Why not?" he asked, already fidgeting on the steps outside the wire-netting cage.

Ah, how she hated these Whys, and Why nots! They tired her utterly. "Because I say so," she snapped.

But he persisted: "I always play there."

"You're getting too big now, and you'll be going to school soon."

Tommy sank onto the steps and remained there, looking away over the great pit to the busy, sunlit compound. He had known this moment was coming, of course. It was a knowledge that was part of the silence. And yet he had not known it. He said: "Why, why, why, why?" singing it out in a persistent wail.

"Because I say so." Then, in tired desperation: "You get sick from the Africans, too."

At this, he switched his large black eyes from the scenery to his mother, and she flushed a little. For they were derisively scornful. Yet she half-believed it herself, or rather, must believe it, for all through the wet season the bush would lie waterlogged and festering with mosquitoes, and nothing could be done about it, and one has to put the blame on something.

She said: "Don't argue. You're not to play with them. You're too big now to play with a lot of dirty kaffirs. When you were little it was different, but now you're a big boy."

Tommy sat on the steps in the sweltering afternoon sun that came thick and yellow through the haze of dust and smoke over the mountains, and he said nothing. He made no attempt to go near the compound, now that his growing to manhood depended on his not playing with the black people. So he had been made to feel. Yet he did not believe a word of it, not really.

Some days later, he was kicking a football by himself around the back of the house when a group of black children called to him from the bush, and he turned away as if he had not seen them. They called again and then ran away. And Tommy wept bitterly, for now he was alone.

He went to the edge of the big pit and lay on his stomach looking down. The sun blazed through him so that his bones ached, and he shook his mass of hair forward over his eyes to shield them. Below, the great pit was so deep that the men working on the bottom of it were like ants. The trucks that climbed up the almost vertical sides were like matchboxes. The system of ladders and steps cut in the earth, which the workers used to climb up and down, seemed so flimsy across the gulf that a stone might dislodge it. Indeed, falling stones often did. Tommy sprawled, gripping the earth tight with tense belly and flung limbs, and stared down. They were all like ants and flies. Mr. Macintosh, too, when he went down, which he did often, for no one could say he was a coward. And his father, and Tommy himself, they were all no bigger than little insects.

It was like an enormous ant-working, as brightly tinted as a fresh antheap. The levels of earth around the mouth of the pit were reddish, then lower down grey and gravelly, and lower still, clear yellow. Heaps of the inert, heavy yellow soil, brought up from the bottom, lay all around him. He stretched out his hand and took some of it. It was unresponsive, lying lifeless and dense on his fingers, a little damp from the rain. He clenched his fist, and loosened it, and now the mass of yellow earth lay shaped on his palm, showing the marks of his fingers. A shape like—what? A bit of root? A fragment of rock rotted by water? He rolled his palms vigorously around it, and it became smooth like a water-ground stone. Then he sat up and took more earth, and formed a pit, and up the sides flying ladders with bits of stick, and little kips of wetted earth for the trucks. Soon the sun dried it, and it all cracked and fell apart. Tommy gave the model a kick and went moodily back to the house. The sun was going down. It seemed that he had left a golden age of freedom behind, and now there was a new country of restrictions and timetables.

His mother saw how he suffered, but thought: Soon he'll go to school and find companions.

But he was only just seven, and very young to go all the way to the city to boarding school. She sent for schoolbooks, and taught him to read. Yet this was for only two or three hours in the day, and for the rest he mooned about, as she complained, gazing away over the gulf to the compound, from where he could hear the noise of the playing children. He was stoical about it, or so it seemed, but underneath he was suffering badly from this new knowledge, which was much more vital than anything he had learned from the schoolbooks. He knew the word loneliness, and lying at the edge of the pit he formed the yellow clay into little figures which he called Betty and Freddy and Dirk. Playmates. Dirk was the name of the boy he liked best among the children in the compound over the gulf.

One day his mother called him to the back door. There stood Dirk, and he was holding between his hands a tiny duiker, the size of a thin cat. Tommy ran forward, and was about to exclaim with Dirk over the little animal, when he remembered his new status. He stopped, stiffened himself, and said: "How much?"

Dirk, keeping his eyes evasive, said: "One shilling, baas."

Tommy glanced at his mother and then said, proudly, his voice high: "Damned cheek, too much."

Annie Clarke flushed. She was ashamed and flustered. She came forward and said quickly: "It's all right, Tommy, I'll give you the shilling." She took the coin from the pocket of her apron and gave it to Tommy, who handed it at once to Dirk. Tommy took the little animal gently in his hands, and his tenderness for this frightened and lonely creature rushed up to his eyes and he turned away so that Dirk couldn't see—he would have been bitterly ashamed to show softness in front of Dirk, who was so tough and fearless.

Dirk stood back, watching, unwilling to see the last of the buck. Then he said: "It's just born, it can die."

Mrs. Clarke said, dismissingly: "Yes, Tommy will look after it." Dirk walked away slowly, fingering the shilling in his pocket, but looking back at where Tommy and his mother were making a nest for the little buck in a packing case. Mrs. Clarke made a feeding bottle with some linen stuffed into the neck of a tomato-sauce bottle and filled it with milk and water and sugar. Tommy knelt by the buck and tried to drip the milk into its mouth.

It lay trembling, lifting its delicate head from the crumpled, huddled limbs, too weak to move, the big eyes dark and forlorn. Then the trembling became a spasm of weakness and the head collapsed with a soft thud against the side of the box, and then slowly, and with a trembling effort, the neck lifted the head again. Tommy tried to push the wad of linen into the soft mouth, and the milk wetted the fur and ran down over the buck's chest, and he wanted to cry.

"But it'll die, Mother, it'll die," he shouted, angrily.

"You mustn't force it," said Annie Clarke, and she went away to her household duties. Tommy knelt there with the bottle, stroking the trembling little buck and suffering every time the thin neck collapsed with weakness, and tried again and again to interest it in the milk. But the buck wouldn't drink at all.

"Why?" shouted Tommy, in the anger of his misery. "Why won't it drink? Why? Why?"

"But it's only just born," said Mrs. Clarke. The cord was still on the creature's navel, like a shrivelling, dark stick.

That night Tommy took the little buck into his room, and secretly in the dark lifted it, folded in a blanket, into his bed. He could feel it trembling fitfully against his chest, and he cried into the dark because he knew it was going to die.

In the morning when he woke, the buck could not lift its head at all, and it was a weak, collapsed weight on Tommy's chest, a chilly weight. The blanket in which it lay was messed with yellow stuff like a scrambled egg. Tommy washed the buck gently, and wrapped it again in new coverings, and laid it on the verandah where the sun could warm it.

Mrs. Clarke gently forced the jaws open and poured down milk until the buck choked. Tommy knelt beside it all morning, suffering as he had never suffered before. The tears ran steadily down his face and he wished he could die too, and Mrs. Clarke wished very much she could catch Dirk and give him a good beating, which would be unjust, but might do something to relieve her feelings. "Besides," she said to her husband, "it's nothing but cruelty, taking a tiny thing like that from its mother."

Late that afternoon the buck died, and Mr. Clarke, who had not seen his son's misery over it, casually threw the tiny, stiff corpse to the cookboy and told him to go and bury it. Tommy stood on the verandah, his face tight and angry, and watched the cookboy shovel his little buck hastily under some bushes, and return whistling.

Then he went into the room where his mother and father were sitting and said: "Why is Dirk yellow and not dark brown like the other kaffirs?"

Silence. Mr. Clarke and Annie Clarke looked at each other. Then Mr. Clarke said: "They come different colours."

Tommy looked forcefully at his mother, who said: "He's a half-caste."

"What's a half-caste?"

"You'll understand when you grow up."

Tommy looked from his father, who was filling his pipe, his eyes lowered to the work, then at his mother, whose cheekbones held that proud, bright flush.

"I understand now," he said, defiantly.

"Then why do you ask?" said Mrs. Clarke, with anger. Why, she was saying, do you infringe the rule of silence?

Tommy went out, and to the brink of the great pit. There he lay, wondering why he had said he understood when he did not. Though in a sense he did. He was remembering, though he had not noticed it before, that among the gang of children in the compound were two yellow children. Dirk was one, and Dirk's sister another. She was a tiny child, who came toddling on the fringe of the older children's games. But Dirk's mother was black, or rather, dark brown like the others. And Dirk was not really yellow, but light copper colour. The colour of this earth, were it a little darker. Tommy's fingers were fiddling with the damp clay. He looked at the little figures he had made, Betty and Freddy. Idly, he smashed them. Then he picked up Dirk and flung him down. But he must have flung him down too carefully, for he did not break, and so he set the figure against the stalk of a weed. He took a lump of clay, and as his fingers experimentally pushed and kneaded it, the shape grew into the shape of a little duiker. But not a sick duiker, which had died because it had been taken from its mother. Not at all, it was a fine strong duiker, standing with one hoof raised and its head listening, ears pricked forward.

Tommy knelt on the verge of the great pit, absorbed, while the duiker grew into its proper form. He became dissatisfied— it was too small. He impatiently smashed what he had done, and taking a big heap of the yellowish, dense soil, shook water on it from an old rusty railway sleeper that had collected rainwater, and made the mass soft and workable. Then he began again. The duiker would be half life-size.

And so his hands worked and his mind worried along its path of questions: Why? Why? Why? And finally: If Dirk is half black, or rather half white and half dark brown, then who is his father?

For a long time his mind hovered on the edge of the answer, but did not finally reach it. But from time to time he looked across the gulf to where Mr. Macintosh was strolling, swinging his big cudgel, and he thought: There are only two white men on this mine.

The buck was now finished, and he wetted his fingers in rusty rainwater, and smoothed down the soft clay to make it glisten like the surfaces of fur, but at once it dried and dulled, and as he knelt there he thought how the sun would crack it and it would fall to pieces, and an angry dissatisfaction filled him and he hung his head and wanted very much to cry. And just as the first tears were coming he heard a soft whistle from behind him, and turned, and there was Dirk, kneeling behind a bush and looking out through the parted leaves.

"Is the buck all right?" asked Dirk.

Tommy said: "It's dead," and he kicked his foot at his model duiker so that the thick clay fell apart in lumps.

Dirk said: "Don't do that, it's nice," and he sprang forward and tried to fit the pieces together.

"It's no good, the sun'll crack it," said Tommy, and he began to cry, although he was so ashamed to cry in front of Dirk. "The buck's dead," he wept, "it's dead."

"I can get you another," said Dirk, looking at Tommy rather surprised. "I killed its mother with a stone. It's easy."

Dirk was seven, like Tommy. He was tall and strong, like Tommy. His eyes were dark and full, but his mouth was not full and soft, but long and narrow, clenched in the middle. His hair was very black and soft and long, falling uncut around his face, and his skin was a smooth, yellowish copper. Tommy stopped crying and looked at Dirk. He said: "It's cruel to kill a buck's mother with a stone." Dirk's mouth parted in surprised laughter over his big white teeth. Tommy watched him laugh, and he thought: Well, now I know who his father is.

He looked away to his home, which was two hundred yards off, exposed to the sun's glare among low bushes of hibiscus and poinsettia. He looked at Mr. Macintosh's house, which was a few hundred yards farther off. Then he looked at Dirk. He was full of anger, which he did not understand, but he did understand that he was also defiant, and this was a moment of decision. After a long time he said: "They can see us from here," and the decision was made.

They got up, but as Dirk rose he saw the little clay figure laid against a stem, and he picked it up. "This is me," he said at once. For crude as the thing was, it was unmistakably Dirk, who smiled with pleasure. "Can I have it?" he asked, and Tommy nodded, equally proud and pleased.

They went off into the bush between the two houses, and then on for perhaps half a mile. This was the deserted part of the hollow in the mountains, no one came here, all the bustle and noise was on the other side. In front of them rose a sharp peak, and low at its foot was a high anthill, draped with Christmas fern and thick with shrub.

The two boys went inside the curtains of fern and sat down. No one could see them here. Dirk carefully put the little clay figure of himself inside a hole in the roots of a tree. Then he said: "Make the buck again." Tommy took his knife and knelt beside a fallen tree, and tried to carve the buck from it. The wood was soft and rotten, and was easily carved, and by night there was the clumsy shape of the buck coming out of the trunk. Dirk said: "Now we've both got something."

The next day the two boys made their way separately to the antheap and played there together, and so it was every day.

Then one evening Mrs. Clarke said to Tommy just as he was going to bed: "I thought I told you not to play with the kaffirs?"

Tommy stood very still. Then he lifted his head and said to her, with a strong look across at his father: "Why shouldn't I play with Mr. Macintosh's son?"

Mrs. Clarke stopped breathing for a moment, and closed her eyes. She opened them in appeal at her husband. But Mr. Clarke was filling his pipe. Tommy waited and then said good night and went to his room.

There he undressed slowly and climbed into the narrow iron bed and lay quietly, listening to the thud, thud, gold, gold, thud, thud, of the mine-stamps. Over in the compound they were dancing, and the tom-toms were beating fast, like the quick beat of the buck's heart that night as it lay on his chest. They were yelling like the wind coming through gaps in a mountain and through the window he could see the high, flaring light of the fires, and the black figures of the dancing people were wild and active against it.

Mrs. Clarke came quickly in. She was crying. "Tommy," she said, sitting on the edge of his bed in the dark.

"Yes?" he said, cautiously.

"You mustn't say that again. Not ever."

He said nothing. His mother's hand was urgently pressing his arm. "Your father might lose his job," said Mrs. Clarke, wildly. "We'd never get this money anywhere else. Never. You must understand, Tommy."

"I do understand," said Tommy, stiffly, very sorry for his mother, but hating her at the same time. "Just don't say it, Tommy, don't ever say it." Then she kissed him in a way that was both fond and appealing, and went out, shutting the door. To her husband she said it was time Tommy went to school, and next day she wrote to make the arrangements.

And so now Tommy made the long journey by car and train into the city four times a year, and four times a year he came back for the holidays. Mr. Macintosh always drove him to the station and gave him ten shillings pocket money, and he came to fetch him in the car with his parents, and he always said: "Well, laddie, and how's school?" And Tommy said: "Fine, Mr. Macintosh." And Mr. Macintosh said: "We'll make a college man of you yet."

When he said this, the flush came bright and proud on Annie Clarke's cheeks, and she looked quickly at Mr. Clarke, who was smiling and embarrassed. But Mr. Macintosh laid his hands on Tommy's shoulders and said: "There's my laddie, there's my laddie," and Tommy kept his shoulders stiff and still. Afterwards, Mrs. Clarke would say, nervously: "He's fond of you, Tommy, he'll do right by you." And once she said: "It's natural, he's got no children of his own." But Tommy scowled at her and she flushed and said: "There's things you don't understand yet, Tommy, and you'll regret it if you throw away your chances." Tommy turned away with an impatient movement. Yet it was not so clear at all, for it was almost as if he were a rich man's son, with all that pocket money, and the parcels of biscuits and sweets that Mr. Macintosh sent into school during the term, and being fetched in the great rich car. And underneath it all he felt as if he were dragged along by the nose. He felt as if he were part of a conspiracy of some kind that no one ever spoke about. Silence. His real feelings were growing up slow and complicated and obstinate underneath that silence.

At school it was not at all complicated, it was the other world. There Tommy did his lessons and played with his friends and did not think of Dirk. Or rather, his thoughts of him were proper for that world. A half-caste, ignorant, living in the kaffir location—he felt ashamed that he played with Dirk in the holidays, and he told no one. Even on the train coming home he would think like that of Dirk, but the nearer he reached home the more his thoughts wavered and darkened. On the first evening at home he would speak of the school, and how he was first in the class, and he played with this boy or that, or went to such fine houses in the city as a guest. The very first morning he would be standing on the verandah looking at the big pit and at the compound away beyond it, and his mother watched him, smiling in nervous supplication. And then he walked down the steps, away from the pit, and into the bush to the antheap. There Dirk was waiting for him. So it was every holiday. Neither of the boys spoke at first of what divided them. But, on the eve of Tommy's return to school after he had been there a year, Dirk said: "You're getting educated, but I've nothing to learn." Tommy said: "I'll bring back books and teach you." He said this in a quick voice, as if ashamed, and Dirk's eyes were accusing and angry. He gave his sarcastic laugh and said: "That's what you say, white boy."

It was not pleasant, but what Tommy said was not pleasant either, like a favour wrung out of a condescending person.

The two boys were sitting on the antheap under the fine lacy curtains of Christmas fern, looking at the rocky peak soaring into the smoky yellowish sky. There was the most unpleasant sort of annoyance in Tommy, and he felt ashamed of it. And on Dirk's face there was an aggressive but ashamed look. They continued to sit there, a little apart, full of dislike for each other, and knowing that the dislike came from the pressure of the outside world. "I said I'd teach you, didn't I?" said Tommy, grandly, shying a stone at a bush so that leaves flew off in all directions. "You white bastard," said Dirk, in a low voice, and he let out that sudden ugly laugh, showing his white teeth. "What did you say?" said Tommy, going pale and jumping to his feet. "You heard," said Dirk, still laughing. He too got up. Then Tommy flung himself on Dirk and they overbalanced and rolled off into the bushes, kicking and scratching. They rolled apart and began fighting properly, with fists. Tommy was better-fed and more healthy. Dirk was tougher. They were a match, and they stopped when they were too tired and battered to go on. They staggered over to the antheap and sat there side by side, panting, wiping the blood off their faces. At last they lay on their backs on the rough slant of the anthill and looked up at the sky. Every trace of dislike had vanished, and they felt easy and quiet. When the sun went down they walked together through the bush to a point where they could not be seen from the houses, and there they said, as always: "See you tomorrow."

When Mr. Macintosh gave him the usual ten shillings, he put them into his pocket thinking he would buy a football, but he did not. The ten shillings stayed unspent until it was nearly the end of term, and then he went to the shops and bought a reader and some exercise books and pencils, and an arithmetic. He hid these at the bottom of his trunk and whipped them out before his mother could see them.

He took them to the antheap next morning, but before he could reach it he saw there was a little shed built on it, and the Christmas fern had been draped like a veil across the roof of the shed. The bushes had been cut on the top of the anthill, but left on the sides, so that the shed looked as if it rose from the tops of the bushes. The shed was of unbarked poles pushed into the earth, the roof was of thatch, and the upper half of the front was left open. Inside there was a bench of poles and a table of planks on poles. There sat Dirk, waiting hungrily, and Tommy went and sat beside him, putting the books and pencils on the table.

"This shed is fine," said Tommy, but Dirk was already looking at the books. So he began to teach Dirk how to read. And for all that holiday they were together in the shed while Dirk pored over the books. He found them more difficult than Tommy did, because they were full of words for things Dirk did not know, like curtains or carpet, and teaching Dirk to read the word "carpet" meant telling him all about carpets and the furnishings of a house. Often Tommy felt bored and restless and said: "Let's play," but Dirk said fiercely: "No, I want to read." Tommy grew fretful, for after all he had been working in the term and now he felt entitled to play. So there was another fight. Dirk said Tommy was a lazy white bastard, and Tommy said Dirk was a dirty half-caste. They fought as before, evenly matched and to no conclusion, and afterwards felt fine and friendly, and even made jokes about the fighting. It was arranged that they should work in the mornings only and leave the afternoons for play. When Tommy went back home that evening his mother saw the scratches on his face and the swollen nose, and said hopefully: "Have you and Dirk been fighting?" But Tommy said no, he had hit his face on a tree.

His parents, of course, knew about the shed in the bush, but did not speak of it to Mr. Macintosh. No one did. For Dirk's very existence was something to be ignored by everyone, and none of the workers, not even the overseers, would dare to mention Dirk's name. When Mr. Macintosh asked Tommy what he had done to his face, he said he had slipped and fallen.

And so their eighth year and their ninth went past. Dirk could read and write and do all the sums that Tommy could do. He was always handicapped by not knowing the different way of living and soon he said, angrily, it wasn't fair, and there was another fight about it, and then Tommy began another way of teaching. He would tell how it was to go to a cinema in the city, every detail of it, how the seats were arranged in such a way, and one paid so much, and the lights were like this, and the picture on the screen worked like that. Or he would describe how at school they ate such things for breakfast and other things for lunch. Or tell how the man had come with picture slides talking about China. The two boys got out an atlas and found China, and Tommy told Dirk every word of what the lecturer had said. Or it might be Italy or some other country. And they would argue that the lecturer should have said this or that, for Dirk was always hotly scornful of the white man's way of looking at things, so arrogant, he said. Soon Tommy saw things through Dirk; he saw the other life in town clear and brightly coloured and a little distorted, as Dirk did.

Soon, at school, Tommy would involuntarily think: I must remember this to tell Dirk. It was impossible for him to do anything, say anything, without being very conscious of just how it happened, as if Dirk's black, sarcastic eye had got inside him, Tommy, and never closed. And a feeling of unwillingness grew in Tommy, because of the strain of fitting these two worlds together. He found himself swearing at niggers or kaffirs like the other boys, and more violently than they did, but immediately afterwards he would find himself thinking: I must remember this so as to tell Dirk. Because of all this thinking, and seeing everything clear all the time, he was very bright at school, and found the work easy. He was two classes ahead of his age.

That was the tenth year, and one day Tommy went to the shed in the bush and Dirk was not waiting for him. It was the first day of the holidays. All the term he had been remembering things to tell Dirk, and now Dirk was not there. A dove was sitting on the Christmas fern, cooing lazily in the hot morning, a sleepy, lonely sound. When Tommy came pushing through the bushes it flew away. The mine-stamps thudded heavily, gold, gold, and Tommy saw that the shed was empty even of books, for the case where they were usually kept was hanging open.

He went running to his mother: "Where's Dirk?" he asked.

"How should I know?" said Annie Clarke, cautiously. She really did not know.

"You do know, you do!" he cried, angrily. And then he went racing off to the big pit. Mr. Macintosh was sitting on an upturned truck on the edge, watching the hundreds of workers below him, moving like ants on the yellow bottom. "Well, laddie?" he asked, amiably, and moved over for Tommy to sit by him.

"Where's Dirk?" asked Tommy, accusingly, standing in front of him.

Mr. Macintosh tipped his old felt hat even further back and scratched at his front hair and looked at Tommy.

"Dirk's working," he said, at last.

"Where?"

Mr. Macintosh pointed at the bottom of the pit. Then he said again: "Sit down, laddie, I want to talk to you."

"I don't want to," said Tommy, and he turned away and went blundering over the veld to the shed. He sat on the bench and cried, and when dinnertime came he did not go home. All that day he sat in the shed, and when he had finished crying he remained on the bench, leaning his back against the poles of the shed, and stared into the bush. The doves cooed and cooed, kru-kruuuu, kru-kruuuu, and a woodpecker tapped, and the mine-stamps thudded. Yet it was very quiet, a hand of silence gripped the bush, and he could hear the borers and the ants at work in the poles of the bench he sat on. He could see that although the anthill seemed dead, a mound of hard, peaked, baked earth, it was very much alive, for there was a fresh outbreak of wet, damp earth in the floor of the shed. There was a fine crust of reddish, lacy earth over the poles of the walls. The shed would have to be built again soon, because the ants and borers would have eaten it through. But what was the use of a shed without Dirk?

All that day he stayed there, and did not return till dark, and when his mother said: "What's the matter with you, why are you crying?" he said angrily, "I don't know," matching her dishonesty with his own. The next day, even before breakfast, he was off to the shed, and did not return until dark, and refused his supper although he had not eaten all day.

And the next day it was the same, but now he was bored and lonely. He took his knife from his pocket and whittled at a stick, and it became a boy, bent and straining under the weight of a heavy load, his arms clenched up to support it. He took the figure home at suppertime and ate with it on the table in front of him.

"What's that?" asked Annie Clarke, and Tommy answered: "Dirk."

He took it to his bedroom, and sat in the soft lamplight, working away with his knife, and he had it in his hand the following morning when he met Mr. Macintosh at the brink of the pit. "What's that, laddie?" asked Mr. Macintosh, and Tommy said: "Dirk."

Mr. Macintosh's mouth went thin, and then he smiled and said: "Let me have it."

"No, it's for Dirk."

Mr. Macintosh took out his wallet and said: "I'll pay you for it."

"I don't want any money," said Tommy, angrily, and Mr. Macintosh, greatly disturbed, put back his wallet. Then Tommy, hesitating, said: "Yes, I do." Mr. Macintosh, his values confirmed, was relieved, and he took out his wallet again and produced a pound note, which seemed to him very generous. "Five pounds," said Tommy, promptly. Mr. Macintosh first scowled, then laughed. He tipped back his head and roared with laughter. "Well, laddie, you'll make a businessman yet. Five pounds for a little bit of wood!"

"Make it for yourself then, if it's just a bit of wood."

Mr. Macintosh counted out five pounds and handed them over. "What are you going to do with that money?" he asked, as he watched Tommy buttoning them carefully into his shirt pocket. "Give them to Dirk," said Tommy, triumphantly, and

Mr. Macintosh's heavy old face went purple. He watched while Tommy walked away from him, sitting on the truck, letting the heavy cudgel swing lightly against his shoes. He solved his immediate problem by thinking: He's a good laddie, he's got a good heart.

That night Mrs. Clarke came over while he was sitting over his roast beef and cabbage, and said: "Mr. Macintosh, I want a word with you." He nodded at a chair, but she did not sit. "Tommy's upset," she said, delicately, "he's been used to Dirk, and now he's got no one to play with."

For a moment Mr. Macintosh kept his eyes lowered, then he said: "It's easily fixed, Annie, don't worry yourself." He spoke heartily, as it was easy for him to do, speaking of a worker, who might be released at his whim for other duties.

That bright protesting flush came on to her cheeks, in spite of herself, and she looked quickly at him, with real indignation. But he ignored it and said; "I'll fix it in the morning, Annie."

She thanked him and went back home, suffering because she had not said those words which had always soothed her conscience in the past: You're nothing but a pig, Mr. Macintosh . . .

As for Tommy, he was sitting in the shed, crying his eyes out. And then, when there were no more tears, there came such a storm of anger and pain that he would never forget it as long as he lived. What for? He did not know, and that was the worst of it. It was not simply Mr. Macintosh, who loved him, and who thus so blackly betrayed his own flesh and blood, nor the silences of his parents. Something deeper, felt working in the substance of life as he could hear those ants working away with those busy jaws at the roots of the poles he sat on, to make new material for their different forms of life. He was testing those words which were used, or not used—merely suggested—all the time, and for a ten-year-old boy it was almost too hard to bear. A child may say of a companion one day that he hates so and so, and the next: He is my friend. That is how a relationship is, shifting and changing, and children are kept safe in their hates and loves by the fabric of social life their parents make over their heads. And middle-aged people say: This is my friend, this is my enemy, including all the shifts and changes of feeling in one word, for the sake of an easy mind. In between these ages, at about twenty perhaps, there is a time when the young people test everything, and accept many hard and cruel truths about living, and that is because they do not know how hard it is to accept them finally, and for the rest of their lives. It is easy to be truthful at twenty.

But it is not easy at ten, a little boy entirely alone, looking at words like friendship. What, then, was friendship? Dirk was his friend, that he knew, but did he like Dirk? Did he love him? Sometimes not at all. He remembered how Dirk had said: "I'll get you another baby buck. I'll kill its mother with a stone." He remembered his feeling of revulsion at the cruelty. Dirk was cruel. But—and here Tommy unexpectedly laughed, and for the first time he understood Dirk's way of laughing. It was really funny to say that Dirk was cruel, when his very existence was a cruelty. Yet Mr. Macintosh laughed in exactly the same way, and his skin was white, or rather, white browned over by the sun. Why was Mr. Macintosh also entitled to laugh, with that same abrupt ugliness? Perhaps somewhere in the beginnings of the rich Mr. Macintosh there had been the same cruelty, and that had worked its way through the life of Mr. Macintosh until it turned into the cruelty of Dirk, the coloured boy, the half-caste? If so, it was all much harder to understand.

And then Tommy thought how Dirk seemed to wait always, as if he, Tommy, were bound to stand by him, as if this were a justice that was perfectly clear to Dirk; and he, Tommy, did in fact fight with Mr. Macintosh for Dirk, and he could behave in no other way. Why? Because Dirk was his friend? Yet there were times when he hated Dirk, and certainly Dirk hated him, and when they fought they could have killed each other easily, and with joy.

Well, then? Well, then? What was friendship, and why were they bound so closely, and by what? Slowly the little boy, sitting alone on his antheap, came to an understanding which is proper to middle-aged people, that resignation in knowledge which is called irony. Such a person may know, for instance, that he is bound most deeply to another person, although he does not like that person, in the way the word is ordinarily used, or the way he talks, or his politics, or anything else. And yet they are friends and will always be friends, and what happens to this bound couple affects each most deeply, even though they may be in different continents, or may never see each other again. Or after twenty years they may meet, and there is no need to say a word, everything is understood. This is one of the ways of friendship, and just as real as amiability or being alike.

Well, then? For it is a hard and difficult knowledge for any little boy to accept. But he accepted it, and knew that he and Dirk were closer than brothers and always would be so. He grew many years older in that day of painful struggle, while he listened to the mine-stamps saying gold, gold, and to the ants working away with their jaws to destroy the bench he sat on, to make food for themselves.

Next morning Dirk came to the shed, and Tommy, looking at him, knew that he, too, had grown years older in the months of working in the great pit. Ten years old—but he had been working with men and he was not a child.

Tommy took out the five pound notes and gave them to Dirk.

Dirk pushed them back. "What for?" he asked.

"I got them from him," said Tommy, and at once Dirk took them as if they were his right.

And at once, inside Tommy, came indignation, for he felt he was being taken for granted, and he said: "Why aren't you working?"

"He said I needn't. He means, while you are having your holidays."

"I got you free," said Tommy, boasting.

Dirk's eyes narrowed in anger. "He's my father," he said, for the first time.

"But he made you work," said Tommy, taunting him. And then: "Why do you work? I wouldn't. I should say no."

"So you would say no?" said Dirk in angry sarcasm.

"There's no law to make you."

"So there's no law, white boy, no law . . ." But Tommy had sprung at him, and they were fighting again, rolling over and over, and this time they fell apart from exhaustion and lay on the ground panting for a long time.

Later Dirk said: "Why do we fight, it's silly?"

"I don't know," said Tommy, and he began to laugh, and Dirk laughed too. They were to fight often in the future, but never with such bitterness, because of the way they were laughing now.

It was the following holidays before they fought again. Dirk was waiting for him in the shed.

"Did he let you go?" asked Tommy at once, putting down new books on the table for Dirk.

"I just came," said Dirk. "I didn't ask."

They sat together on the bench, and at once a leg gave way and they rolled off on the floor laughing. "We must mend it," said Tommy. "Let's build the shed again."

"No," said Dirk at once, "don't let's waste time on the shed. You can teach me while you're here, and I can make the shed when you've gone back to school."

Tommy slowly got up from the floor, frowning. Again he felt he was being taken for granted. "Aren't you going to work on the mine during the term?"

"No, I'm not going to work on the mine again. I told him I wouldn't."

"You've got to work," said Tommy, grandly.

"So I've got to work," said Dirk, threateningly. "You can go to school, white boy, but I've got to work, and in the holidays I can just take time off to please you."

They fought until they were tired, and five minutes afterwards they were seated on the anthill talking. "What did you do with the five pounds?" asked Tommy.

"I gave them to my mother."

"What did she do with them?"

"She bought herself a dress, and then food for us all, and bought me these trousers, and she put the rest away to keep."

A pause. Then, deeply ashamed, Tommy asked, "Doesn't he give her any money?"

"He doesn't come any more. Not for more than a year."

"Oh, I thought he did still," said Tommy casually, whistling.

"No." Then, fiercely, in a low voice: "There'll be some more half-castes in the compound soon."

Dirk sat crouching, his fierce black eyes on Tommy, ready to spring at him. But Tommy was sitting with his head bowed, looking at the ground. "It's not fair," he said. "It's not fair."

"So you've discovered that, white boy?" said Dirk. It was said good-naturedly, and there was no need to fight. They went to their books and Tommy taught Dirk some new sums.

But they never spoke of what Dirk would do in the future, how he would use all this schooling. They did not dare.

That was the eleventh year.

When they were twelve, Tommy returned from school to be greeted by the words: "Have you heard the news?"

"What news?"

They were sitting as usual on the bench. The shed was newly built, with strong thatch, and good walls, plastered this time with mud, so as to make it harder for the ants.

"They are saying you are going to be sent away."

"Who says so?"

"Oh, everyone," said Dirk, stirring his feet about vaguely under the table. This was because it was the first few minutes after the return from school, and he was always cautious, until he was sure Tommy had not changed towards him. And that "everyone" was explosive. Tommy nodded, however, and asked apprehensively: "Where to?"

"To the sea."

"How do they know?" Tommy scarcely breathed the word "they."

"Your cook heard your mother say so . . ." And then Dirk added with a grin, forcing the issue: "Cheek, dirty kaffirs talking about white men."

Tommy smiled obligingly, and asked: "How, to the sea, what does it mean?"

"How should we know, dirty kaffirs."

"Oh, shut up," said Tommy, angrily. They glared at each other, their muscles tensed. But they sighed and looked away. At twelve it was not easy to fight, it was all too serious.

That night Tommy said to his parents: "They say I'm going to sea. Is it true?"

His mother asked quickly: "Who said so?"

"But is it true?" Then, derisively: "Cheek, dirty kaffirs talking about us."

"Please don't talk like that, Tommy, it's not right."

"Oh, mother, please, how am I going to sea?"

"But be sensible Tommy, it's not settled, but Mr. Macintosh . . ."

"So it's Mr. Macintosh!"

Mrs. Clarke looked at her husband, who came forward and sat down and settled his elbows on the table. A family conference. Tommy also sat down.

"Now listen, son. Mr. Macintosh has a soft spot for you. You should be grateful to him. He can do a lot for you."

"But why should I go to sea?"

"You don't have to. He suggested it—he was in the Merchant Navy himself once."

"So I've got to go just because he did."

"He's offered to pay for you to go to college in England, and give you money until you're in the Navy."

"But I don't want to be a sailor. I've never even seen the sea."

"But you're good at your figures, and you have to be, so why not?"

"I won't," said Tommy, angrily. "I won't, I won't." He glared at them through tears. "You want to get rid of me, that's all it is. You want me to go away from here, from . . ."

The parents looked at each other and sighed.

"Well, if you don't want to, you don't have to. But it's not every boy who has a chance like this."

"Why doesn't he send Dirk?" asked Tommy, aggressively.

"Tommy," cried Annie Clarke, in great distress.

"Well, why doesn't he? He's much better than me at figures."

"Go to bed," said Mr. Clarke suddenly, in a fit of temper. "Go to bed."

Tommy went out of the room, slamming the door hard. He must be grown-up. His father had never spoken to him like that. He sat on the edge of the bed in stubborn rebellion, listening to the thudding of the stamps. And down in the compound they were dancing, the lights of the fires flickered red on his windowpane.

He wondered if Dirk were there, leaping around the fires with the others.

Next day he asked him: "Do you dance with the others?" At once he knew he had blundered. When Dirk was angry, his eyes darkened and narrowed. When he was hurt, his mouth set in a way which made the flesh pinch thinly under his nose. So he looked now.

"Listen, white boy. White people don't like us half-castes. Neither do the blacks like us. No one does. And so I don't dance with them."

"Let's do some lessons," said Tommy, quickly. And they went to their books, dropping the subject.

Later Mr. Macintosh came to the Clarkes' house and asked for Tommy. The parents watched Mr. Macintosh and their son walk together along the edge of the great pit. They stood at the window and watched, but they did not speak.

Mr. Macintosh was saying easily: "Well, laddie, and so you don't want to be a sailor."

"No, Mr. Macintosh."

"I went to sea when I was fifteen. It's hard, but you aren't afraid of that. Besides, you'd be an officer."

Tommy said nothing.

"You don't like the idea?"

"No."

Mr. Macintosh stopped and looked down into the pit. The earth at the bottom was as yellow as it had been when Tommy was seven, but now it was much deeper. Mr. Macintosh did not know how deep, because he had not measured it. Far below, in this man-made valley, the workers were moving and shifting like black seeds tilted on a piece of paper.

"Your father worked on the mines and he became an engineer working at nights, did you know that?"

"Yes."

"It was very hard for him. He was thirty before he was qualified, and then he earned twenty-five pounds a month until he came to this mine."

"Yes."

"You don't want to do that, do you?"

"I will if I have to," muttered Tommy, defiantly.

Mr. Macintosh's face was swelling and purpling. The veins along his nose and forehead were black. Mr. Macintosh was asking himself why this lad treated him like dirt, when he was offering to do him an immense favour. And yet, in spite of the look of sullen indifference which was so ugly on that young face, he could not help loving him. He was a fine boy, tall, strong, and his hair was the soft, bright brown, and his eyes clear and black. A much better man than his father, who was rough and marked by the long struggle of his youth. He said: "Well, you don't have to be a sailor, perhaps you'd like to go to university and be a scholar."

"I don't know," said Tommy, unwillingly, although his heart had moved suddenly. Pleasure—he was weakening. Then he said suddenly: "Mr. Macintosh, why do you want to send me to college?"

And Mr. Macintosh fell right into the trap. "I have no children," he said, sentimentally. "I feel for you like my own son." He stopped. Tommy was looking away towards the compound, and his intention was clear.

"Very well then," said Mr. Macintosh, harshly. "If you want to be a fool."

Tommy stood with his eyes lowered and he knew quite well he was a fool. Yet he could not have behaved in any other way.

"Don't be hasty," said Mr. Macintosh, after a pause. "Don't throw away your chances, laddie. You're nothing but a lad, yet.

Take your time." And with this tone, he changed all the emphasis of the conflict, and made it simply a question of waiting. Tommy did not move, so Mr. Macintosh went on quickly: "Yes, that's right, you just think it over." He hastily slipped a pound note from his pocket and put it into the boy's hand.

"You know what I'm going to do with it?" said Tommy, laughing suddenly, and not at all pleasantly.

"Do what you like, do just as you like, it's your money," said Mr. Macintosh, turning away so as not to have to understand.

Tommy took the money to Dirk, who received it as if it were his right, a feeling in which Tommy was now an accomplice, and they sat together in the shed. "I've got to be something," said Tommy angrily. "They're going to make me be something."

"They wouldn't have to make me be anything," said Dirk, sardonically. "I know what I'd be."

"What?" asked Tommy, enviously.

"An engineer."

"How do you know what you've got to do?"

"That's what I want," said Dirk, stubbornly.

After a while Tommy said: "If you went to the city, there's a school for coloured children."

"I wouldn't see my mother again."

"Why not?"

"There's laws, white boy, laws. Anyone who lives with and after the fashion of the natives is a native. Therefore I'm a native, and I'm not entitled to go to school with the half-castes."

"If you went to the town, you'd not be living with the natives so you'd be classed as a coloured."

"But then I couldn't see my mother, because if she came to town she'd still be a native."

There was a triumphant conclusiveness in this that made Tommy think: He intends to get what he wants another way . . . And then: Through me . . . But he had accepted that justice a long time ago, and now he looked at his own arm that lay on the rough plank of the table. The outer side was burnt dark and dry with the sun, and the hair glinted on it like fine copper. It was no darker than Dirk's brown arm, and no lighter. He turned it over. Inside, the skin was smooth, dusky white, the veins running blue and strong across the wrist. He looked at Dirk, grinning, who promptly turned his own arm over, in a challenging way. Tommy said, unhappily: "You can't go to school properly because the inside of your arm is brown. And that's that!" Dirk's tight and bitter mouth expanded into the grin that was also his father's, and he said: "That is so, white boy, that is so."

"Well, it's not my fault," said Tommy, aggressively, closing his fingers and banging the fist down again and again.

"I didn't say it was your fault," said Dirk at once.

Tommy said, in that uneasy, aggressive tone: "I've never even seen your mother."

To this, Dirk merely laughed, as if to say: You have never wanted to.

Tommy said, after a pause: "Let me come and see her now."

Then Dirk said, in a tone which was uncomfortable, almost like compassion: "You don't have to."

"Yes," insisted Tommy. "Yes, now." He got up, and Dirk rose too. "She won't know what to say," warned Dirk. "She doesn't speak English." He did not really want Tommy to go to the compound; Tommy did not really want to go. Yet they went.

In silence they moved along the path between the trees, in silence skirted the edge of the pit, in silence entered the trees on the other side, and moved along the paths to the compound. It was big, spread over many acres, and the huts were in all stages of growth and decay, some new, with shining thatch, some tumble-down, with dulled and sagging thatch, some in the process of being built, the peeled wands of the roof frames gleaming like milk in the sun.

Dirk led the way to a big square hut. Tommy could see people watching him walking with the coloured boy, and turning to laugh and whisper. Dirk's face was proud and tight, and he could feel the same look on his own face. Outside the square hut sat a little girl of about ten. She was bronze, Dirk's colour. Another little girl, quite black, perhaps six years old, was squatted on a log, finger in mouth, watching them. A baby, still unsteady on its feet, came staggering out of the doorway and collapsed, chuckling, against Dirk's knees. Its skin was almost white. Then Dirk's mother came out of the hut after the baby, smiled when she saw Dirk, but went anxious and bashful when she saw Tommy. She made a little bobbing curtsey, and took the baby from Dirk, for the sake of something to hold in her awkward and shy hands.

"This is Baas Tommy," said Dirk. He sounded very embarrassed.

She made another little curtsey and stood smiling.

She was a large woman, round and smooth all over, but her legs were slender, and her arms, wound around the child, thin and knotted. Her round face had a bashful curiosity, and her eyes moved quickly from Dirk to Tommy and back, while she smiled and smiled, biting her lips with strong teeth, and smiled again.

Tommy said: "Good morning," and she laughed and said "Good morning."

Then Dirk said: "Enough now, let's go." He sounded very angry. Tommy said: "Goodbye." Dirk's mother said: "Goodbye," and made her little bobbing curtsey, and she moved her child from one arm to another and bit her lip anxiously over her gleaming smile.

Tommy and Dirk went away from the square mud hut where the variously-coloured children stood staring after them.

"There now," said Dirk, angrily. "You've seen my mother."

"I'm sorry," said Tommy uncomfortably, feeling as if the responsibility for the whole thing rested on him. But Dirk laughed suddenly and said: "Oh, all right, all right, white boy, it's not your fault."

All the same, he seemed pleased that Tommy was upset.

Later, with an affectation of indifference, Tommy asked, thinking of those new children: "Does Mr. Macintosh come to your mother again now?"

And Dirk answered "Yes," just one word.

In the shed Dirk studied from a geography book, while Tommy sat idle and thought bitterly that they wanted him to be a sailor. Then his idle hands protested, and he took a knife and began slashing at the edge of the table. When the gashes showed a whiteness from the core of the wood, he took a stick lying on the floor and whittled at it, and when it snapped from thinness he went out to the trees, picked up a lump of old wood from the ground, and brought it back to the shed. He worked on it with his knife, not knowing what it was he made, until a curve under his knife reminded him of Dirk's sister squatting at the hut door, and then he directed his knife with a purpose. For several days he fought with the lump of wood, while Dirk studied. Then he brought a tin of boot polish from the house, and worked the bright brown wax into the creamy white wood, and soon there was a bronze-coloured figure of the little girl, staring with big, curious eyes while she squatted on spindly legs.

Tommy put it in front of Dirk, who turned it around, grinning a little. "It's like her," he said at last. "You can have it if you like," said Tommy. Dirk's teeth flashed, he hesitated, and then reached into his pocket and took out a bundle of dirty cloth. He undid it, and Tommy saw the little clay figure he had made of Dirk years ago. It was crumbling, almost worn to a lump of mud, but in it was still the vigorous challenge of Dirk's body. Tommy's mind signalled recognition—for he had forgotten he had ever made it—and he picked it up. "You kept it?" he asked shyly, and Dirk smiled. They looked at each other, smiling. It was a moment of warm, close feeling, and yet in it was the pain that neither of them understood, and also the cruelty and challenge that made them fight. They lowered their eyes unhappily. "I'll do your mother," said Tommy, getting up and running away into the trees in order to escape from the challenging closeness. He searched until he found a thorn tree, which is so hard it turns the edge of an axe, and then he took an axe and worked at the felling of the tree until the sun went down. A big stone near him was kept wet to sharpen the axe, and next day he worked on until the tree fell. He sharpened the worn axe again, and cut a length of tree about two feet, and split off the tough bark, and brought it back to the shed. Dirk had fitted a shelf against the logs of the wall at the back. On it he had set the tiny, crumbling figure of himself, and the new bronze shape of his little sister. There was a space left for the new statue. Tommy said, shyly: "I'll do it as quickly as I can so that it will be done before the term starts." Then, lowering his eyes, which suffered under this new contract of shared feeling, he examined the piece of wood. It was not pale and gleaming like almonds, as was the softer wood. It was a gingery brown, a close-fibred, knotted wood, and down its centre, as he knew, was a hard black spine. He turned it between his hands and thought that this was more difficult than anything he had ever done. For the first time he studied a piece of wood before starting on it, with a desired shape in his mind, trying to see how what he wanted would grow out of the dense mass of material he held.

Then he tried his knife on it and it broke. He asked Dirk for his knife. It was a long piece of metal, taken from a pile of scrap mining machinery, sharpened on stone until it was razor-fine. The handle was cloth wrapped tight around.

With this new and unwieldy tool Tommy fought with the wood for many days. When the holidays were ending, the shape was there, but the face was blank. Dirk's mother was full-bodied, with soft, heavy flesh and full, naked shoulders above a tight, sideways draped cloth. The slender legs were planted firm on naked feet, and the thin arms, knotted with work, were lifted to the weight of a child who, a small, helpless creature swaddled in cloth, looked out with large, curious eyes. But the mother's face was not yet there.

"I'll finish it next holidays," said Tommy, and Dirk set it carefully beside the other figures on the shelf. With his back turned he asked cautiously: "Perhaps you won't be here next holidays?"

"Yes I will," said Tommy, after a pause. "Yes I will."

It was a promise, and they gave each other that small, warm, unwilling smile, and turned away, Dirk back to the compound and Tommy to the house, where his trunk was packed for school.

That night Mr. Macintosh came over to the Clarkes' house and spoke with the parents in the front room. Tommy, who was asleep, woke to find Mr. Macintosh beside him. He sat on the foot of the bed and said: "I want to talk to you, laddie." Tommy turned the wick of the oil lamp, and now he could see in the shadowy light that Mr. Macintosh had a look of uneasiness about him. He was sitting with his strong old body balanced behind the big stomach, hands laid on his knees, and his grey Scots eyes were watchful.

"I want you to think about what I said," said Mr. Macintosh, in a quick, bluff good-humour. "Your mother says in two years' time you will have matriculated, you're doing fine at school. And after that you can go to college."

Tommy lay on his elbow, and in the silence the drums came tapping from the compound, and he said: "But Mr. Macintosh, I'm not the only one who's good at his books."

Mr. Macintosh stirred, but said bluffly: "Well, but I'm talking about you."

Tommy was silent, because as usual these opponents were so much stronger than was reasonable, simply because of their ability to make words mean something else. And then, his heart painfully beating, he said: "Why don't you send Dirk to college? You're so rich, and Dirk knows everything I know. He's better than me at figures. He's a whole book ahead of me, and he can do sums I can't."

Mr. Macintosh crossed his legs impatiently, uncrossed them, and said: "Now why should I send Dirk to college?" For now Tommy would have to put into precise words what he meant, and this Mr. Macintosh was quite sure he would not do. But to make certain, he lowered his voice and said: "Think of your mother, laddie, she's worrying about you, and you don't want to make her worried, do you?"

Tommy looked towards the door, under it came a thick yellow streak of light: in that room his mother and his father were waiting in silence for Mr. Macintosh to emerge with news of Tommy's sure and wonderful future.

"You know why Dirk should go to college," said Tommy in despair, shifting his body unhappily under the sheets, and Mr. Macintosh chose not to hear it. He got up, and said quickly: "You just think it over, laddie. There's no hurry, but by next holidays I want to know." And he went out of the room. As he opened the door, a brightly lit, painful scene was presented to Tommy: his father and mother sat, smiling in embarrassed entreaty at Mr. Macintosh. The door shut, and Tommy turned down the light, and there was darkness.

He went to school next day. Mrs. Clarke, turning out Mr. Macintosh's house as usual, said unhappily: "I think you'll find everything in its proper place," and slipped away, as if she were ashamed.

As for Mr. Macintosh, he was in a mood which made others, besides Annie Clarke, speak to him carefully. His cookboy, who had worked for him twelve years, gave notice that month. He had been knocked down twice by that powerful, hairy fist, and he was not a slave, after all, to remain bound to a bad-tempered master. And when a load of rock slipped and crushed the skulls of two workers, and the police came out for an investigation, Mr. Macintosh met them irritably, and told them to mind their own business. For the first time in that mine's history of scandalous recklessness, after many such accidents, Mr. Macintosh heard the indignant words from the police officer: "You speak as if you were above the law, Mr. Macintosh. If this happens again, you'll see . . ."

Worst of all, he ordered Dirk to go back to work in the pit, and Dirk refused.

"You can't make me," said Dirk.

"Who's the boss on this mine?" shouted Mr. Macintosh.

"There's no law to make children work," said the thirteen-year-old, who stood as tall as his father, a straight, lithe youth against the bulky strength of the old man.

The word "law" whipped the anger in Mr. Macintosh to the point where he could feel his eyes go dark, and the blood pounding in that hot darkness in his head. In fact, it was the power of this anger that sobered him, for he had been very young when he had learned to fear his own temper. And above all, he was a shrewd man. He waited until his sight was clear again, and then asked, reasonably: "Why do you want to loaf around the compound, why not work and earn money?"

Dirk said: "I can read and write, and I know my figures better than Tommy—Baas Tommy," he added, in a way which made the anger rise again in Mr. Macintosh, so that he had to make a fresh effort to subdue it.

But Tommy was a point of weakness in Mr. Macintosh, and it was then that he spoke the words which afterwards made him wonder if he'd gone suddenly crazy. For he said: "Very well, when you're sixteen you can come and do my books and write the letters for the mine."

Dirk said: "All right," as if this were no more than his due, and walked off, leaving Mr. Macintosh impotently furious with himself. For how could anyone but himself see the books? Such a person would be his master. It was impossible, he had no intention of ever letting Dirk, or anyone else, see them. Yet he had made the promise. And so he would have to find another way of using Dirk, or—and the words came involuntarily— getting rid of him.

From a mood of settled bad temper, Mr. Macintosh dropped into one of sullen thoughtfulness, which was entirely foreign to his character. Being shrewd is quite different from the processes of thinking. Shrewdness, particularly the money-making shrewdness, is a kind of instinct. While Mr. Macintosh had always known what he wanted to do, and how to do it, that did not mean he had known why he wanted so much money, or why he had chosen these ways of making it. Mr. Macintosh felt like a cat whose nose has been rubbed into its own dirt, and for many nights he sat in the hot little house, which vibrated continually from the noise of the mine-stamps, most uncomfortably considering himself and his life. He reminded himself, for instance, that he was sixty, and presumably had not more than ten or fifteen years to live. It was not a thought that an unreflective man enjoys, particularly when he had never considered his age at all. He was so healthy, strong, tough. But he was sixty nevertheless, and what would be his monument? An enormous pit in the earth, and a million pounds' worth of property. Then how should he spend ten or fifteen years? Exactly as he had the preceding sixty, for he hated being away from this place, and this gave him a caged and useless sensation, for it had never entered his head before that he was not as free as he felt himself to be.

Well, then—and this thought gnawed most closely to Mr. Macintosh's pain—why had he not married? For he considered himself a marrying sort of man, and had always intended to find himself the right sort of woman and marry her. Yet he was already sixty. The truth was that Mr. Macintosh had no idea at all why he had not married and got himself sons; and in these slow, uncomfortable ponderings the thought of Dirk's mother intruded itself only to be hastily thrust away. Mr. Macintosh, the sensualist, had a taste for dark-skinned women; and now it was certainly too late to admit as a permanent feature of his character something he had always considered as a sort of temporary whim, or makeshift, like someone who learns to enjoy an inferior brand of tobacco when better brands are not available.

He thought of Tommy, of whom he had been used to say: "I've taken a fancy to the laddie." Now it was not so much a fancy as a deep, grieving love. And Tommy was the son of his employee, and looked at him with contempt, and he, Mr. Macintosh, reacted with angry shame as if he were guilty of something. Of what? It was ridiculous.

The whole situation was ridiculous, and so Mr. Macintosh allowed himself to slide back into his usual frame of mind. Tommy's only a boy, he thought, and he'll see reason in a year or so. And as for Dirk, I'll find him some kind of a job when the time comes . . .

At the end of the term, when Tommy came home, Mr. Macintosh asked, as usual, to see the school report, which usually filled him with pride. Instead of heading the class with approbation from the teachers and high marks in all subjects,

Tommy was near the bottom, with such remarks as Slovenly, and Lazy, and Bad-mannered. The only subject in which he got any marks at all was that called Art, which Mr. Macintosh did not take into account.

When Tommy was asked by his parents why he was not working, he replied, impatiently: "I don't know," which was quite true; and at once escaped to the anthill. Dirk was there, waiting for the books Tommy always brought for him. Tommy reached at once up to the shelf where stood the figure of Dirk's mother, lifted it down and examined the unworked space which would be the face. "I know how to do it," he said to Dirk, and took out some knives and chisels he had brought from the city.

That was how he spent the three weeks of that holiday, and when he met Mr. Macintosh he was sullen and uncomfortable. "You'll have to be working a bit better," he said, before Tommy went back, to which he received no answer but an unwilling smile.

During that term Tommy distinguished himself in two ways besides being steadily at the bottom of the class he had so recently led. He made a fiery speech in the debating society on the iniquity of the colour bar, which rather pleased his teachers, since it is a well-known fact that the young must pass through these phases of rebellion before settling down to conformity. In fact, the greater the verbal rebellion, the more settled was the conformity likely to be. In secret, Tommy got books from the city library such as are not usually read by boys of his age, on the history of Africa, and on comparative anthropology, and passed from there to the history of the moment—he ordered papers from the Government Stationery Office, the laws of the country. Most particularly those affecting the relations between black and white and coloured. These he bought in order to take back to Dirk. But in addition to all this ferment, there was that subject Art, which in this school meant a drawing lesson twice a week, copying busts of Julius Caesar, or it might be Nelson, or shading in fronds of fern or leaves, or copying a large vase or a table standing diagonally to the class, thus learning what he was told were the laws of Perspective. There was no modelling, nothing approaching sculpture in this school, but this was the nearest thing to it, and that mysterious prohibition which forbade him to distinguish himself in Geometry or English, was silent when it came to using the pencil.

At the end of the term his report was very bad, but it admitted that he had An Interest in Current Events, and a Talent for Art.

And now this word Art, coming at the end of two successive terms, disturbed his parents and forced itself on Mr. Macintosh. He said to Annie Clarke: "It's a nice thing to make pictures, but the lad won't earn a living by it." And Mrs. Clarke said reproachfully to Tommy: "It's all very well, Tommy, but you aren't going to earn a living drawing pictures."

"I didn't say I wanted to earn a living with it," shouted Tommy, miserably. "Why have I got to be something, you're always wanting me to be something."

That holiday Dirk spent studying the Acts of Parliament and the Reports of Commissions and Sub-Committees which Tommy had brought him, while Tommy attempted something new. There was a square piece of soft white wood which Dirk had pilfered from the mine, thinking Tommy might use it. And Tommy set it against the walls of the shed, and knelt before it and attempted a frieze or engraving—he did not know the words for what he was doing. He cut out a great pit, surrounded by mounds of earth and rock, with the peaks of great mountains beyond, and at the edge of the pit stood a big man carrying a stick, and over the edge of the pit wound a file of black figures, tumbling into the gulf. From the pit came flames and smoke. Tommy took green ooze from leaves and mixed clay to colour the mountains and edges of the pit, and he made the little figures black with charcoal, and he made the flames writhing up out of the pit red with the paint used for parts of the mining machinery.

"If you leave it here, the ants'll eat it," said Dirk, looking with grim pleasure at the crude but effective picture.

To which Tommy shrugged. For while he was always solemnly intent on a piece of work in hand, afraid of anything that might mar it, or even distract his attention from it, once it was finished he cared for it not at all.

It was Dirk who had painted the shelf which held the other figures with a mixture that discouraged ants, and it was now Dirk who set the piece of square wood on a sheet of tin smeared with the same mixture, and balanced it in a way so it should not touch any part of the walls of the shed, where the ants might climb up.

And so Tommy went back to school, still in that mood of obstinate disaffection, to make more copies of Julius Caesar and vases of flowers, and Dirk remained with his books and his Acts of Parliament. They would be fourteen before they met again, and both knew that crises and decisions faced them. Yet they said no more than the usual: Well, so long, before they parted. Nor did they ever write to each other, although this term Tommy had a commission to send certain books and other Acts of Parliament for a purpose which he entirely approved.

Dirk had built himself a new hut in the compound, where he lived alone, in the compound but not of it, affectionate to his mother, but apart from her. And to this hut at night came certain of the workers who forgot their dislike of the half-caste, that cuckoo in their nest, in their common interest in what he told them of the Acts and Reports. What he told them was what he had learnt himself in the proud loneliness of his isolation. "Education," he said, "education, that's the key"—and Tommy agreed with him, although he had, or so one might suppose from the way he was behaving, abandoned all idea of getting an education for himself. All that term parcels came to "Dirk, c/o Mr. Macintosh," and Mr. Macintosh delivered them to Dirk without any questions.

In the dim and smoky hut every night, half a dozen of the workers laboured with stubs of pencil and the exercise books sent by Tommy, to learn to write and do sums and understand the Laws.

One night Mr. Macintosh came rather late out of that other hut, and saw the red light from a fire moving softly on the rough ground outside the door of Dirk's hut. All the others were dark. He moved cautiously among them until he stood in the shadows outside the door, and looked in. Dirk was squatting on the floor, surrounded by half a dozen men, looking at a newspaper.

Mr. Macintosh walked thoughtfully home in the starlight. Dirk, had he known what Mr. Macintosh was thinking, would have been very angry, for all his flaming rebellion, his words of resentment were directed against Mr. Macintosh and his tyranny. Yet for the first time Mr. Macintosh was thinking of Dirk with a certain rough, amused pride. Perhaps it was because he was a Scot, after all, and in everyone of his nation is an instinctive respect for learning and people with the determination to "get on." A chip off the old block, thought Mr. Macintosh, remembering how he, as a boy, had laboured to get a bit of education. And if the chip was the wrong colour—well, he would do something for Dirk. Something, he would decide when the time came. As for the others who were with Dirk, there was nothing easier than to sack a worker and engage another. Mr. Macintosh went to his bed, dressed as usual in vest and pyjama trousers, unwashed and thrifty in candlelight.

In the morning he gave orders to one of the overseers that Dirk should be summoned. His heart was already soft with thinking about the generous scene which would shortly take place. He was going to suggest that Dirk should teach all the overseers to read and write—on a salary from himself, of course—in order that these same overseers should be more useful in the work. They might learn to mark pay sheets, for instance.

The overseer said that Baas Dirk spent his days studying in Baas Tommy's hut—with the suggestion in his manner that Baas Dirk could not be disturbed while so occupied, and that this was on Tommy's account.

The man, closely studying the effect of his words, saw how Mr. Macintosh's big, veiny face swelled, and he stepped back a pace. He was not one of Dirk's admirers.

Mr. Macintosh, after some moments of heavy breathing, allowed his shrewdness to direct his anger. He dismissed the man, and turned away.

During that morning he left his great pit and walked off into the bush in the direction of the towering blue peak. He had heard vaguely that Tommy had some kind of a hut, but imagined it as a child's thing. He was still very angry because of that calculated "Baas Dirk." He walked for a while along a smooth path through the trees, and came to a clearing. On the other side was an anthill, and on the anthill a well-built hut, draped with Christmas fern around the open front, like curtains. In the opening sat Dirk. He wore a clean white shirt, and long smooth trousers. His head, oiled and brushed close, was bent over books. The hand that turned the pages of the books had a brass ring on the little finger. He was the very image of an aspiring clerk: that form of humanity which Mr. Macintosh despised most.

Mr. Macintosh remained on the edge of the clearing for some time, vaguely waiting for something to happen, so that he might fling himself, armoured and directed by his contemptuous anger, into a crisis which would destroy Dirk forever. But nothing did happen. Dirk continued to turn the pages of the book, so Mr. Macintosh went back to his house, where he ate boiled beef and carrots for his dinner.

Afterwards he went to a certain drawer in his bedroom, and from it took an object carelessly wrapped in cloth which, exposed, showed itself as that figure of Dirk the boy Tommy had made and sold for five pounds. And Mr. Macintosh turned and handled and pored over that crude wooden image of Dirk in a passion of curiosity, just as if the boy did not live on the same square mile of soil with him, fully available to his scrutiny at most hours of the day.

If one imagines a Judgment Day with the graves giving up their dead impartially, black, white, bronze, and yellow, to a happy reunion, one of the pleasures of that reunion might well be that people who have lived on the same acre or street all their lives will look at each other with incredulous recognition. "So that is what you were like," might be the gathering murmur around God's heaven. For the glass wall between colour and colour is not only a barrier against touch, but has become thick and distorted, so that black men, white men, see each other through it, but see—what? Mr. Macintosh examined the image of Dirk as if searching for some final revelation, but the thought that came persistently to his mind was that the statue might be of himself as a lad of twelve. So after a few moments he rolled it again in the cloth and tossed it back into the corner of a drawer, out of sight, and with it the unwelcome and tormenting knowledge.

Late that afternoon he left his house again and made his way towards the hut on the antheap. It was empty, and he walked through the knee-high grass and bushes till he could climb up the hard, slippery walls of the antheap and so into the hut.

First he looked at the books in the case. The longer he looked, the faster faded that picture of Dirk as an oiled and mincing clerk, which he had been clinging to ever since he threw the other image into the back of a drawer. Respect for Dirk was reborn. Complicated mathematics, much more advanced than he had ever done. Geography. History. "The Development of the Slave Trade in the Eighteenth Century." "The Growth of Parliamentary Institutions in Great Britain." This title made Mr. Macintosh smile—the freebooting buccaneer examining a coastguard's notice perhaps. Mr. Macintosh lifted down one book after another and smiled. Then, beside these books, he saw a pile of slight, blue pamphlets, and he examined them. "The Natives Employment Act." "The Natives Juvenile Employment Act." "The Native Passes Act." And Mr. Macintosh flipped over the leaves and laughed, and had Dirk heard that laugh it would have been worse to him than any whip.

For as he patiently explained these laws and others like them to his bitter allies in the hut at night, it seemed to him that every word he spoke was like a stone thrown at Mr. Macintosh, his father. Yet Mr. Macintosh laughed, since he despised these laws, although in a different way, as much as Dirk did. When Mr. Macintosh, on his rare trips to the city, happened to drive past the House of Parliament, he turned on it a tolerant and appreciative gaze. "Well, why not?" he seemed to be saying. "It's an occupation, like any other."

So to Dirk's desperate act of retaliation he responded with a smile, and tossed back the books and pamphlets on the shelf. And then he turned to look at the other things in the shed, and for the first time he saw the high shelf where the statuettes were arranged. He looked, and felt his face swelling with that fatal rage. There was Dirk's mother, peering at him in bashful sensuality from over the baby's head, there the little girl, his daughter, squatting on spindly legs and staring. And there, on the edge of the shelf, a small, worn shape of clay which still held the vigorous strength of Dirk. Mr. Macintosh, breathing heavily, holding down his anger, stepped back to gain a clearer view of those figures, and his heel slipped on a slanting piece of wood. He turned to look, and there was the picture Tommy had carved and coloured of his mine. Mr. Macintosh saw the great pit, the black little figures tumbling and sprawling over into the flames, and he saw himself, stick in hand, astride on his two legs at the edge of the pit, his hat on the back of his head.

And now Mr. Macintosh was so disturbed and angry that he was driven out of the hut and into the clearing, where he walked back and forth through the grass, looking at the hut while his anger growled and moved inside him. After some time he came close to the hut again and peered in. Yes, there was Dirk's mother, peering bashfully from her shelf, as if to say: Yes, it's me, remember? And there on the floor was the square tinted piece of wood which said what Tommy thought of him and his life. Mr. Macintosh took a box of matches from his pocket. He lit a match. He understood he was standing in the hut with a lit match in his hand to no purpose. He dropped the match and ground it out with his foot. Then he put a pipe in his mouth, filled it and lit it, gazing all the time at the shelf and at the square carving. The second match fell to the floor and lay spurting a small white flame. He ground his heel hard on it. Anger heaved up in him beyond all sanity, and he lit another match, pushed it into the thatch of the hut, and walked out of it and so into the clearing and away into the bush. Without looking behind him he walked back to his house where his supper of boiled beef and carrots was waiting for him. He was amazed, angry, resentful. Finally he felt aggrieved, and wanted to explain to someone what a monstrous injustice was Tommy's view of him. But there was no one to explain it to; and he slowly quietened to a steady dulled sadness, and for some days remained so, until time restored him to normal. From this condition he looked back at his behaviour and did not like it. Not that he regretted burning the hut, it seemed to him unimportant. He was angry at himself for allowing his anger to dictate his actions. Also he knew that such an act brings its own results.

So he waited, and thought mainly of the cruelty of fate in denying him a son who might carry on his work—for he certainly thought of his work as something to be continued. He thought sadly of Tommy, who denied him. And so, his affection for Tommy was sprung again by thinking of him, and he waited, thinking of reproachful things to say to him.

When Tommy returned from school he went straight to the clearing and found a mound of ash on the antheap that was already sifted and swept by the wind. He found Dirk, sitting on a tree trunk in the bush waiting for him.

"What happened?" asked Tommy. And then, at once: "Did you save your books?"

Dirk said: "He burnt it."

"How do you know?"

"I know."

Tommy nodded. "All your books have gone," he said, very grieved, and as guilty as if he had burnt them himself.

"Your carvings and your statues are burnt too."

But at this Tommy shrugged, since he could not care about his things once they were finished. "Shall we build the hut again now?" he suggested.

"My books are burnt," said Dirk, in a low voice, and Tommy, looking at him, saw how his hands were clenched. He instinctively moved a little aside to give his friend's anger space.

"When I grow up I'll clear you all out, all of you, there won't be one white man left in Africa, not one."

Tommy's face had a small, half-scared smile on it. The hatred Dirk was directing against him was so strong he nearly went away. He sat beside Dirk on the tree trunk and said: "I'll try and get you more books."

"And then he'll burn them again."

"But you've already got what was in them inside your head," said Tommy, consolingly. Dirk said nothing, but sat like a clenched fist, and so they remained on the tree trunk in the quiet bush while the doves cooed and the mine-stamps thudded, all that hot morning. When they had to separate at midday to return to their different worlds, it was with deep sadness, knowing that their childhood was finished, and their playing, and something new was ahead.

And at the meal Tommy's mother and father had his school report on the table, and they were reproachful. Tommy was at the foot of his class, and he would not matriculate this year. Or any year if he went on like this.

"You used to be such a clever boy," mourned his mother, "and now what's happened to you?"

Tommy, sitting silent at the table, moved his shoulders in a hunched, irritable way, as if to say: Leave me alone. Nor did he feel himself to be stupid and lazy, as the report said he was.

In his room were drawing blocks and pencils and hammers and chisels. He had never said to himself he had exchanged one purpose for another, for he had no purpose. How could he, when he had never been offered a future he could accept? Now, at this time, in his fifteenth year, with his reproachful parents deepening their reproach, and the knowledge that Mr. Macintosh would soon see that report, all he felt was a locked stubbornness, and a deep strength.

In the afternoon he went back to the clearing, and he took his chisels with him. On the old, soft, rotted tree trunk that he sat on that morning, he sat again, waiting for Dirk. But Dirk did not come. Putting himself in his friend's place he understood that Dirk could not endure to be with a white-skinned person—a white face, even that of his oldest friend, was too much the enemy. But he waited, sitting on the tree trunk all through the afternoon, with his chisels and hammers in a little box at his feet in the grass, and he fingered the soft, warm wood he sat on, letting the shape and texture of it come into the knowledge of his fingers.

Next day, there was still no Dirk.

Tommy began walking around the fallen tree, studying it. It was very thick, and its roots twisted and slanted into the air to the height of his shoulder. He began to carve the root. It would be Dirk again.

That night Mr. Macintosh came to the Clarkes' house and read the report. He went back to his own, and sat wondering why Tommy was set so bitterly against him. The next day he went to the Clarkes' house again to find Tommy, but the boy was not there.

He therefore walked through the thick bush to the antheap, and found Tommy kneeling in the grass working on the tree root.

Tommy said: "Good morning," and went on working, and Mr. Macintosh sat on the trunk and watched.

"What are you making?" asked Mr. Macintosh.

"Dirk," said Tommy, and Mr. Macintosh went purple and almost sprang up and away from the tree trunk. But Tommy was not looking at him. So Mr. Macintosh remained, in silence. And then the useless vigour of Tommy's concentration on that rotting bit of root goaded him, and his mind moved naturally to a new decision.

"Would you like to be an artist?" he suggested.

Tommy allowed his chisel to rest, and looked at Mr. Macintosh as if this were a fresh trap. He shrugged, and with the appearance of anger, went on with his work.

"If you've a real gift, you can earn money by that sort of thing. I had a cousin back in Scotland who did it. He made souvenirs, you know, for travellers." He spoke in a soothing and jolly way.

Tommy let the souvenirs slide by him, as another of these impositions on his independence. He said: "Why did you burn Dirk's books?"

But Mr. Macintosh laughed in relief. "Why should I burn his books?" It really seemed ridiculous to him, his rage had been against Tommy's work, not Dirk's.

"I know you did," said Tommy. "I know it. And Dirk does too."

Mr. Macintosh lit his pipe in good humour. For now things seemed much easier. Tommy did not know why he had set fire to the hut, and that was the main thing. He puffed smoke for a few moments and said: "Why should you think I don't want Dirk to study? It's a good thing, a bit of education."

Tommy stared disbelievingly at him.

"I asked Dirk to use his education, I asked him to teach some of the others. But he wouldn't have any of it. Is that my fault?"

Now Tommy's face was completely incredulous. Then he went scarlet, which Mr. Macintosh did not understand. Why should the boy be looking so foolish? But Tommy was thinking: We were on the wrong track . . . And then he imagined what his offer must have done to Dirk's angry, rebellious pride, and he suddenly understood. His face still crimson, he laughed. It was a bitter, ironical laugh, and Mr. Macintosh was upset—it was not a boy's laugh at all.

Tommy's face slowly faded from crimson, and he went back to work with his chisel. He said, after a pause: "Why don't you send Dirk to college instead of me? He's much more clever than me. I'm not clever, look at my report."

"Well, laddie . . ." began Mr. Macintosh reproachfully—he had been going to say: "Are you being lazy at school simply to force my hand over Dirk?" He wondered at his own impulse to say it; and slid off into the familiar obliqueness which Tommy ignored: "But you know how things are, or you ought to by now. You talk as if you didn't understand."

But Tommy was kneeling with his back to Mr. Macintosh, working at the root, so Mr. Macintosh continued to smoke. Next day he returned and sat on the tree trunk and watched. Tommy looked at him as if he considered his presence an unwelcome gift, but he did not say anything.

Slowly, the big fanged root which rose from the trunk was taking Dirk's shape. Mr. Macintosh watched with uneasy loathing. He did not like it, but he could not stop watching. Once he said: "But if there's a veld fire, it'll get burnt. And the ants'll eat it in any case." Tommy shrugged. It was the making of it that mattered, not what happened to it afterwards, and this attitude was so foreign to Mr. Macintosh's accumulating nature that it seemed to him that Tommy was touched in the head. He said: "Why don't you work on something that'll last? Or even if you studied like Dirk it would be better."

Tommy said: "I like doing it."

"But look, the ants are already at the trunk—by the time you get back from your school next time there'll be nothing left of it."

"Or someone might set fire to it," suggested Tommy. He looked steadily at Mr. Macintosh's reddening face with triumph. Mr. Macintosh found the words too near the truth. For certainly, as the days passed, he was looking at the new work with hatred and fear and dislike. It was nearly finished. Even if nothing more were done to it, it could stand as it was, complete.

Dirk's long, powerful body came writhing out of the wood like something struggling free. The head was clenched back, in the agony of the birth, eyes narrowed and desperate, the mouth—Mr. Macintosh's mouth—tightened in obstinate purpose. The shoulders were free, but the hands were held; they could not pull themselves out of the dense wood, they were imprisoned. His body was free to the knees, but below them the human limbs were uncreated, the natural shapes of the wood swelled to the perfect muscled knees.

Mr. Macintosh did not like it. He did not know what art was, but he knew he did not like this at all, it disturbed him deeply, so that when he looked at it he wanted to take an axe and cut it to pieces. Or burn it, perhaps . . .

As for Tommy, the uneasiness of this elderly man who watched him all day was a deep triumph. Slowly, and for the first time, he saw that perhaps this was not a sort of game that he played, it might be something else. A weapon—he watched Mr. Macintosh's reluctant face, and a new respect for himself and what he was doing grew in him.

At night, Mr. Macintosh sat in his candlelit room and he thought, or rather *felt,* his way to a decision.

There was no denying the power of Tommy's gift. Therefore, it was a question of finding the way to turn it into money. He knew nothing about these matters, however, and it was Tommy himself who directed him, for towards the end of the holidays he said: "When you're so rich you can do anything. You could send Dirk to college and not even notice it."

Mr. Macintosh, in the reasonable and persuasive voice he now always used, said, "But you know these coloured people have nowhere to go."

Tommy said: "You could send him to the Cape. There are coloured people in the university there. Or Johannesburg." And he insisted against Mr. Macintosh's silence: "You're so rich you can do anything you like."

But Mr. Macintosh, like most rich people, thought not of money as things to buy, things to do, but rather how it was tied up in buildings and land.

"It would cost thousands," he said. "Thousands for a coloured boy."

But Tommy's scornful look silenced him, and he said hastily: "I'll think about it." But he was thinking not of Dirk, but of Tommy. Sitting alone in his room he told himself it was simply a question of paying for knowledge.

So next morning he made his preparations for a trip to town. He shaved, and over his cotton singlet he put a striped jacket, which half concealed his long, stained khaki trousers. This was as far as he ever went in concessions to the city life he despised. He got into his big American car and set off.

In the city he took the simplest route to knowledge.

He went to the Education Department, and said he wanted to see the Minister of Education. "I'm Macintosh," he said, with perfect confidence; and the pretty secretary who had been patronising his clothes, went at once to the Minister and said: "There is a Mr. Macintosh to see you." She described him as an old, fat, dirty man with a large stomach, and soon the doors opened and Mr. Macintosh was with the spring of knowledge.

He emerged five minutes later with what he wanted, the name of a certain expert. He drove through the deep green avenues of the city to the house he had been told to go to, which was a large and well-kept one, and comforted Mr. Macintosh in his faith that art properly used could make money. He parked his car in the road and walked in.

On the verandah, behind a table heaped with books, sat a middle-aged man with spectacles. Mr. Tomlinson was essentially a scholar with working hours he respected, and he lifted his eyes to see a big, dirty man with black hair showing above the dirty whiteness of his vest, and he said sharply: "What do you want?"

"Wait a minute, laddie," said Mr. Macintosh easily, and he held out a note from the Minister of Education, and Mr. Tomlinson took it and read it, feeling reassured. It was worded in such a way that his seeing Mr. Macintosh could be felt as a favour he was personally doing the Minister.

"I'll make it worth your while," said Mr. Macintosh, and at once distaste flooded Mr. Tomlinson, and he went pink, and said: "I'm afraid I haven't the time."

"Damn it, man, it's your job, isn't it? Or so Wentworth said."

"No," said Mr. Tomlinson, making each word clear, "I advise on ancient Monuments."

Mr. Macintosh stared, then laughed, and said: "Wentworth said you'd do, but it doesn't matter, I'll get someone else." And he left.

Mr. Tomlinson watched this hobo go off the verandah and into a magnificent car, and his thought was: "He must have stolen it." Then, puzzled and upset, he went to the telephone. But in a few moments he was smiling. Finally he laughed. Mr. Macintosh was *the* Mr. Macintosh, a genuine specimen of the old-timer. It was the phrase "old-timer" that made it possible for Mr. Tomlinson to relent. He therefore rang the hotel at which Mr. Macintosh, as a rich man, would be bound to be staying, and he said he had made an error, he would be free the following day to accompany Mr. Macintosh.

And so next morning Mr. Macintosh, not at all surprised that the expert was at his service after all, with Mr. Tomlinson, who preserved a tolerant smile, drove out to the mine.

They drove very fast in the powerful car, and Mr. Tomlinson held himself steady while they jolted and bounced, and listened to Mr. Macintosh's tales of Australia and New Zealand, and thought of him rather as he would of an ancient Monument.

At last the long plain ended, and foothills of greenish scrub heaped themselves around the car, and then high mountains piled with granite boulders, and the heat came in thick, slow waves into the car, and Mr. Tomlinson thought: I'll be glad when we're through the mountains into the plain. But instead they turned into a high, enclosed place with mountains all around, and suddenly there was an enormous gulf in the ground, and on one side of it were two tiny tin-roofed houses, and on the other acres of kaffir huts. The mine-stamps thudded regularly, like a pulse of the heart, and Mr. Tomlinson wondered how anybody, white or black, could bear to live in such a place.

He ate boiled beef and carrots and greasy potatoes with one of the richest men in the subcontinent, and thought how well and intelligently he would use such money if he had it—which is the only consolation left to the cultivated man of moderate income. After lunch, Mr. Macintosh said: "And now, let's get it over."

Mr. Tomlinson expressed his willingness, and, smiling to himself, followed Mr. Macintosh off into the bush on a kaffir path. He did not know what he was going to see. Mr. Macintosh had said: "Can you tell if a youngster has got any talent just by looking at a piece of wood he has carved?"

Mr. Tomlinson said he would do his best.

Then they were beside a fallen tree trunk, and in the grass knelt a big lad, with untidy brown hair falling over his face, labouring at the wood with a large chisel.

"This is a friend of mine," said Mr. Macintosh to Tommy, who got to his feet and stood uncomfortably, wondering what was happening. "Do you mind if Mr. Tomlinson sees what you are doing?"

Tommy made a shrugging movement and felt that things were going beyond his control. He looked in awed amazement at Mr. Tomlinson, who seemed to him rather like a teacher or professor, and certainly not at all what he imagined an artist to be.

"Well?" said Mr. Macintosh to Mr. Tomlinson, after a space of half a minute.

Mr. Tomlinson laughed in a way which said: "Now don't be in such a hurry." He walked around the carved tree root, looking at the figure of Dirk from this angle and that.

Then he asked Tommy: "Why do you make these carvings?"

Tommy very uncomfortably shrugged, as if to say: What a silly question; and Mr. Macintosh hastily said: "He gets high marks for Art at school."

Mr. Tomlinson smiled again and walked around to the other side of the trunk. From here he could see Dirk's face, flattened back on the neck, eyes half-closed and strained, the muscles of the neck shaped from natural veins of the wood.

"Is this someone you know?" he asked Tommy in an easy, intimate way, one artist to another.

"Yes," said Tommy, briefly; he resented the question.

Mr. Tomlinson looked at the face and then at Mr. Macintosh. "It has a look of you," he observed dispassionately, and coloured himself as he saw Mr. Macintosh grow angry. He walked well away from the group, to give Mr. Macintosh space to hide his embarrassment. When he returned, he asked Tommy: "And so you want to be a sculptor?"

"I don't know," said Tommy, defiantly.

Mr. Tomlinson shrugged rather impatiently, and with a nod at Mr. Macintosh suggested it was enough. He said goodbye to Tommy, and went back to the house with Mr. Macintosh.

There he was offered tea and biscuits, and Mr. Macintosh asked: "Well, what do you think?"

But by now Mr. Tomlinson was certainly offended at this casual cash-on-delivery approach to art, and he said: "Well, that rather depends, doesn't it?"

"On what?" demanded Mr. Macintosh.

"He seems to have talent," conceded Mr. Tomlinson.

"That's all I want to know," said Mr. Macintosh, and suggested that now he could run Mr. Tomlinson back to town.

But Mr. Tomlinson did not feel it was enough, and he said: "It's quite interesting, that statue. I suppose he's seen pictures in magazines. It has quite a modern feeling."

"Modern?" said Mr. Macintosh. "What do you mean?"

Mr. Tomlinson shrugged again, giving it up. "Well," he said, practically, "what do you mean to do?"

"If you say he has talent, I'll send him to the university and he can study art."

After a long pause, Mr. Tomlinson murmured: "What a fortunate boy he is." He meant to convey depths of disillusionment and irony, but Mr. Macintosh said: "I always did have a fancy for him."

He took Mr. Tomlinson back to the city, and as he dropped him on his verandah, presented him with a cheque for fifty pounds, which Mr. Tomlinson most indignantly returned. "Oh, give it to charity," said Mr. Macintosh impatiently, and went to his car, leaving Mr. Tomlinson to heal his susceptibilities in any way he chose.

When Mr. Macintosh reached his mine again it was midnight, and there were no lights in the Clarkes' house, and so his need to be generous must be stifled until the morning.

Then he went to Annie Clarke and told her he would send Tommy to university, where he could be an artist, and Mrs.

Clarke wept with gratitude, and said that Mr. Macintosh was much kinder than Tommy deserved, and perhaps he would learn sense yet and go back to his books.

As far as Mr. Macintosh was concerned it was all settled.

He set off through the trees to find Tommy and announce his future to him.

But when he arrived at seeing distance there were two figures, Dirk and Tommy, seated on the trunk talking, and Mr. Macintosh stopped among the trees, filled with such bitter anger at this fresh check to his plans that he could not trust himself to go on. So he returned to his house, and brooded angrily—he knew exactly what was going to happen when he spoke to Tommy, and now he must make up his mind, there was no escape from a decision.

And while Mr. Macintosh mused bitterly in his house, Tommy and Dirk waited for him; it was now all as clear to them as it was to him.

Dirk had come out of the trees to Tommy the moment the two men left the day before. Tommy was standing by the fanged root, looking at the shape of Dirk in it, trying to under-stand what was going to be demanded of him. The word "artist" was on his tongue, and he tasted it, trying to make the strangeness of it fit that powerful shape struggling out of the wood. He did not like it. He did not want—but what did he want? He felt pressure on himself, the faint beginnings of something that would one day be like a tunnel of birth from which he must fight to emerge; he felt the obligations working within himself like a goad which would one day be a whip perpetually falling behind him so that he must perpetually move onwards.

His sense of fetters and debts was confirmed when Dirk came to stand by him. First he asked: "What did they want?"

"They want me to be an artist, they always want me to be something," said Tommy sullenly. He began throwing stones at the tree and shying them off along the tops of the grass. Then one hit the figure of Dirk, and he stopped.

Dirk was looking at himself. "Why do you make me like that?" he asked. The narrow, strong face expressed nothing but that familiar, sardonic antagonism, as if he said: "You, too—just like the rest!"

"Why, what's the matter with it?" challenged Tommy at once.

Dirk walked around it, then back. "You're just like all the rest," he said.

"Why? Why don't you like it?" Tommy was really distressed. Also, his feeling was: What's it got to do with him? Slowly he understood that his emotion was that belief in his right to freedom which Dirk always felt immediately, and he said in a different voice: "Tell me what's wrong with it?"

"Why do I have to come out of the wood? Why haven't I any hands or feet?"

"You have, but don't you see . . ." But Tommy looked at Dirk standing in front of him and suddenly gave an impatient movement: "Well, it doesn't matter, it's only a statue."

He sat on the trunk and Dirk beside him. After a while he said: "How should you be, then?"

"If you made yourself, would you be half wood?"

Tommy made an effort to feel this, but failed. "But it's not me, it's you." He spoke with difficulty, and thought: But it's important, I shall have to think about it later. He almost groaned with the knowledge that here it was, the first debt, presented for payment.

Dirk said suddenly: "Surely it needn't be wood. You could do the same thing if you put handcuffs on my wrists." Tommy lifted his head and gave a short, astonished laugh. "Well, what's funny?" said Dirk, aggressively. "You can't do it the easy way, you have to make me half wood, as if I was more a tree than a human being."

Tommy laughed again, but unhappily. "Oh, I'll do it again," he acknowledged at last. "Don't fuss about that one, it's finished. I'll do another."

There was a silence.

Dirk said: "What did that man say about you?"

"How do I know?"

"Does he know about art?"

"I suppose so."

"Perhaps you'll be famous," said Dirk at last. "In that book you gave me, it said about painters. Perhaps you'll be like that."

"Oh, shut up," said Tommy, roughly. "You're just as bad as he is."

"Well, what's the matter with it?"

"Why have I got to be something? First it was a sailor, and then it was a scholar, and now it's an artist."

"They wouldn't have to make me be anything," said Dirk sarcastically.

"I know," admitted Tommy grudgingly. And then, passionately: "I shan't go to university unless he sends you too."

"I know," said Dirk at once, "I know you won't."

They smiled at each other, that small, shy, revealed smile, which was so hard for them because it pledged them to such a struggle in the future.

Then Tommy asked: "Why didn't you come near me all this time?"

"I get sick of you," said Dirk. "I sometimes feel I don't want to see a white face again, not ever. I feel that I hate you all, every one."

"I know," said Tommy, grinning. Then they laughed, and the last strain of dislike between them vanished.

They began to talk, for the first time, of what their lives would be.

Tommy said: "But when you've finished training to be an engineer, what will you do? They don't let coloured people be engineers."

"Things aren't always going to be like that," said Dirk.

"It's going to be very hard," said Tommy, looking at him questioningly, and was at once reassured when Dirk said, sarcastically: "Hard, it's going to be hard? Isn't it hard now, white boy?"

Later that day Mr. Macintosh came towards them from his house.

He stood in front of them, that big, shrewd, rich man, with his small, clever grey eyes, and his narrow, loveless mouth; and he said aggressively to Tommy: "Do you want to go to the university and be an artist?"

"If Dirk comes too," said Tommy immediately.

"What do you want to study?" Mr. Macintosh asked Dirk, direct.

"I want to be an engineer," said Dirk at once.

"If I pay your way through the university then at the end of it I'm finished with you. I never want to hear from you and you are never to come back to this mine once you leave it."

Dirk and Tommy both nodded, and the instinctive agreement between them fed Mr. Macintosh's bitter unwillingness in the choice, so that he ground out viciously: "Do you think you two can be together in the university? You don't understand. You'll be living separate, and you can't go around together just as you like."

The boys looked at each other, and then, as if some sort of pact had been made between them, simply nodded.

"You can't go to university anyway, Tommy, until you've done a bit better at school. If you go back for another year and work you can pass your matric, and go to university, but you can't go now, right at the bottom of the class."

Tommy said: "I'll work." He added at once: "Dirk'll need more books to study here till we can go."

The anger was beginning to swell Mr. Macintosh's face, but Tommy said: "It's only fair. You burnt them, and now he hasn't any at all."

"Well," said Mr. Macintosh heavily. "Well, so that's how it is!"

He looked at the two boys, seated together on the tree trunk. Tommy was leaning forward, eyes lowered, a troubled but determined look on his face. Dirk was sitting erect, looking straight at his father with eyes filled with hate.

"Well," said Mr. Macintosh, with an effort at raillery which sounded harsh to them all: "Well, I send you both to university and you don't give me so much as a thank-you!"

At this, both faced towards him, with such bitter astonishment that he flushed.

"Well, well," he said. "Well, well . . ." And then he turned to leave the clearing, and cried out as he went, so as to give the appearance of dominance: "Remember, laddie, I'm not sending you unless you do well at school this year . . ."

And so he left them and went back to his house, an angry old man, defeated by something he did not begin to understand.

As for the boys, they were silent when he had gone.

The victory was entirely theirs, but now they had to begin again, in the long and difficult struggle to understand what they had won and how they would use it. ∽

INTERPRETIVE QUESTIONS
FOR DISCUSSION

Why does Tommy bind his own fate to that of Dirk, refusing to go to the university unless Dirk is sent, too?

1. Why does Tommy not just know, but accept, that "he and Dirk were closer than brothers and always would be so"? (174)

2. Why does the sheltered Tommy feel that he belongs to the world of the noisy and cheerful compound as much as he belongs to the world of his "equable, silent parents"? (155)

3. Why is Tommy full of an anger he doesn't understand when he realizes that Mr. Macintosh is Dirk's father? Why does this anger enable him to defy his parents and begin playing secretly with Dirk? (163)

4. Why don't the attitudes about kaffirs and half-castes that Tommy adopts at school prevent him from immediately picking up his friendship with Dirk when he returns home for the holidays? (166)

5. Why is it "in a quick voice, as if ashamed" that Tommy tells Dirk that he will bring back books from school and teach him? (166) Why does Dirk respond by laughing sarcastically and calling Tommy a "white bastard"? (167)

6. After teaching Dirk about his life in the city, why is Tommy compelled to remember things at school in order to later relate them to Dirk? Why is it impossible for Tommy to "do anything,

say anything, without being very conscious of just how it happened, as if Dirk's black, sarcastic eye had got inside him . . . and never closed"? (169)

7. Why does Tommy find relief from the strain of fitting his two worlds together by "swearing at niggers or kaffirs like the other boys, and more violently than they did"? Why are even these shameful incidents things that Tommy resolves to "remember . . . so as to tell Dirk"? (169)

8. Why does Tommy insist on meeting Dirk's mother even though he doesn't really want to go to the compound and Dirk doesn't really want to take him there? (181)

9. When Dirk angrily says, "You've seen my mother," why does Tommy apologize and feel "as if the responsibility for the whole thing rested on him"? What does Tommy mean by "the whole thing"? (182)

10. Why does Mr. Macintosh's burning of the hut mark for Tommy and Dirk the end of their childhood, the end of their playing? (197)

11. What is it that Tommy finally realizes when he imagines what Mr. Macintosh's offer to pay Dirk to teach the overseers "must have done to Dirk's angry, rebellious pride"? Why is Tommy's realization followed by a "bitter, ironical laugh" that "was not a boy's laugh at all"? (199)

12. Why can't Tommy, who realizes he's being a fool, keep from forcing Mr. Macintosh to consider his responsibility for Dirk? (179)

Suggested textual analyses

Pages 166–169: beginning, "At school it was not at all complicated," and ending, "He was two classes ahead of his age."

Pages 196–199: beginning, "When Tommy returned from school," and ending, "I'm not clever, look at my report."

Why do Tommy's carvings lead to a "new contract of shared feeling" between Tommy and Dirk?

1. Why does Tommy include himself when he thinks of the workers, Mr. Macintosh, and his father as ants and flies on an enormous antheap? (158) Why does this thought prompt Tommy to mold a miniature version of the working pit out of the heavy yellow soil brought up from the bottom of the mine? (158–159)

2. When he is forbidden to play with the children of the compound, why does Tommy soothe his loneliness by forming clay figures of his former playmates? (159)

3. Why does Dirk keep the clay figure that Tommy had made of him years before, even though it is worn almost to a lump of mud? (183)

4. Why does Tommy channel his artistic energy into making carvings of the members of Dirk's family? (183–184)

5. Why is the "mysterious prohibition," which forbids Tommy to distinguish himself in geometry or English, silent when it comes to his art classes? (190)

6. Why does Mr. and Mrs. Clarke's insistence that Tommy think about a profession and "be something" make the boy so miserable? (190)

7. Why is Dirk so careful to preserve Tommy's sculptures, while Tommy cares not at all about a piece once it is finished? (190–191)

8. Why does Tommy gain a "new respect for himself" when he realizes that his sculpture of Dirk makes Mr. Macintosh uneasy— that his woodcarving is not a game, but a potential "weapon"? (201)

9. Why does the thought of being an artist give Tommy a feeling of "fetters and debts"? Why are we told that Tommy experiences this sense of pressure on himself as "the faint beginnings of

something that would one day be like a tunnel of birth from which he must fight to emerge," an image that recalls his carving of Dirk in the struggle of birth? (206)

10. Why isn't the art expert, Mr. Tomlinson, impressed when Mr. Macintosh tells him that he will send Tommy to the university to study art? Why are we told that, intending to convey depths of disillusionment and irony, Mr. Tomlinson murmurs, "What a fortunate boy he is"? (205)

11. Why is Tommy unable to explain to Dirk why he has sculpted him as emerging from the tree root? Is there a latent racism in the carving, as Dirk suggests when he asks Tommy, "If you made yourself, would you be half wood?" (207)

12. Having made a promise to himself to think about Dirk's objection to the tree-root carving, why does Tommy almost groan with the knowledge that "here it was, the first debt, presented for payment"? (207)

Suggested textual analyses

Pages 182–184: beginning, "In the shed," and ending, "where his trunk was packed for school."

Pages 204–207: beginning, "Mr. Tomlinson smiled again," and ending, "Don't fuss about that one, it's finished. I'll do another."

Why does Mr. Macintosh give in and decide to send Dirk, as well as Tommy, to the university?

1. Why does Mr. Macintosh feel a "deep, grieving love" for Tommy, despite the fact that the boy holds him in contempt? (188) Why does Mr. Macintosh consider Tommy not just a "fine boy," but a "much better man than his father, who was rough and marked by the long struggle of his youth"? (179)

2. Why is Dirk able to defy Mr. Macintosh and tell him that he won't work on the mine again? (186)

3. Why are we told that Tommy wonders if there might have been cruelty in "the beginnings of the rich Mr. Macintosh . . . that had worked its way through the life of Mr. Macintosh until it turned into the cruelty of Dirk, the coloured boy, the half-caste"? (173)

4. Why does Mr. Macintosh's weakness for Tommy prompt him to promise Dirk that when he is sixteen he can do the books and write the letters for the mine? (187)

5. Why is it Mr. Macintosh's rough, amused pride in Dirk's efforts to "get on" that finally sparks a desire to "do something" for his son, even though Dirk is the "wrong colour"? (192)

6. When Mr. Macintosh goes off in search of Dirk at the hut, why does he stand on the edge of the clearing, "vaguely waiting for something to happen," rather than confront the boy directly? Why does he long to destroy Dirk forever? (193)

7. What is the "final revelation" that Mr. Macintosh is searching for when he turns and pores over the crude wooden image of Dirk that Tommy had made and sold to him for five pounds? Why is Mr. Macintosh tormented by the knowledge that the "statue might be of himself as a lad of twelve"? (194)

8. Why is Mr. Macintosh unfazed when he discovers Dirk's political pamphlets, but enraged when he sees the statues of Dirk and his family displayed in the hut on the antheap? (194–195)

9. Why is it Tommy's view of Mr. Macintosh and his life—as expressed in his carving of the pit—that fuels Mr. Macintosh's rage to the point that he burns down the hut? (195–196)

10. Why does Tommy's sculpture of Dirk writhing out of the wood of the tree root fill Mr. Macintosh with hatred and fear? Why, despite his uneasy loathing, can't Mr. Macintosh stop watching Tommy carve the sculpture? (200)

11. Why are Tommy and Dirk able to overcome Mr. Macintosh's "bitter unwillingness" to send them both to the university? (209) What is the "something" Mr. Macintosh is defeated by that "he did not begin to understand"? (210)

12. Why are we told that, although the victory was entirely theirs, Tommy and Dirk "had to begin again, in the long and difficult struggle to understand what they had won and how they would use it"? What don't the boys yet understand about what they have won? (210)

Suggested textual analyses

Pages 192–196: beginning, "One night Mr. Macintosh came rather late," and ending, "thinking of reproachful things to say to him."

Pages 209–210: from "Later that day Mr. Macintosh came towards them," to the end of the story.

FOR FURTHER REFLECTION

1. Where does the deep conviction that one is entitled to freedom come from when a person has been marginalized or exploited by society since birth?

2. Is learning to value the "other"—accepting that we are all members of the human family—something that can be learned with the mind?

3. Are children less susceptible to racism than adults are?

4. Do artists lead the way in bringing about social change?

5. Given the history of racism in our society, is anger an inevitable component of any relationship between blacks and whites? If so, how can this anger be acknowledged, and overcome, so that relationships between black people and white people can develop and endure?

A Voyage to the Country of the Houyhnhnms

Jonathan Swift

JONATHAN SWIFT (1667–1745) was born
in Dublin, Ireland, to English parents.
Swift's father died a few months before his
birth, and he was raised by his mother and
uncles. They sent him to an excellent Irish
preparatory school and to Trinity College,
where he earned his B.A. in 1686. In 1689,
Swift left Ireland for England and became
secretary to Sir William Temple, a "man of
culture" and former diplomat. Swift aided
Temple with the writing of essays and
memoirs and read widely in Temple's
personal library. During this time, Swift also
wrote poetry, and he discovered his gifts as
a writer of satire. Returning to Ireland in
1699, Swift served in the Irish church
hierarchy and became a highly respected
political pamphleteer in both Ireland and
England. His appointment as Dean of
St. Patrick's Cathedral in Dublin in 1713
was made as a political favor for his writing
on behalf of England's Tories. *Gulliver's
Travels,* which includes "A Voyage to the
Country of the Houyhnhnms," was
published in 1726.

I
1

I CONTINUED AT HOME with my wife and children about
five months in a very happy condition, if I could have learned
the lesson of knowing when I was well. I left my poor wife big
with child, and accepted an advantageous offer made me to be
Captain of the *Adventure,* a stout merchantman of 350 tons: for
I understood navigation well, and being grown weary of a surgeon's employment at sea, which however I could exercise upon
occasion, I took a skilful young man of that calling, one Robert
Purefoy, into my ship. We set sail from Portsmouth upon the
seventh day of August, 1710; on the fourteenth we met with
Captain Pocock of Bristol, at Tenerife, who was going to the Bay
of Campeche, to cut logwood. On the sixteenth he was parted
from us by a storm; I heard since my return that his ship
foundered, and none escaped but one cabin boy. He was an honest man, and a good sailor, but a little too positive in his own
opinions, which was the cause of his destruction, as it hath been
of several others. For if he had followed my advice, he might have
been safe at home with his family at this time, as well as myself.

I had several men died in my ship of calentures, so that I was forced to get recruits out of Barbados, and the Leeward Island, where I touched by the direction of the merchants who employed me, which I had soon too much cause to repent: for I found afterwards that most of them had been buccaneers. I had fifty hands on board, and my orders were that I should trade with the Indians in the South Sea, and make what discoveries I could. These rogues whom I had picked up debauched my other men, and they all formed a conspiracy to seize the ship and secure me; which they did one morning, rushing into my cabin, and binding me hand and foot, threatening to throw me overboard, if I offered to stir. I told them I was their prisoner and would submit. This they made me swear to do, and then they unbound me, only fastening one of my legs with a chain near my bed, and placed a sentry at my door with his piece charged, who was commanded to shoot me dead, if I attempted my liberty. They sent me down victuals and drink, and took the government of the ship to themselves. Their design was to turn pirates, and plunder the Spaniards, which they could not do, till they got more men. But first they resolved to sell the goods in the ship, and then go to Madagascar for recruits, several among them having died since my confinement. They sailed many weeks, and traded with the Indians, but I knew not what course they took, being kept a close prisoner in my cabin, and expecting nothing less than to be murdered, as they often threatened me.

Upon the ninth day of May, 1711, one James Welch came down to my cabin; and said he had orders from the Captain to set me ashore. I expostulated with him but in vain; neither would he so much as tell me who their new Captain was. They forced me into the longboat, letting me put on my best suit of clothes, which were as good as new, and a small bundle of linen, but no arms except my hanger; and they were so civil as not to search my pockets, into which I conveyed what money I had, with some other little necessaries. They rowed about a league, and then set me down on a strand. I desired them to tell me what country it was. They all swore they knew no more than myself, but said that the Captain (as they called him) was resolved, after they had sold the lading, to get rid of me in the first place where they could discover land. They pushed off immediately, advising me to make haste, for fear of being overtaken by the tide, and so bade me farewell.

In this desolate condition I advanced forward, and soon got upon firm ground, where I sat down on a bank to rest myself, and consider what I had best to do. When I was a little refreshed I went up into the country, resolving to deliver myself to the first savages I should meet, and purchase my life from them by some bracelets, glass rings, and other toys which sailors usually provide themselves with in those voyages, and whereof I had some about me. The land was divided by long rows of trees, not regularly planted, but naturally growing; there was plenty of grass, and several fields of oats. I walked very circumspectly for fear of being surprised, or suddenly shot with an arrow from behind or on either side. I fell into a beaten road, where I saw many tracks of human feet, and some of cows, but most of horses. At last I beheld several animals in a field, and one or two of the same kind sitting in trees. Their shape was very singular and deformed, which a little discomposed me, so that I lay down behind a thicket to observe them better. Some of them coming forward near the place where I lay, gave me an opportunity of distinctly marking their form. Their heads and breasts were covered with a thick hair, some frizzled and others lank; they had beards like goats, and a long ridge of hair down their backs and the foreparts of their legs and feet, but the rest of their bodies were bare, so that I might see their skins, which were of a brown buff colour. They had no tails, nor any hair at all on their buttocks, except about the anus; which, I presume, nature had placed there to defend them as they sat on the ground; for this posture they used, as well as lying down, and often stood on their hind feet. They climbed high trees, as nimbly as a squirrel, for they had strong extended claws before and behind, terminating in sharp points, and hooked. They would often spring and bound and leap with prodigious agility. The females were not so large as the males; they had long lank hair on their heads, but none on their faces, nor any thing more than a sort of down on the rest of their bodies, except about the anus, and pudenda. Their dugs hung between their forefeet, and often reached almost to the ground as they walked. The hair of both sexes was of several colours, brown, red, black, and yellow. Upon the whole, I never beheld in all my travels so disagreeable an animal, nor one against which I naturally conceived so strong an antipathy. So that thinking I had seen enough, full of contempt and aversion, I got up and pursued the beaten road, hoping it might direct me to the cabin of some Indian. I had not got far when I met one of these creatures full in my way, and coming up directly to me. The ugly monster, when he saw me, distorted several ways every feature of his visage, and stared as at an object he had never seen before; then approaching nearer, lifted up his forepaw, whether out of curiosity or mischief, I could not tell. But I drew my hanger, and gave him a good blow with the flat side of it, for I durst not strike him with the edge, fearing the inhabitants might be provoked against me, if they should come to know that I had killed or maimed any of their cattle. When the beast felt the smart, he drew back, and roared so loud that a herd of at least forty came flocking about me from the next field, howling and making odious faces; but I ran to the body of a tree, and leaning my back against it, kept them off by waving my hanger. Several of this cursed brood, getting hold of the branches behind, leapt up into the tree, from whence they began to discharge their excrements on my head; however, I escaped pretty well, by sticking close to the stem of the tree, but was almost stifled with the filth, which fell about me on every side.

In the midst of this distress, I observed them all to run away on a sudden as fast as they could, at which I ventured to leave the tree, and pursue the road, wondering what it was that could put them into this fright. But looking on my left, I saw a horse walking softly in the field; which my persecutors having sooner discovered, was the cause of their flight. The horse started a little when he came near me, but soon recovering himself, looked full in my face with manifest tokens of wonder; he viewed my hands and feet, walking round me several times. I would have pursued my journey, but he placed himself directly in the way, yet looking with a very mild aspect, never offering the least violence. We stood gazing at each other for some time; at last I took the boldness to reach my hand towards his neck, with a design to stroke it, using the common style and whistle of jockeys when they are going to handle a strange horse. But this animal, seeming to receive my civilities with disdain, shook his head, and bent his brows, softly raising up his right forefoot to remove my hand. Then he neighed three or four times, but in so different a cadence, that I almost began to think he was speaking to himself in some language of his own.

While he and I were thus employed, another horse came up: who applying himself to the first in a very formal manner, they gently struck each other's right hoof before, neighing several times by turns, and varying the sound, which seemed to be almost articulate. They went some paces off, as if it were to confer together, walking side by side, backward and forward, like persons deliberating upon some affair of weight, but often turning their eyes towards me, as it were to watch that I might not escape. I was amazed to see such actions and behaviour in brute beasts, and concluded with myself, that if the inhabitants of this country were endued with a proportionable degree of reason, they must needs be the wisest people upon earth. This thought gave me so much comfort, that I resolved to go forward until I could discover some house or village, or meet with any of the natives, leaving the two horses to discourse together as they pleased. But the first, who was a dapple gray, observing me to steal off, neighed after me in so expressive a tone, that I fancied myself to understand what he meant; whereupon I turned back, and came near him, to expect his farther commands, but concealing my fear as much as I could, for I began to be in some pain, how this adventure might terminate; and the reader will easily believe I did not much like my present situation.

The two horses came up close to me, looking with great earnestness upon my face and hands. The gray steed rubbed my hat all round with his right forehoof, and discomposed it so much that I was forced to adjust it better, by taking it off, and settling it again; whereat both he and his companion (who was a brown bay) appeared to be much surprised; the latter felt the lappet of my coat, and finding it to hang loose about me, they both looked with new signs of wonder. He stroked my right hand, seeming to admire the softness and colour; but he squeezed it so hard between his hoof and his pastern, that I was forced to roar; after which they both touched me with all possible tenderness. They were under great perplexity about my shoes and stockings, which they felt very often, neighing to each other, and using various gestures, not unlike those of a philosopher, when he would attempt to solve some new and difficult phenomenon.

Upon the whole, the behaviour of these animals was so orderly and rational, so acute and judicious, that I at last concluded they must needs be magicians, who had thus metamorphosed themselves upon some design, and seeing a stranger in the way, were resolved to divert themselves with him; or perhaps were really amazed at the sight of a man so very different in habit, feature, and complexion from those who might probably live in so remote a climate. Upon the strength of this reasoning, I ventured to address them in the following manner: Gentlemen, if you be conjurers, as I have good cause to believe, you can understand any language; therefore I make bold to let your worships know that I am a poor distressed Englishman, driven by his misfortunes upon your coast, and I entreat one of you, to let me ride upon his back, as if he were a real horse, to some house or village where I can be relieved. In return of which favour I will make you a present of this knife and bracelet (taking them out of my pocket). The two creatures stood silent while I spoke, seeming to listen with great attention; and when I had ended, they neighed frequently towards each other, as if they were engaged in serious conversation. I plainly observed, that their language expressed the passions very well, and the words might with little pains be resolved into an alphabet more easily than the Chinese.

I could frequently distinguish the word *Yahoo,* which was repeated by each of them several times; and although it was impossible for me to conjecture what it meant, yet while the two horses were busy in conversation, I endeavoured to practise this word upon my tongue; and as soon as they were silent, I boldly pronounced *Yahoo* in a loud voice, imitating, at the same time, as near as I could, the neighing of a horse; at which they were both visibly surprised, and the gray repeated the same word twice, as if he meant to teach me the right accent, wherein I spoke after him as well as I could, and found myself perceivably to improve every time, though very far from any degree of perfection. Then the bay tried me with a second word, much harder to be pronounced; but reducing it to the English orthography, may be spelt thus, *Houyhnhnm.* I did not succeed in this so well as the former, but after two or three farther trials, I had better fortune; and they both appeared amazed at my capacity.

After some further discourse, which I then conjectured might relate to me, the two friends took their leaves, with the same compliment of striking each other's hoof; and the gray made me signs that I should walk before him, wherein I thought it prudent to comply, till I could find a better director. When I offered to slacken my pace, he would cry *Hhuun, Hhuun;* I guessed his meaning, and gave him to understand as well as I could, that I was weary, and not able to walk faster; upon which he would stand a while to let me rest.

2

Having travelled about three miles, we came to a long kind of building, made of timber stuck in the ground, and wattled across; the roof was low, and covered with straw. I now began to be a little comforted, and took out some toys, which travellers usually carry for presents to the savage Indians of America and other parts, in hopes the people of the house would be thereby encouraged to receive me kindly. The horse made me a sign to go in first; it was a large room with a smooth clay floor, and a rack and manger extending the whole length on one side. There were three nags, and two mares, not eating, but some of them sitting down upon their hams, which I very much wondered at; but wondered more to see the rest employed in domestic business. These seemed but ordinary cattle; however, this confirmed my first opinion, that a people who could so far civilize brute animals, must needs excel in wisdom all the nations of the world. The gray came in just after, and thereby prevented any ill treatment which the others might have given me. He neighed to them several times in a style of authority, and received answers.

Beyond this room there were three others, reaching the length of the house, to which you passed through three doors, opposite to each other, in the manner of a vista; we went through the second room towards the third; here the gray walked in first, beckoning me to attend: I waited in the second room, and got ready my presents for the master and mistress of the house: they were two knives, three bracelets of false pearl, a small looking glass, and a bead necklace. The horse neighed three or four times, and I waited to hear some answers in a human voice, but I heard no other returns than in the same dialect, only one or two a little shriller than his. I began to think that this house must belong to some person of great note among them, because there appeared so much ceremony before I could gain admittance. But, that a man of quality should be served all by horses, was beyond my comprehension. I feared my brain was disturbed by my sufferings and misfortunes: I roused myself, and looked about me in the room where I was left alone; this was furnished like the first, only after a more elegant manner. I rubbed my eyes often, but the same objects still occurred. I pinched my arms and sides to awake myself, hoping I might be in a dream. I then absolutely concluded, that all these appearances could be nothing else but necromancy and magic. But I had no time to pursue these reflections; for the gray horse came to the door, and made me a sign to follow him into the third room, where I saw a very comely mare, together with a colt and foal, sitting on their haunches, upon mats of straw, not unartfully made, and perfectly neat and clean.

The mare, soon after my entrance, rose from her mat, and coming up close, after having nicely observed my hands and face, gave me a most contemptuous look; then turning to the horse, I heard the word *Yahoo* often repeated betwixt them; the meaning of which word I could not then comprehend, although it were the first I had learned to pronounce; but I was soon better informed, to my everlasting mortification: for the horse beckoning to me with his head, and repeating the word *Hhuun, Hhuun,* as he did upon the road, which I understood was to attend him, led me out into a kind of court, where was another building at some distance from the house. Here we entered, and I saw three of these detestable creatures, whom I first met after my landing, feeding upon roots, and the flesh of some animals, which I afterwards found to be that of asses and dogs, and now and then a cow dead by accident or disease. They were all tied by the neck with strong withes, fastened to a beam; they held their food between the claws of their forefeet, and tore it with their teeth.

The master horse ordered a sorrel nag, one of his servants, to untie the largest of these animals, and take him into the yard. The beast and I were brought close together, and our countenances diligently compared, both by master and servant, who thereupon repeated several times the word *Yahoo*. My horror and astonishment are not to be described, when I observed in this abominable animal a perfect human figure: the face of it indeed was flat and broad, the nose depressed, the lips large, and the mouth wide. But these differences are common to all savage nations, where the lineaments of the countenance are distorted by the natives suffering their infants to lie grovelling on the earth, or by carrying them on their backs, nuzzling with their face against the mother's shoulders. The forefeet of the Yahoo differed from my hands in nothing else but the length of the nails, the coarseness and brownness of the palms, and the hairiness on the backs. There was the same resemblance between our feet, with the same differences, which I knew very well, though the horses did not, because of my shoes and stockings; the same in every part of our bodies, except as to hairiness and colour, which I have already described.

The great difficulty that seemed to stick with the two horses, was to see the rest of my body so very different from that of a Yahoo, for which I was obliged to my clothes, whereof they had no conception. The sorrel nag offered me a root, which he held (after their manner, as we shall describe in its proper place) between his hoof and pastern; I took it in my hand, and having smelt it, returned it to him as civilly as I could. He brought out of the Yahoo's kennel a piece of ass's flesh, but it smelt so offensively that I turned from it with loathing: he then threw it to the Yahoo, by whom it was greedily devoured. He afterwards showed me a wisp of hay, and a fetlock full of oats; but I shook my head, to signify that neither of these were food for me. And indeed, I now apprehended that I must absolutely starve, if I did not get to some of my own species; for as to those filthy Yahoos, although there were few greater lovers of mankind, at that time, than myself, yet I confess I never saw any sensitive being so detestable on all accounts; and the more I came near them, the more hateful they grew, while I stayed in that country. This the master horse observed by my behaviour, and therefore sent the Yahoo back to his kennel. He then put his forehoof to his mouth, at which I was much surprised, although he did it with ease, and with a motion that appeared perfectly natural, and made other signs to know what I would eat; but I could not return him such an answer as he was able to apprehend; and if he had understood me, I did not see how it was possible to contrive any way for finding myself nourishment. While we were thus engaged, I observed a cow passing by, whereupon I pointed to her, and expressed a desire to let me go and milk her. This had its effect; for he led me back into the house, and ordered a mare-servant to open a room, where a good store of milk lay in earthen and wooden vessels, after a very orderly and cleanly manner. She gave me a large bowl full, of which I drank very heartily, and found myself well refreshed.

About noon I saw coming towards the house a kind of vehicle, drawn like a sledge by four Yahoos. There was in it an old steed, who seemed to be of quality; he alighted with his hindfeet forward, having by accident got a hurt in his left forefoot. He came to dine with our horse, who received him with great civility. They dined in the best room, and had oats boiled in milk for the second course, which the old horse ate warm, but the rest cold. Their mangers were placed circular in the middle of the room, and divided into several partitions, round which they sat on their haunches upon bosses of straw. In the middle was a large rack with angles answering to every partition of the manger; so that each horse and mare ate their own hay, and their own mash of oats and milk, with much decency and regularity. The behaviour of the young colt and foal appeared very modest, and that of the master and mistress extremely cheerful and complaisant to their guest. The gray ordered me to stand by him, and much discourse passed between him and his friend concerning me, as I found by the stranger's often looking on me, and the frequent repetition of the word *Yahoo*.

I happened to wear my gloves, which the master gray observing, seemed perplexed, discovering signs of wonder what I had done to my forefeet; he put his hoof three or four times to them, as if he would signify that I should reduce them to their former shape, which I presently did, pulling off both my gloves, and putting them into my pocket. This occasioned farther talk, and I saw the company was pleased with my behaviour, whereof I soon found the good effects. I was ordered to speak the few words I understood, and while they were at dinner the master taught me the names for oats, milk, fire, water, and some others; which I could readily pronounce after him, having from my youth a great facility in learning languages.

When dinner was done the master horse took me aside, and by signs and words made me understand the concern that he was in, that I had nothing to eat. Oats in their tongue are called *blunnh*. This word I pronounced two or three times; for although I had refused them at first, yet upon second thoughts I considered that I could contrive to make of them a kind of bread, which might be sufficient with milk to keep me alive, till I could make my escape to some other country and to creatures of my own species. The horse immediately ordered a white mare-servant of his family to bring me a good quantity of oats in a sort of wooden tray. These I heated before the fire as well as I could, and rubbed them till the husks came off, which I made a shift to winnow from the grain; I ground and beat them between two stones, then took water, and made them into a paste or cake, which I toasted at the fire, and ate warm with milk. It was at first a very insipid diet, though common enough in many parts of Europe, but grew tolerable by time; and having been often reduced to hard fare in my life, this was not the first experiment I had made how easily nature is satisfied. And I cannot but observe, that I never had one hour's sickness while I stayed in this island. 'Tis true, I sometimes made a shift to catch a rabbit or bird by springes made of Yahoos' hairs, and I often gathered wholesome herbs, which I boiled, or ate as salads with my bread, and now and then, for a rarity, I made a little butter, and drank the whey. I was at first at a great loss for salt; but custom soon reconciled the want of it; and I am confident that the frequent use of salt among us is an effect of luxury, and was first introduced only as a provocative to drink; except where it is necessary for preserving of flesh in long voyages, or in places remote from great markets. For we observe no animal to be fond of it but man: and as to myself, when I left this country, it was a great while before I could endure the taste of it in anything that I ate.

This is enough to say upon the subject of my diet, wherewith other travellers fill their books, as if the readers were personally concerned whether we fared well or ill. However, it was necessary to mention this matter, lest the world should think it impossible that I could find sustenance for three years in such a country, and among such inhabitants.

When it grew towards evening, the master horse ordered a place for me to lodge in; it was but six yards from the house, and separated from the stable of the Yahoos. Here I got some straw, and covering myself with my own clothes, slept very sound. But I was in a short time better accommodated, as the reader shall know hereafter, when I come to treat more particularly about my way of living.

3

My principal endeavour was to learn the language, which my master (for so I shall henceforth call him), and his children, and every servant of his house, were desirous to teach me. For they looked upon it as a prodigy that a brute animal should discover such marks of a rational creature. I pointed to every thing and enquired the name of it, which I wrote down in my journal-book when I was alone, and corrected my bad accent by desiring those of the family to pronounce it often. In this employment, a sorrel nag, one of the underservants, was ready to assist me.

In speaking they pronounce through the nose and throat, and their language approaches nearest to the High Dutch or German of any I know in Europe; but is much more graceful and significant. The Emperor Charles V made almost the same observation, when he said that if he were to speak to his horse it should be in High Dutch.

The curiosity and impatience of my master were so great, that he spent many hours of his leisure to instruct me. He was convinced (as he afterwards told me) that I must be a Yahoo, but my teachableness, civility, and cleanliness astonished him; which were qualities altogether so opposite to those animals. He was most perplexed about my clothes, reasoning sometimes with himself whether they were a part of my body; for I never pulled them off till the family were asleep, and got them on before they waked in the morning. My master was eager to learn from whence I came; how I acquired those appearances of reason, which I discovered in all my actions; and to know my story from my own mouth, which he hoped he should soon do by the great proficiency I made in learning and pronouncing their words and sentences. To help my memory, I formed all I learned into the English alphabet, and writ the words down with the translations. The last after some time I ventured to do in my master's presence. It cost me much trouble to explain to him what I was doing; for the inhabitants have not the least idea of books or literature.

In about ten weeks' time I was able to understand most of his questions, and in three months could give him some tolerable answers. He was extremely curious to know from what part of the country I came, and how I was taught to imitate a rational creature; because the Yahoos (whom he saw I exactly resembled in my head, hands, and face, that were only visible), with some appearance of cunning, and the strongest disposition to mischief, were observed to be the most unteachable of all brutes. I answered that I came over the sea from a far place, with many others of my own kind, in a great hollow vessel made of the bodies of trees. That my companions forced me to land on this coast, and then left me to shift for myself. It was with some difficulty, and by the help of many signs, that I brought him to understand me. He replied, that I must needs be mistaken, or that I *said the thing which was not*. (For they have no word in their language to express lying or falsehood.) He knew it was impossible that there could be a country beyond the sea, or that a parcel of brutes could move a wooden vessel whither they pleased upon water. He was sure no Houyhnhnm alive could make such a vessel, nor would trust Yahoos to manage it.

The word *Houyhnhnm,* in their tongue, signifies a *horse,* and in its etymology, *the perfection of nature*. I told my master, that I was at a loss for expression, but would improve as fast as I could; and hoped in a short time I should be able to tell him wonders: he was pleased to direct his own mare, his colt and foal, and the servants of the family, to take all opportunities of instructing me, and every day for two or three hours he was at the same pains himself. Several horses and mares of quality in the neighbourhood came often to our house upon the report spread of a wonderful Yahoo, that could speak like a Houyhnhnm, and seemed in his words and actions to discover some glimmerings of reason. These delighted to converse with me: they put many questions, and received such answers as I was able to return. By all these advantages I made so great a progress that in five months from my arrival I understood whatever was spoke, and could express myself tolerably well.

The Houyhnhnms who came to visit my master out of a design of seeing and talking with me, could hardly believe me to be a right Yahoo, because my body had a different covering from others of my kind. They were astonished to observe me without the usual hair or skin, except on my head, face, and hands; but I discovered that secret to my master, upon an accident which happened about a fortnight before.

I have already told the reader, that every night when the family were gone to bed it was my custom to strip and cover myself with my clothes. It happened one morning early that my master sent for me by the sorrel nag, who was his valet; when he came I was fast asleep, my clothes fallen off on one side, and my shirt above my waist. I awaked at the noise he made, and observed him to deliver his message in some disorder; after which he went to my master, and in a great fright gave him a very confused account of what he had seen. This I presently discovered; for going as soon as I was dressed to pay my attendance upon his Honour, he asked me the meaning of what his servant had reported, that I was not the same thing when I slept as I appeared to be at other times; that his valet assured him, some part of me was white, some yellow, at least not so white, and some brown.

I had hitherto concealed the secret of my dress, in order to distinguish myself as much as possible from that cursed race of Yahoos; but now I found it in vain to do so any longer. Besides,

I considered that my clothes and shoes would soon wear out, which already were in a declining condition, and must be supplied by some contrivance from the hides of Yahoos or other brutes; whereby the whole secret would be known. I therefore told my master that in the country from whence I came those of my kind always covered their bodies with the hairs of certain animals prepared by art, as well for decency as to avoid the inclemencies of air, both hot and cold; of which, as to my own person, I would give him immediate conviction, if he pleased to command me; only desiring his excuse, if I did not expose those parts that nature taught us to conceal. He said my discourse was all very strange, but especially the last part; for he could not understand why nature should teach us to conceal what nature had given. That neither himself nor family were ashamed of any parts of their bodies; but however I might do as I pleased. Whereupon I first unbuttoned my coat and pulled it off. I did the same with my waistcoat; I drew off my shoes, stockings, and breeches. I let my shirt down to my waist, and drew up the bottom, fastening it like a girdle about my middle to hide my nakedness.

My master observed the whole performance with great signs of curiosity and admiration. He took up all my clothes in his pastern, one piece after another, and examined them diligently; he then stroked my body very gently and looked round me several times, after which he said it was plain I must be a perfect Yahoo; but that I differed very much from the rest of my species, in the softness and whiteness and smoothness of my skin, my want of hair in several parts of my body, the shape and shortness of my claws behind and before, and my affectation of walking continually on my two hinderfeet. He desired to see no more, and gave me leave to put on my clothes again, for I was shuddering with cold.

I expressed my uneasiness at his giving me so often the appellation of Yahoo, an odious animal for which I had so utter a hatred and contempt. I begged he would forbear applying that word to me, and take the same order in his family, and among his friends whom he suffered to see me. I requested likewise that the secret of my having a false covering to my body might be known to none but himself, at least as long as my present clothing should last; for as to what the sorrel nag his valet had observed, his Honour might command him to conceal it.

All this my master very graciously consented to, and thus the secret was kept till my clothes began to wear out, which I was forced to supply by several contrivances that shall hereafter be mentioned. In the meantime he desired I would go on with my utmost diligence to learn their language, because he was more astonished at my capacity for speech and reason than at the figure of my body, whether it were covered or no; adding that he waited with some impatience to hear the wonders which I promised to tell him.

From thenceforward he doubled the pains he had been at to instruct me; he brought me into all company, and made them treat me with civility, because, as he told them privately, this would put me into good humour and make me more diverting.

Every day when I waited on him, beside the trouble he was at in teaching, he would ask me several questions concerning myself, which I answered as well as I could; and by these means he had already received some general ideas, though very imperfect. It would be tedious to relate the several steps by which I advanced to a more regular conversation: but the first account I gave of myself in any order and length, was to this purpose:

That I came from a very far country, as I already had attempted to tell him, with about fifty more of my own species; that we travelled upon the seas, in a great hollow vessel made of wood, and larger than his Honour's house. I described the ship to him in the best terms I could, and explained by the help of my handkerchief displayed, how it was driven forward by the wind. That upon a quarrel among us, I was set on shore on this coast, where I walked forward without knowing whither, till he delivered me from the persecution of those execrable Yahoos. He asked me who made the ship, and how it was possible that the Houyhnhnms of my country would leave it to the

management of brutes? My answer was that I durst proceed no
further in my relation, unless he would give me his word and
honour that he would not be offended, and then I would tell
him the wonders I had so often promised. He agreed; and I went
on by assuring him that the ship was made by creatures like
myself, who in all the countries I had travelled, as well as in
my own, were the only governing, rational animals; and that
upon my arrival hither I was as much astonished to see the
Houyhnhnms act like rational beings, as he or his friends could
be in finding some marks of reason in a creature he was pleased
to call a Yahoo, to which I owned my resemblance in every part,
but could not account for their degenerate and brutal nature. I
said farther that if good fortune ever restored me to my native
country, to relate my travels hither, as I resolved to do, every
body would believe that I *said the thing which was not;* that I
invented the story out of my own head; and with all possible
respect to himself, his family and friends, and under his promise
of not being offended, our countrymen would hardly think it
probable, that a Houyhnhnm should be the presiding creature
of a nation, and a Yahoo the brute.

4

My master heard me with great appearances of uneasiness in his
countenance, because *doubting,* or *not believing,* are so little
known in this country, that the inhabitants cannot tell how to
behave themselves under such circumstances. And I remember
in frequent discourses with my master concerning the nature of
manhood in other parts of the world, having occasion to talk of
lying and *false representation,* it was with much difficulty that
he comprehended what I meant, although he had otherwise a
most acute judgment. For he argued thus: that the use of speech
was to make us understand one another, and to receive information of facts; now if one *said the thing which was not,* these
ends were defeated; because I cannot properly be said to understand him; and I am so far from receiving information, that he

leaves me worse than in ignorance, for I am led to believe a thing black when it is white, and short when it is long. And these were all the notions he had concerning that faculty of *lying,* so perfectly well understood among human creatures.

To return from this digression; when I asserted that the Yahoos were the only governing animals in my country, which my master said was altogether past his conception, he desired to know whether we had Houyhnhnms among us, and what was their employment: I told him we had great numbers, that in summer they grazed in the fields, and in winter were kept in houses, with hay and oats, where Yahoo servants were employed to rub their skins smooth, comb their manes, pick their feet, serve them with food, and make their beds. I understand you well, said my master, it is now very plain, from all you have spoken, that whatever share of reason the Yahoos pretend to, the Houyhnhnms are your masters; I heartily wish our Yahoos would be so tractable. I begged his Honour would please to excuse me from proceeding any farther, because I was very certain that the account he expected from me would be highly displeasing. But he insisted in commanding me to let him know the best and the worst: I told him he should be obeyed. I owned that the Houyhnhnms among us, whom we called horses, were the most generous and comely animals we had, that they excelled in strength and swiftness; and when they belonged to persons of quality, employed in travelling, racing, or drawing chariots, they were treated with much kindness and care, till they fell into disease or became foundered in the feet; and then they were sold, and used to all kind of drudgery till they died; after which their skins were stripped and sold for what they were worth, and their bodies left to be devoured by dogs and birds of prey. But the common race of horses had not so good fortune, being kept by farmers and carriers, and other mean people, who put them to great labour, and fed them worse. I described, as well as I could, our way of riding, the shape and use of a bridle, a saddle, a spur, and a whip, of harness and wheels. I added that we fastened plates of a certain hard substance called iron at the bottom of their feet, to preserve their hoofs from being broken by the stony ways on which we often travelled.

My master, after some expressions of great indignation, wondered how we dared to venture upon a Houyhnhnm's back, for he was sure that the weakest servant in his house would be able to shake off the strongest Yahoo, or by lying down and rolling on his back squeeze the brute to death. I answered that our horses were trained up from three or four years old to the several uses we intended them for; that if any of them proved intolerably vicious, they were employed for carriages; that they were severely beaten while they were young, for any mischievous tricks; that the males, designed for common use of riding or draught, were generally castrated about two years after their birth, to take down their spirits and make them more tame and gentle; that they were indeed sensible of rewards and punishments; but his Honour would please to consider, that they had not the least tincture of reason any more than the Yahoos in this country.

It put me to the pains of many circumlocutions to give my master a right idea of what I spoke; for their language doth not abound in variety of words, because their wants and passions are fewer than among us. But it is impossible to represent his noble resentment at our savage treatment of the Houyhnhnm race, particularly after I had explained the manner and use of castrating horses among us, to hinder them from propagating their kind, and to render them more servile. He said if it were possible there could be any country where Yahoos alone were endued with reason, they certainly must be the governing animal, because reason will in time always prevail against brutal strength. But considering the frame of our bodies, and especially of mine, he thought no creature of equal bulk was so ill contrived, for employing that reason in the common offices of life; whereupon he desired to know whether those among whom I lived resembled me or the Yahoos of his country. I assured him, that I was as well shaped as most of my age; but the younger and the females were much more soft and tender, and the skins of the latter generally as white as milk. He said I differed indeed from other Yahoos, being much more cleanly, and not altogether so deformed, but in point of real advantage he thought I differed for the worse. That my nails were of no use either to my fore or hinderfeet; as to my forefeet, he could not properly call them by that name, for he never observed me to walk upon them; that they were too soft to bear the ground; that I generally went with them uncovered, neither was the covering I sometimes wore on them of the same shape or so strong as that on my feet behind. That I could not walk with any security, for if either of my hinderfeet slipped, I must inevitably fall. He then began to find fault with other parts of my body, the flatness of my face, the prominence of my nose, my eyes placed directly in front, so that I could not look on either side without turning my head; that I was not able to feed myself without lifting one of my forefeet to my mouth; and therefore nature had placed those joints to answer that necessity. He knew not what could be the use of those several clefts and divisions in my feet behind; that these were too soft to bear the hardness and sharpness of stones without a covering made from the skin of some other brute; that my whole body wanted a fence against heat and cold, which I was forced to put on and off every day with tediousness and trouble. And lastly that he observed every animal in this country naturally to abhor the Yahoos, whom the weaker avoided and the stronger drove from them. So that supposing us to have the gift of reason, he could not see how it were possible to cure that natural antipathy which every creature discovered against us; nor consequently, how we could tame and render them serviceable. However, he would (as he said) debate the matter no farther, because he was more desirous to know my own story, the country where I was born, and the several actions and events of my life before I came hither.

I assured him how extremely desirous I was that he should be satisfied on every point; but I doubted much whether it would be possible for me to explain myself on several subjects whereof his Honour could have no conception, because I saw nothing in his country to which I could resemble them. That however I would do my best, and strive to express myself by similitudes, humbly desiring his assistance when I wanted proper words; which he was pleased to promise me.

I said my birth was of honest parents in an island called England, which was remote from this country, as many days' journey as the strongest of his Honour's servants could travel in the annual course of the sun. That I was bred a surgeon, whose trade it is to cure wounds and hurts in the body, got by accident or violence; that my country was governed by a female man, whom we called a Queen. That I left it to get riches, whereby I might maintain myself and family when I should return. That in my last voyage I was Commander of the ship, and had about fifty Yahoos under me, many of which died at sea, and I was forced to supply them by others picked out from several nations. That our ship was twice in danger of being sunk; the first time by a great storm, and the second, by striking against a rock. Here my master interposed, by asking me how I could persuade strangers out of different countries to venture with me, after the losses I had sustained, and the hazards I had run. I said they were fellows of desperate fortunes, forced to fly from the places of their birth, on account of their poverty or their crimes. Some were undone by lawsuits; others spent all they had in drinking, whoring, and gaming; others fled for treason; many for murder, theft, poisoning, robbery, perjury, forgery, coining false money, for committing rapes or sodomy, for flying from their colours, or deserting to the enemy, and most of them had broken prison; none of these durst return to their native countries for fear of being hanged, or of starving in a jail; and therefore were under the necessity of seeking a livelihood in other places.

During this discourse my master was pleased to interrupt me several times; I had made use of many circumlocutions in describing to him the nature of the several crimes, for which most of our crew had been forced to fly their country. This labour took up several days' conversation before he was able to comprehend me. He was wholly at a loss to know what could be the use or necessity of practising those vices. To clear up which I endeavoured to give some ideas of the desire of power and riches, of the terrible effects of lust, intemperance, malice, and envy. All this I was forced to define and describe by putting of cases, and making of suppositions. After which, like one whose imagination was struck with something never seen or heard of before, he would lift up his eyes with amazement and indignation. Power, government, war, law, punishment, and a thousand other things had no terms wherein that language could express them, which made the difficulty almost insuperable to give my master any conception of what I meant. But being of an excellent understanding, much improved by contemplation and converse, he at last arrived at a competent knowledge of what human nature in our parts of the world is capable to perform, and desired I would give him some particular account of that land which we call Europe, but especially of my own country.

5

The reader may please to observe, that the following extract of many conversations I had with my master, contains a summary of the most material points which were discoursed at several times for above two years; his Honour often desiring fuller satisfaction as I farther improved in the Houyhnhnm tongue. I laid before him, as well as I could, the whole state of Europe; I discoursed of trade and manufactures, of arts and sciences; and the answers I gave to all the questions he made, as they arose upon several subjects, were a fund of conversation not to be exhausted. But I shall here only set down the substance of what passed between us concerning my own country, reducing it into order as well as I can, without any regard to time or other circumstances, while I strictly adhere to truth. My only concern is that I shall hardly be able to do justice to my master's arguments and expressions, which must needs suffer by my want of capacity, as well as by a translation into our barbarous English.

In obedience therefore to his Honour's commands, I related to him the Revolution under the Prince of Orange; the long war with France entered into by the said prince, and renewed by his successor the present Queen, wherein the greatest powers of Christendom were engaged, and which still continued: I computed at his request that about a million of Yahoos might have been killed in the whole progress of it, and perhaps a hundred or more cities taken, and thrice as many ships burnt or sunk.

He asked me what were the usual causes or motives that made one country go to war with another. I answered they were innumerable, but I should only mention a few of the chief. Sometimes the ambition of princes, who never think they have land or people enough to govern; sometimes the corruption of ministers, who engage their master in a war in order to stifle or divert the clamour of the subjects against their evil administration. Difference in opinions hath cost many millions of lives: for instance, whether flesh be bread, or bread be flesh; whether the juice of a certain berry be blood or wine; whether whistling be a vice or a virtue; whether it be better to kiss a post, or throw it into the fire; what is the best colour for a coat, whether black, white, red, or gray; and whether it should be long or short, narrow or wide, dirty or clean; with many more. Neither are any wars so furious and bloody, or of so long continuance, as those occasioned by difference in opinion, especially if it be in things indifferent.

Sometimes the quarrel between two princes is to decide which of them shall dispossess a third of his dominions, where neither of them pretend to any right. Sometimes one prince quarrelleth with another, for fear the other should quarrel with him. Sometimes a war is entered upon, because the enemy is too strong, and sometimes because he is too weak. Sometimes our neighbours want the things which we have, or have the things which we want; and we both fight, till they take ours or give us theirs. It is a very justifiable cause of a war to invade a country after the people have been wasted by famine, destroyed by pestilence, or embroiled by factions among themselves. It is justifiable to enter into war against our nearest ally, when one of his towns lies convenient for us, or a territory of land, that would render our dominions round and complete. If a prince sends forces into a nation where the people are poor and ignorant, he may lawfully put half of them to death, and make slaves of the rest, in order to civilize and reduce them from their barbarous way of living. It is a very kingly, honourable, and frequent practice, when one prince desires the assistance of another to secure him against an invasion, that the assistant, when he hath driven out the invader, should seize on the dominions himself, and kill, imprison, or banish the prince he came to relieve. Alliance by blood or marriage is a frequent cause of war between princes; and the nearer the kindred is, the greater is their disposition to quarrel: poor nations are hungry, and rich nations are proud; and pride and hunger will ever be at variance. For these reasons, the trade of a soldier is held the most honourable of all others; because a soldier is a Yahoo hired to kill in cold blood as many of his own species, who have never offended him, as possibly he can.

There is likewise a kind of beggarly princes in Europe, not able to make war by themselves, who hire out their troops to richer nations, for so much a day to each man; of which they keep three-fourths to themselves, and it is the best part of their maintenance; such are those in Germany and other northern parts of Europe.

What you have told me (said my master) upon the subject of war, does indeed discover most admirably the effects of that reason you pretend to: however, it is happy that the shame is greater than the danger; and that nature hath left you utterly uncapable of doing much mischief.

For your mouths lying flat with your faces, you can hardly bite each other to any purpose, unless by consent. Then as to the claws upon your feet before and behind, they are so short and tender, that one of our Yahoos would drive a dozen of yours before him. And therefore in recounting the numbers of those who have been killed in battle, I cannot but think that you have *said the thing which is not.*

I could not forbear shaking my head and smiling a little at his ignorance. And being no stranger to the art of war, I gave him a description of cannons, culverins, muskets, carabines, pistols, bullets, powder, swords, bayonets, battles, sieges, retreats, attacks, undermines, countermines, bombardments, sea fights; ships sunk with a thousand men, twenty thousand killed on each side; dying groans, limbs flying in the air, smoke, noise, confusion, trampling to death under horses' feet; flight, pursuit, victory; fields strewed with carcasses left for food to dogs, and wolves, and birds of prey; plundering, stripping, ravishing, burning, and destroying. And to set forth the valour of my own dear countrymen, I assured him that I had seen them blow up a hundred enemies at once in a siege, and as many in a ship, and beheld the dead bodies come down in pieces from the clouds, to the great diversion of the spectators.

I was going on to more particulars, when my master commanded me silence. He said whoever understood the nature of Yahoos might easily believe it possible for so vile an animal to be capable of every action I had named, if their strength and cunning equalled their malice. But as my discourse had increased his abhorrence of the whole species, so he found it gave him a disturbance in his mind, to which he was wholly a stranger before. He thought his ears being used to such abominable words, might by degrees admit them with less detestation. That although he hated the Yahoos of this country, yet he no more blamed them for their odious qualities, than he did a *gnnayh* (a bird of prey) for its cruelty, or a sharp stone for cutting his hoof. But when a creature pretending to reason could be capable of such enormities, he dreaded lest the corruption of that faculty might be worse than brutality itself. He seemed therefore confident, that instead of reason, we were only possessed of some quality fitted to increase our natural vices; as the reflection from a troubled stream returns the image of an ill-shapen body, not only larger, but more distorted.

He added, that he had heard too much upon the subject of war, both in this and some former discourses. There was another point which a little perplexed him at present. I had informed him, that some of our crew left their country on account of being ruined by *Law;* that I had already explained the meaning of the word; but he was at a loss how it should come to pass, that the law which was intended for every man's preservation, should be any man's ruin. Therefore he desired to be farther satisfied what I meant by law, and the dispensers thereof, according to the present practice in my own country; because he thought nature and reason were sufficient guides for a reasonable animal, as we pretended to be, in showing us what we ought to do, and what to avoid.

I assured his Honour that law was a science wherein I had not much conversed, further than by employing advocates, in vain, upon some injustices that had been done me: however, I would give him all the satisfaction I was able.

I said there was a society of men among us, bred up from their youth in the art of proving by words multiplied for the purpose, that white is black, and black is white, according as they are paid. To this society all the rest of the people are slaves. For example, if my neighbour hath a mind to my cow, he hires a lawyer to prove that he ought to have my cow from me. I must then hire another to defend my right, it being against all rules of law that any man should be allowed to speak for himself. Now in this case I who am the right owner lie under two great disadvantages. First, my lawyer, being practised almost from his cradle in defending falsehood, is quite out of his element when he would be an advocate for justice, which as an office unnatural, he always attempts with ill will. The second disadvantage is that my lawyer must proceed with great caution, or else he will be reprimanded by the judges, and abhorred by his brethren, as one that would lessen the practice of the law. And therefore I have but two methods to preserve my cow. The first is to gain over my adversary's lawyer with a double fee, who will then betray his client by insinuating that he hath justice on his side. The second way is for my lawyer to make my cause appear as unjust as he can, by allowing the cow to belong to my adversary: and this, if it be skilfully done, will certainly bespeak the favour of the bench.

Now, your Honour is to know that these judges are persons appointed to decide all controversies of property, as well as for the trial of criminals, and picked out from the most dexterous lawyers, who are grown old or lazy, and having been biassed all their lives against truth and equity, are under such a fatal necessity of favouring fraud, perjury, and oppression, that I have known several of them refuse a large bribe from the side where justice lay, rather than injure the faculty, by doing any thing unbecoming their nature or their office.

It is a maxim among these lawyers, that whatever hath been done before may legally be done again: and therefore they take special care to record all the decisions formerly made against common justice and the general reason of mankind. These, under the name of *precedents,* they produce as authorities, to justify the most iniquitous opinions; and the judges never fail of directing accordingly.

In pleading they studiously avoid entering into the merits of the cause, but are loud, violent, and tedious in dwelling upon all circumstances which are not to the purpose. For instance, in the case already mentioned, they never desire to know what claim or title my adversary hath to my cow; but whether the said cow were red or black, her horns long or short, whether the field I graze her in be round or square, whether she was milked at home or abroad, what diseases she is subject to, and the like; after which they consult precedents, adjourn the cause from time to time, and in ten, twenty, or thirty years, come to an issue.

It is likewise to be observed, that this society hath a peculiar cant and jargon of their own, that no other mortal can understand, and wherein all their laws are written, which they take special care to multiply; whereby they have wholly confounded the very essence of truth and falsehood, or right and wrong; so that it will take thirty years to decide whether the field left me by my ancestors for six generations belongs to me, or to a stranger three hundred miles off.

In the trial of persons accused for crimes against the state the method is much more short and commendable: the judge first sends to sound the disposition of those in power, after which he can easily hang or save the criminal, strictly preserving all due forms of law.

Here my master interposing, said it was a pity that creatures endowed with such prodigious abilities of mind as these lawyers, by the description I gave of them, must certainly be, were not rather encouraged to be instructors of others in wisdom and knowledge. In answer to which I assured his Honour that in all points out of their own trade, they were the most ignorant and stupid generation among us, the most despicable in common conversation, avowed enemies to all knowledge and learning, and equally disposed to pervert the general reason of mankind in every other subject of discourse, as in that of their own profession.

6

My master was yet wholly at a loss to understand what motives could incite this race of lawyers to perplex, disquiet, and weary themselves, and engage in a confederacy of injustice, merely for the sake of injuring their fellow-animals; neither could he comprehend what I meant in saying they did it for hire. Whereupon I was at much pains to describe to him the use of money, the materials it was made of, and the value of the metals; that when a Yahoo had got a great store of this precious substance, he was able to purchase whatever he had a mind to; the finest clothing, the noblest houses, great tracts of land, the most costly meats and drinks, and have his choice of the most beautiful females. Therefore since money alone was able to perform all these feats, our Yahoos thought they could never have enough of it to spend or save, as they found themselves inclined from their natural bent either to profusion or avarice. That the rich man enjoyed the fruit of the poor man's labour, and the latter were a thousand to one in proportion to the former. That the bulk of our people were forced to live miserably, by labouring every day for small wages to make a few live plentifully. I enlarged myself much on these and many other particulars to the same purpose; but his Honour was still to seek; for he went upon a supposition that all animals had a title to their share in the productions of the earth, and especially those who presided over the rest. Therefore he desired I would let him know what these costly meats were, and how any of us happened to want them. Whereupon I enumerated as many sorts as came into my head, with the various methods of dressing them, which could not be done without sending vessels by sea to every part of the world, as well for liquors to drink, as for sauces, and innumerable other conveniences. I assured him that this whole globe of earth must be at least three times gone round, before one of our better female Yahoos could get her breakfast or a cup to put it in. He said that must needs be a miserable country which cannot furnish food for its own inhabitants. But what he chiefly wondered at, was how such vast tracts of ground as I described should be wholly without fresh water, and the people put to the necessity of sending over the sea for drink. I replied that England (the dear place of my nativity) was computed to produce three times the quantity of food, more than its inhabitants are able to consume, as well as liquors extracted from grain, or pressed out of the fruit of certain trees, which made excellent drink, and the same proportion in every other convenience of life. But, in order to feed the luxury and intemperance of the males, and the vanity of the females, we sent away the greatest part of our necessary things to other countries, from whence in return we brought the materials of diseases, folly, and vice, to spend among ourselves. Hence it follows of necessity that vast numbers of our people are compelled to seek their livelihood by begging, robbing, stealing, cheating, pimping, forswearing, flattering, suborning, forging, gaming, lying, fawning, hectoring, voting, scribbling, stargazing, poisoning, whoring, canting, libelling, freethinking, and the like occupations: every one of which terms, I was at much pains to make him understand.

That wine was not imported among us from foreign countries, to supply the want of water or other drinks, but because it was a sort of liquid which made us merry by putting us out of our senses, diverted all melancholy thoughts, begat wild extravagant imaginations in the brain, raised our hopes, and banished our fears, suspended every office of reason for a time, and deprived us of the use of our limbs, till we fell into a profound sleep; although it must be confessed, that we always awaked sick and dispirited and that the use of this liquor filled us with diseases, which made our lives uncomfortable and short.

But beside all this, the bulk of our people supported themselves by furnishing the necessities or conveniences of life to the rich, and to each other. For instance, when I am at home and dressed as I ought to be, I carry on my body the workmanship of a hundred tradesmen; the building and furniture of my house employ as many more, and five times the number to adorn my wife.

I was going on to tell him of another sort of people, who get their livelihood by attending the sick, having upon some occasions informed his Honour that many of my crew had died of diseases. But here it was with the utmost difficulty that I brought him to apprehend what I meant. He could easily conceive that a Houyhnhnm grew weak and heavy a few days before his death, or by some accident might hurt a limb. But that nature, who works all things to perfection, should suffer any pains to breed in our bodies, he thought impossible, and desired to know the reason of so unaccountable an evil. I told him we fed on a thousand things which operated contrary to each other; that we ate when we were not hungry, and drank without the provocation of thirst; that we sat whole nights drinking strong liquors without eating a bit, which disposed us to sloth, inflamed our bodies, and precipitated or prevented digestion. That prostitute female Yahoos acquired a certain malady, which bred rottenness in the bones of those who fell into their embraces; that this and many other diseases were propagated from father to son, so that great numbers come into the world with complicated maladies upon them; that it would be endless to give him a catalogue of all diseases incident to human bodies; for they could not be fewer than five or six hundred, spread over every limb and joint; in short, every part, external and intestine, having diseases appropriated to them. To remedy which there was a sort of people bred up among us, in the profession of pretence of curing the sick. And because I had some skill in the faculty, I would in gratitude to his Honour let him know the whole mystery and method by which they proceed.

Their fundamental is that all diseases arise from repletion, from whence they conclude that a great evacuation of the body is necessary, either through the natural passage or upwards at the mouth. Their next business is from herbs, minerals, gums, oils, shells, salts, juices, seaweed, excrements, barks of trees, serpents, toads, frogs, spiders, dead men's flesh and bones, birds, beasts, and fishes, to form a composition for smell and taste the most abominable, nauseous, and detestable they can possibly contrive, which the stomach immediately rejects with loathing; and this they call a vomit; or else from the same storehouse, with some other poisonous additions, they command us to take in at the orifice above or below (just as the physician then happens to be disposed) a medicine equally annoying and disgustful to the bowels; which relaxing the belly, drives down all before it, and this they call a purge or a clyster. For nature (as the physicians allege) having intended the superior anterior orifice only for the intromission of solids and liquids, and the inferior posterior for ejection, these artists ingeniously considering that in all diseases nature is forced out of her seat, therefore to replace her in it the body must be treated in a manner directly contrary, by interchanging the use of each orifice, forcing solids and liquids in at the anus, and making evacuations at the mouth.

But besides real diseases we are subject to many that are only imaginary, for which the physicians have invented imaginary cures; these have their several names, and so have the drugs that are proper for them, and with these our female Yahoos are always infested.

One great excellency in this tribe is their skill at prognostics, wherein they seldom fail; their predictions in real diseases, when they rise to any degree of malignity, generally portending death, which is always in their power, when recovery is not: and therefore, upon any unexpected signs of amendment, after they have pronounced their sentence, rather than be accused as false prophets, they know how to approve their sagacity to the world by a seasonable dose.

They are likewise of special use to husbands and wives who are grown weary of their mates, to eldest sons, to great ministers of state, and often to princes.

I had formerly upon occasion discoursed with my master upon the nature of government in general, and particularly of our own excellent constitution, deservedly the wonder and envy of the whole world. But having here accidentally mentioned a minister of state, he commanded me some time after to inform him what species of Yahoo I particularly meant by that appellation.

I told him that a First or Chief Minister of State, who was the person I intended to describe, was a creature wholly exempt from joy and grief, love and hatred, pity and anger; at least made use of no other passions but a violent desire of wealth, power, and titles; that he applies his words to all uses, except to the indication of his mind; that he never tells a truth but with an intent that you should take it for a lie; nor a lie but with a design that you should take it for a truth; that those he speaks worst of behind their backs are in the surest way of preferment; and whenever he begins to praise you to others or to yourself, you are from that day forlorn. The worst mark you can receive is a promise, especially when it is confirmed with an oath; after which every wise man retires, and gives over all hopes.

There are three methods by which a man may rise to be chief minister: the first is by knowing how with prudence to dispose of a wife, a daughter, or a sister: the second, by betraying or undermining his predecessor: and the third is by a furious zeal in public assemblies against the corruptions of the court. But a wise prince would rather choose to employ those who practise the last of these methods; because such zealots prove always the most obsequious and subservient to the will and passions of their master. That these ministers having all employments at their disposal, preserve themselves in power by bribing the majority of a senate or great council; and at last, by an expedient called an Act of Indemnity (whereof I described the nature to him) they secure themselves from after-reckonings, and retire from the public, laden with the spoils of the nation.

The palace of a chief minister is a seminary to breed up others in his own trade: the pages, lackeys, and porter, by imitating their master, become ministers of state in their several districts, and learn to excel in the three principal ingredients, of insolence, lying, and bribery. Accordingly they have a subaltern court paid to them by persons of the best rank, and sometimes by the force of dexterity and impudence arrive through several gradations to be successors to their lord.

He is usually governed by a decayed wench or favourite footman, who are the tunnels through which all graces are conveyed, and may properly be called, in the last resort, the governors of the kingdom.

One day in discourse my master, having heard me mention the nobility of my country, was pleased to make me a compliment which I could not pretend to deserve: that he was sure I must have been born of some noble family, because I far exceeded in shape, colour, and cleanliness, all the Yahoos of his nation, although I seemed to fail in strength and agility, which must be imputed to my different way of living from those other brutes; and besides I was not only endowed with the faculty of speech, but likewise with some rudiments of reason, to a degree that with all his acquaintance I passed for a prodigy.

He made me observe, that among the Houyhnhnms, the white, the sorrel, and the iron gray were not so exactly shaped as the bay, the dapple gray, and the black; nor born with equal talents of the mind, or a capacity to improve them; and therefore continued always in the condition of servants, without ever aspiring to match out of their own race, which in that country would be reckoned monstrous and unnatural.

I made his Honour my most humble acknowledgments for the good opinion he was pleased to conceive of me; but assured him at the same time that my birth was of the lower sort, having been born of plain honest parents, who were just able to give me a tolerable education; that nobility among us was altogether a different thing from the idea he had of it; that our young noblemen are bred from their childhood in idleness and luxury; that as soon as years will permit, they consume their vigour and contract odious diseases among lewd females; and when their fortunes are almost ruined, they marry some woman of mean birth, disagreeable person, and unsound constitution, merely for the sake of money, whom they hate and despise. That the productions of such marriages are generally scrofulous, rickety, or deformed children; by which means the family seldom continues above three generations, unless the wife takes care to provide a healthy father among her neighbours or domestics, in order to improve and continue the breed. That a weak diseased body, a meagre countenance, and sallow complexion, are the true marks of noble blood; and a healthy robust appearance is so disgraceful in a man of quality, that the world concludes his real father to have been a groom or a coachman. The imperfections of his mind run parallel with those of his body, being a composition of spleen, dullness, ignorance, caprice, sensuality, and pride.

Without the consent of this illustrious body no law can be enacted, repealed, or altered; and these have the decision of all our possessions without appeal.

7

The reader may be disposed to wonder how I could prevail on myself to give so free a representation of my own species, among a race of mortals who were already too apt to conceive the vilest opinion of humankind, from that entire congruity betwixt me and their Yahoos. But I must freely confess that the many virtues of those excellent quadrupeds placed in opposite view to human corruptions, had so far opened my eyes and enlarged my understanding, that I began to view the actions and passions of man in a very different light, and to think the honour of my own kind not worth managing; which, besides, it was impossible for me to do before a person of so acute a judgment as my master, who daily convinced me of a thousand faults in myself, whereof I had not the least perception before, and which among us would never be numbered even among human infirmities. I had likewise learned from his example an utter detestation of all falsehood or disguise, and truth appeared so amiable to me, that I determined upon sacrificing every thing to it.

Let me deal so candidly with the reader as to confess that there was yet a much stronger motive for the freedom I took in my representation of things. I had not been a year in this country before I contracted such a love and veneration for the inhabitants, that I entered on a firm resolution never to return to humankind, but to pass the rest of my life among these admirable Houyhnhnms in the contemplation and practice of every virtue; where I could have no example or incitement to vice. But it was decreed by fortune, my perpetual enemy, that so great a felicity should not fall to my share. However, it is now some comfort to reflect that in what I said of my countrymen I extenuated their faults as much as I durst before so strict an examiner, and upon every article gave as favourable a turn as the matter would bear. For indeed who is there alive that will not be swayed by his bias and partiality to the place of his birth?

I have related the substance of several conversations I had with my master, during the greatest part of the time I had the honour to be in his service, but have indeed for brevity sake omitted much more than is here set down.

When I had answered all his questions, and his curiosity seemed to be fully satisfied, he sent for me one morning early, and commanding me to sit down at some distance (an honour which he had never before conferred upon me), he said he had been very seriously considering my whole story, as far as it related both to myself and my country; that he looked upon us as a sort of animals to whose share, by what accident he could not conjecture, some small pittance of reason had fallen, whereof we made no other use than by its assistance to aggravate our natural corruptions, and to acquire new ones which nature had not given us. That we disarmed ourselves of the few abilities she had bestowed, had been very successful in multiplying our original wants, and seemed to spend our whole lives in vain endeavours to supply them by our own inventions. That as to myself, it was manifest I had neither the strength nor agility of a common Yahoo, that I walked infirmly on my hinderfeet, had found out a contrivance to make my claws of no use or defence, and to remove the hair from my chin, which was intended as a shelter from the sun and the weather. Lastly, that I could neither run with speed, nor climb trees like my brethren (as he called them) the Yahoos in this country.

That our institutions of government and law were plainly owing to our gross defects in reason, and by consequence, in virtue; because reason alone is sufficient to govern a rational creature; which was therefore a character we had no pretence to challenge, even from the account I had given of my own people; although he manifestly perceived that in order to favour them I had concealed many particulars, and often *said the thing which was not.*

He was the more confirmed in this opinion, because he observed that as I agreed in every feature of my body with other Yahoos, except where it was to my real disadvantage in point of strength, speed, and activity, the shortness of my claws, and some other particulars where nature had no part; so from the representation I had given him of our lives, our manners, and our actions, he found as near a resemblance in the disposition of our minds. He said the Yahoos were known to hate one another more than they did any different species of animals; and the reason usually assigned was the odiousness of their own shapes, which all could see in the rest, but not in themselves.

He had therefore begun to think it not unwise in us to cover our bodies, and by that invention conceal many of our own deformities from each other, which would else be hardly supportable. But he now found he had been mistaken, and that the dissensions of those brutes in his country were owing to the same cause with ours, as I had described them. For if (said he) you throw among five Yahoos as much food as would be sufficient for fifty, they will, instead of eating peaceably, fall together by the ears, each single one impatient to have all to itself; and therefore a servant was usually employed to stand by while they were feeding abroad, and those kept at home were tied at a distance from each other: that if a cow died of age or accident, before a Houyhnhnm could secure it for his own Yahoos, those in the neighbourhood would come in herds to seize it, and then would ensue such a battle as I had described, with terrible wounds made by their claws on both sides, although they seldom were able to kill one another, for want of such convenient instruments of death as we had invented. At other times the like battles have been fought between the Yahoos of several neighbourhoods without any visible cause; those of one district watching all opportunities to surprise the next before they are prepared. But if they find their project hath miscarried, they return home, and, for want of enemies, engage in what I call a civil war among themselves.

That in some fields of his country there are certain shining stones of several colours, whereof the Yahoos are violently fond, and when part of these stones is fixed in the earth, as it sometimes happeneth, they will dig with their claws for whole days to get them out, then carry them away, and hide them by heaps in their kennels; but still looking round with great caution, for fear their comrades should find out their treasure. My master said he could never discover the reason of this unnatural appetite, or how these stones could be of any use to a Yahoo; but now he believed it might proceed from the same principle of avarice which I had ascribed to mankind: that he had once, by way of experiment, privately removed a heap of these stones from the place where one of his Yahoos had buried it: whereupon the sordid animal missing his treasure, by his loud lamenting brought the whole herd to the place, there miserably howled, then fell to biting and tearing the rest, began to pine away, would neither eat nor sleep nor work, till he ordered a servant privately to convey the stones into the same hole and hide them as before; which when his Yahoo had found, he presently recovered his spirits and good humour, but took good care to remove them to a better hiding place, and hath ever since been a very serviceable brute.

My master farther assured me, which I also observed myself, that in the fields where these shining stones abound, the fiercest and most frequent battles are fought, occasioned by perpetual inroads of the neighbouring Yahoos.

He said it was common when two Yahoos discovered such a stone in a field, and were contending which of them should be the proprietor, a third would take the advantage, and carry it away from them both; which my master would needs contend to have some kind of resemblance with our suits at law; wherein I thought it for our credit not to undeceive him; since the decision he mentioned was much more equitable than many decrees among us; because the plaintiff and defendant there lost nothing beside the stone they contended for, whereas our courts of equity would never have dismissed the cause while either of them had any thing left.

My master continuing his discourse, said there was nothing that rendered the Yahoos more odious than their undistinguishing appetite to devour every thing that came in their way, whether herbs, roots, berries, the corrupted flesh of animals, or all mingled together; and it was peculiar in their temper that they were fonder of what they could get by rapine or stealth at a greater distance than much better food provided for them at home. If their prey held out, they would eat till they were ready to burst, after which nature had pointed out to them a certain root that gave them a general evacuation.

There was also another kind of root very juicy, but somewhat rare and difficult to be found, which the Yahoos sought for with much eagerness, and would suck it with great delight; and it produced in them the same effects that wine hath upon us. It would make them sometimes hug, and sometimes tear one another; they would howl and grin, and chatter, and reel, and tumble, and then fall asleep in the dirt.

I did indeed observe that the Yahoos were the only animals in this country subject to any diseases; which, however, were much fewer than horses have among us, and contracted not by any ill-treatment they meet with, but by the nastiness and greediness of that sordid brute. Neither has their language any more than a general appellation for those maladies, which is borrowed from the name of the beast, and called *Hnea Yahoo,* or the *Yahoo's Evil,* and the cure prescribed is a mixture of their own dung and urine forcibly put down the Yahoo's throat. This I have since often known to have been taken with success, and do freely recommend it to my countrymen, for the public good, as an admirable specific against all diseases produced by repletion.

As to learning, government, arts, manufactures, and the like, my master confessed he could find little or no resemblance between the Yahoos of that country and those in ours. For he only meant to observe what parity there was in our natures. He had heard indeed some curious Houyhnhnms observe that in most herds there was a sort of ruling Yahoo (as among us there is generally some leading or principal stag in a park), who was always more deformed in body and mischievous in disposition than any of the rest. That this leader had usually a favourite as like himself as he could get, whose employment was to lick his master's feet and posteriors, and drive the female Yahoos to his kennel; for which he was now and then rewarded with a piece of ass's flesh. This favourite is hated by the whole herd, and therefore to protect himself, keeps always near the person of his leader. He usually continues in office till a worse can be found; but the very moment he is discarded, his successor, at the head of all the Yahoos in that district, young and old, male and female, come in a body, and discharge their excrements upon him from head to foot. But how far this might be applicable to

our courts and favourites, and ministers of state, my master said
I could best determine.

I durst make no return to this malicious insinuation, which
debased human understanding below the sagacity of a common
hound, who has judgment enough to distinguish and follow the
cry of the ablest dog in the pack, without being ever mistaken.

My master told me there were some qualities remarkable
in the Yahoos, which he had not observed me to mention, or
at least very slightly, in the accounts I had given him of
humankind. He said those animals, like other brutes, had their
females in common; but in this they differed, that the she-Yahoo
would admit the male while she was pregnant; and that the hes
would quarrel and fight with the females as fiercely as with each
other. Both which practices were such degrees of brutality, that
no other sensitive creature ever arrived at.

Another thing he wondered at in the Yahoos was their
strange disposition to nastiness and dirt, whereas there appears
to be a natural love of cleanliness in all other animals. As to the
former accusation, I was glad to let it pass without any reply,
because I had not a word to offer upon it in defence of my
species, which otherwise I certainly had done from my own
inclinations. But I could have easily vindicated humankind from
the imputation of singularity upon the last article, if there had
been any swine in that country (as unluckily for me there were
not), which although it may be a sweeter quadruped than a
Yahoo, cannot I humbly conceive in justice pretend to more
cleanliness; and so his Honour himself must have owned, if he
had seen their filthy way of feeding, and their custom of wal-
lowing and sleeping in the mud.

My master likewise mentioned another quality which his servants had discovered in several Yahoos, and to him was wholly
unaccountable. He said, a fancy would sometimes take a Yahoo
to retire into a corner, to lie down and howl and groan, and
spurn away all that came near him, although he were young
and fat, wanted neither food nor water; nor did the servants
imagine what could possibly ail him. And the only remedy they

found was to set him to hard work, after which he would infallibly come to himself. To this I was silent out of partiality to my own kind; yet here I could plainly discover the true seeds of spleen, which only seizeth on the lazy, the luxurious, and the rich; who, if they were forced to undergo the same regimen, I would undertake for the cure.

His Honour had further observed that a female Yahoo would often stand behind a bank or bush, to gaze on the young males passing by, and then appear, and hide, using many antic gestures and grimaces, at which time it was observed that she had a most offensive smell; and when any of the males advanced, would slowly retire, looking often back, and with a counterfeit show of fear, run off into some convenient place where she knew the male would follow her.

At other times if a female stranger came among them, three or four of her own sex would get about her, and stare and chatter, and grin, and smell her all over; and then turn off with gestures that seemed to express contempt and disdain.

Perhaps my master might refine a little in these speculations, which he had drawn from what he observed himself, or had been told him by others; however, I could not reflect without some amazement, and much sorrow, that the rudiments of coquetry, censure, and scandal, should have place by instinct in womankind.

I expected every moment that my master would accuse the Yahoos of those unnatural appetites in both sexes, so common among us. But nature, it seems, hath not been so expert a schoolmistress; and these politer pleasures are entirely the productions of art and reason, on our side of the globe.

8

As I ought to have understood human nature much better than I supposed it possible for my master to do, so it was easy to apply the character he gave of the Yahoos to myself and my countrymen; and I believed I could yet make farther discoveries from my own observation. I therefore often begged his favour to let me go among the herds of Yahoos in the neighbourhood, to which he always very graciously consented, being perfectly convinced that the hatred I bore those brutes would never suffer me to be corrupted by them; and his Honour ordered one of his servants, a strong sorrel nag, very honest and good-natured, to be my guard, without whose protection I durst not undertake such adventures. For I have already told the reader how much I was pestered by those odious animals upon my first arrival. And I afterwards failed very narrowly three or four times of falling into their clutches, when I happened to stray at any distance without my hanger. And I have reason to believe they had some imagination that I was of their own species, which I often assisted myself, by stripping up my sleeves, and showing my naked arms and breast in their sight, when my protector was with me. At which times they would approach as near as they durst, and imitate my actions after the manner of monkeys, but ever with great signs of hatred; as a tame jackdaw with cap and stockings is always persecuted by the wild ones, when he happens to be got among them.

They are prodigiously nimble from their infancy; however, I once caught a young male of three years old, and endeavoured by all marks of tenderness to make it quiet; but the little imp fell a squalling and scratching and biting with such violence that I was forced to let it go; and it was high time, for a whole troop of old ones came about us at the noise, but finding the cub safe (for away it ran), and my sorrel nag being by, they durst not venture near us. I observed the young animal's flesh to smell very rank, and the stink was somewhat between a weasel and a fox, but much more disagreeable. I forgot another circumstance (and perhaps I might have the reader's pardon if it were wholly omitted), that while I held the odious vermin in my hands, it voided its filthy excrements of a yellow liquid substance, all over my clothes; but by good fortune there was a small brook hard by, where I washed myself as clean as I could; although I durst not come into my master's presence, until I were sufficiently aired.

By what I could discover, the Yahoos appear to be the most unteachable of all animals, their capacities never reaching higher than to draw or carry burdens. Yet I am of opinion this defect ariseth chiefly from a perverse, restive disposition. For they are cunning, malicious, treacherous, and revengeful. They are strong and hardy, but of a cowardly spirit, and by consequence, insolent, abject, and cruel. It is observed that the red-haired of both sexes are more libidinous and mischievous than the rest, whom yet they much exceed in strength and activity.

The Houyhnhnms keep the Yahoos for present use in huts not far from the house; but the rest are sent abroad to certain fields, where they dig up roots, eat several kinds of herbs, and search about for carrion, or sometimes catch weasels and *luhimuhs* (a sort of wild rat), which they greedily devour. Nature hath taught them to dig deep holes with their nails on the side of a rising ground, wherein they lie by themselves; only the kennels of the females are larger, sufficient to hold two or three cubs.

They swim from their infancy like frogs, and are able to continue long under water, where they often take fish, which the females carry home to their young. And upon this occasion, I hope the reader will pardon my relating an odd adventure.

Being one day abroad with my protector the sorrel nag, and the weather exceeding hot, I entreated him to let me bathe in a river that was near. He consented, and I immediately stripped myself stark naked, and went down softly into the stream. It happened that a young female Yahoo, standing behind a bank, saw the whole proceeding, and inflamed by desire, as the nag and I conjectured, came running with all speed, and leaped into the water, within five yards of the place where I bathed. I was never in my life so terribly frighted; the nag was grazing at some distance, not suspecting any harm. She embraced me after a most fulsome manner; I roared as loud as I could, and the nag came galloping towards me, whereupon she quitted her grasp, with the utmost reluctancy, and leaped upon the opposite bank, where she stood gazing and howling all the time I was putting on my clothes.

This was matter of diversion to my master and his family, as well as of mortification to myself. For now I could no longer deny that I was a real Yahoo in every limb and feature, since the females had a natural propensity to me, as one of their own species. Neither was the hair of this brute of a red colour (which might have been some excuse for an appetite a little irregular), but black as a sloe, and her countenance did not make an appearance altogether so hideous as the rest of the kind; for, I think, she could not be above eleven years old.

Having lived three years in this country, the reader I suppose will expect that I should, like other travellers, give him some account of the manners and customs of its inhabitants, which it was indeed my principal study to learn.

As these noble Houyhnhnms are endowed by nature with a general disposition to all virtues, and have no conceptions or ideas of what is evil in a rational creature, so their grand maxim is to cultivate reason, and to be wholly governed by it. Neither is reason among them a point problematical as with us, where men can argue with plausibility on both sides of the question; but strikes you with immediate conviction; as it must needs do where it is not mingled, obscured, or discoloured by passion and interest. I remember it was with extreme difficulty that I could bring my master to understand the meaning of the word *opinion,* or how a point could be disputable; because reason taught us to affirm or deny only where we are certain, and beyond our knowledge we cannot do either. So that controversies, wranglings, disputes, and positiveness in false or dubious propositions, are evils unknown among the Houyhnhnms. In the like manner when I used to explain to him our several systems of natural philosophy, he would laugh that a creature pretending to reason should value itself upon the knowledge of other people's conjectures, and in things where that knowledge, if it were certain, could be of no use. Wherein he agreed entirely with the sentiments of Socrates, as Plato delivers them; which I mention as the highest honour I can do that prince of philosophers. I have often since reflected what destruction such a doctrine

Jonathan Swift

would make in the libraries of Europe, and how many paths to
fame would be then shut up in the learned world.

Friendship and benevolence are the two principal virtues
among the Houyhnhnms, and these not confined to particular
objects, but universal to the whole race. For a stranger from the
remotest part is equally treated with the nearest neighbour, and
wherever he goes looks upon himself as at home. They preserve
decency and civility in the highest degrees, but are altogether
ignorant of ceremony. They have no fondness for their colts
or foals, but the care they take in educating them proceeds
entirely from the dictates of reason. And I observed my master
to show the same affection to his neighbour's issue that he had
for his own. They will have it that nature teaches them to love
the whole species, and it is reason only that maketh a distinction of persons, where there is a superior degree of virtue.

When the matron Houyhnhnms have produced one of each
sex, they no longer accompany with their consorts, except
they lose one of their issue by some casualty, which very seldom
happens; but in such a case they meet again; or when the like
accident befalls a person whose wife is past bearing, some
other couple bestow him one of their own colts, and then go
together again till the mother is pregnant. This caution is necessary to prevent the country from being over-burthened with
numbers. But the race of inferior Houyhnhnms bred up to be
servants is not so strictly limited upon this article; these are
allowed to produce three of each sex, to be domestics in the
noble families.

In their marriages they are exactly careful to choose such
colours as will not make any disagreeable mixture in the
breed. Strength is chiefly valued in the male, and comeliness
in the female; not upon the account of love, but to preserve the
race from degenerating; for where a female happens to excel
in strength, a consort is chosen with regard to comeliness.
Courtship, love, presents, jointures, settlements, have no place
in their thoughts, or terms whereby to express them in their
language. The young couple meet and are joined, merely because

it is the determination of their parents and friends: it is what they see done every day, and they look upon it as one of the necessary actions of a rational being. But the violation of marriage, or any other unchastity, was never heard of; and the married pair pass their lives with the same friendship and mutual benevolence that they bear to all others of the same species who come in their way; without jealousy, fondness, quarrelling, or discontent.

In educating the youth of both sexes, their method is admirable, and highly deserves our imitation. These are not suffered to taste a grain of oats, except upon certain days, till eighteen years old; nor milk, but very rarely; and in summer they graze two hours in the morning, and as long in the evening, which their parents likewise observe; but the servants are not allowed above half that time, and a great part of their grass is brought home, which they eat at the most convenient hours, when they can be best spared from work.

Temperance, industry, exercise, and cleanliness, are the lessons equally enjoined to the young ones of both sexes; and my master thought it monstrous in us to give the females a different kind of education from the males, except in some articles of domestic management; whereby, as he truly observed, one half of our natives were good for nothing but bringing children into the world; and to trust the care of our children to such useless animals, he said, was yet a greater instance of brutality.

But the Houyhnhnms train up their youth to strength, speed, and hardiness, by exercising them in running races up and down steep hills, and over hard stony grounds; and when they are all in a sweat, they are ordered to leap over head and ears into a pond or river. Four times a year the youth of a certain district meet to show their proficiency in running and leaping, and other feats of strength and agility; where the victor is rewarded with a song made in his or her praise. On this festival the servants drive a herd of Yahoos into the field, laden with hay and oats and milk, for a repast to the Houyhnhnms; after which these brutes are immediately driven back again, for fear of being noisome to the assembly.

Every fourth year, at the vernal equinox, there is a representative council of the whole nation, which meets in a plain about twenty miles from our house, and continues about five or six days. Here they enquire into the state and condition of the several districts; whether they abound or be deficient in hay or oats, or cows or Yahoos. And wherever there is any want (which is but seldom) it is immediately supplied by unanimous consent and contributions. Here likewise the regulation of children is settled: as for instance, if a Houyhnhnm hath two males, he changeth one of them with another that hath two females; and when a child hath been lost by any casualty, where the mother is past breeding, it is determined what family in the district shall breed another to supply the loss.

9

One of these grand assemblies was held in my time, about three months before my departure, whither my master went as the representative of our district. In this council was resumed their old debate, and indeed, the only debate which ever happened in that country; whereof my master after his return gave me a very particular account.

The question to be debated was whether the Yahoos should be exterminated from the face of the earth. One of the members for the affirmative offered several arguments of great strength and weight, alleging that as the Yahoos were the most filthy, noisome, and deformed animal which nature ever produced, so they were the most restive and indocible, mischievous and malicious: they would privately suck the teats of the Houyhnhnms' cows, kill and devour their cats, trample down their oats and grass, if they were not continually watched, and commit a thousand other extravagancies. He took notice of a general tradition, that Yahoos had not been always in that country; but that many ages ago two of these brutes appeared together upon a mountain, whether produced by the heat of the sun upon corrupted mud and slime, or from the ooze and froth of the sea, was never known. That these Yahoos engendered, and their brood in a short time grew so numerous as to overrun and infest the whole nation. That the Houyhnhnms to get rid of this evil, made a general hunting, and at last enclosed the whole herd; and destroying the elder, every Houyhnhnm kept two young ones in a kennel, and brought them to such a degree of tameness, as an animal so savage by nature can be capable of acquiring; using them for draught and carriage. That there seemed to be much truth in this tradition, and that those creatures could not be *Ylnhniamshy* (or *aborigines* of the land), because of the violent hatred the Houyhnhnms, as well as all other animals, bore them; which although their evil disposition sufficiently deserved, could never have arrived at so high a degree, if they had been aborigines, or else they would have long since been rooted out. That the inhabitants taking a fancy to use the service of the Yahoos, had very imprudently neglected to cultivate the breed of asses, which were a comely animal, easily kept, more tame and orderly, without any offensive smell, strong enough for labour, although they yield to the other in agility of body; and if their braying be no agreeable sound, it is far preferable to the horrible howlings of the Yahoos.

Several others declared their sentiments to the same purpose, when my master proposed an expedient to the assembly, whereof he had indeed borrowed the hint from me. He approved of the tradition mentioned by the honourable member who spoke before, and affirmed that the two Yahoos said to be first seen among them had been driven thither over the sea; that coming to land and being forsaken by their companions they retired to the mountains, and degenerating by degrees, became in process of time, much more savage than those of their own species in the country from whence these two originals came. The reason of his assertion was that he had now in his possession a certain wonderful Yahoo (meaning myself), which most of them had heard of, and many of them had seen. He then related to them how he first found me; that my body was all covered with an artificial composure of the skins and hairs of other animals; that

I spoke in a language of my own, and had thoroughly learned theirs; that I had related to him the accidents which brought me thither; that when he saw me without my covering I was an exact Yahoo in every part, only of a whiter colour, less hairy, and with shorter claws. He added how I had endeavoured to persuade him that in my own and other countries the Yahoos acted as the governing, rational animal, and held the Houyhnhnms in servitude; that he observed in me all the qualities of a Yahoo, only a little more civilized by some tincture of reason, which however was in a degree as far inferior to the Houyhnhnm race as the Yahoos of their country were to me; that among other things I mentioned a custom we had of castrating Houyhnhnms when they were young, in order to render them tame; that the operation was easy and safe; that it was no shame to learn wisdom from brutes, as industry is taught by the ant, and building by the swallow. (For so I translate the word *lyhannh,* although it be a much larger fowl.) That this invention might be practised upon the younger Yahoos here, which, besides rendering them tractable and fitter for use, would in an age put an end to the whole species without destroying life. That in the meantime the Houyhnhnms should be exhorted to cultivate the breed of asses, which, as they are in all respects more valuable brutes, so they have this advantage, to be fit for service at five years old, which the others are not till twelve.

This was all my master thought fit to tell me at that time of what passed in the grand council. But he was pleased to conceal one particular, which related personally to myself, whereof I soon felt the unhappy effect, as the reader will know in its proper place, and from whence I date all the succeeding misfortunes of my life.

The Houyhnhnms have no letters, and consequently their knowledge is traditional. But there happening few events of any moment among a people so well united, naturally disposed to every virtue, wholly governed by reason, and cut off from all commerce with other nations, the historical part is easily preserved without burthening their memories. I have already observed that they are subject to no diseases, and therefore can have no need of physicians. However, they have excellent medicines composed of herbs, to cure accidental bruises and cuts in the pastern or frog of the foot by sharp stones, as well as other maims and hurts in the several parts of the body.

They calculate the year by the revolution of the sun and the moon, but use no subdivisions into weeks. They are well enough acquainted with the motions of those two luminaries, and understand the nature of eclipses; and this is the utmost progress of their astronomy.

In poetry they must be allowed to excel all other mortals; wherein the justness of their similes, and the minuteness, as well as exactness of their descriptions, are indeed inimitable. Their verses abound very much in both of these, and usually contain either some exalted notions of friendship and benevolence, or the praises of those who were victors in races and other bodily exercises. Their buildings, although very rude and simple, are not inconvenient, but well contrived to defend them from all injuries of cold and heat. They have a kind of tree, which at forty years old loosens in the root, and falls with the first storm: they grow very straight, and being pointed like stakes with a sharp stone (for the Houyhnhnms know not the use of iron), they stick them erect in the ground about ten inches asunder, and then weave in oat straw, or sometimes wattles betwixt them. The roof is made after the same manner, and so are the doors.

The Houyhnhnms use the hollow part between the pastern and the hoof of their forefeet as we do our hands, and this with greater dexterity than I could at first imagine. I have seen a white mare of our family thread a needle (which I lent her on purpose) with that joint. They milk their cows, reap their oats, and do all the work which requires hands, in the same manner. They have a kind of hard flints, which by grinding against other stones, they form into instruments, that serve instead of wedges, axes, and hammers. With tools made of these flints they likewise cut their hay and reap their oats, which there groweth naturally in several fields: the Yahoos draw home the sheaves in carriages, and the servants tread them in certain covered huts, to get out the grain, which is kept in stores. They make a rude kind of earthen and wooden vessels, and bake the former in the sun.

If they can avoid casualties, they die only of old age, and are buried in the obscurest places that can be found, their friends and relations expressing neither joy nor grief at their departure; nor does the dying person discover the least regret that he is leaving the world, any more than if he were upon returning home from a visit to one of his neighbours. I remember my master having once made an appointment with a friend and his family to come to his house upon some affair of importance, on the day fixed the mistress and her two children came very late; she made two excuses, first for her husband, who, as she said, happened that very morning to *shnuwnh*. The word is strongly expressive in their language, but not easily rendered into English; it signifies, *to retire to his first mother.* Her excuse for not coming sooner was that her husband dying late in the morning, she was a good while consulting her servants about a convenient place where his body should be laid; and I observed she behaved herself at our house as cheerfully as the rest, and died about three months later.

They live generally to seventy or seventy-five years, very seldom to fourscore: some weeks before their death they feel a gradual decay, but without pain. During this time they are much visited by their friends, because they cannot go abroad with their usual ease and satisfaction. However, about ten days before their death, which they seldom fail in computing, they return the visits that have been made them by those who are nearest in the neighbourhood, being carried in a convenient sledge drawn by Yahoos; which vehicle they use, not only upon this occasion, but when they grow old, upon long journeys, or when they are lamed by any accident. And therefore when the dying Houyhnhnms return those visits, they take a solemn leave of their friends, as if they were going to some remote part of the country, where they designed to pass the rest of their lives.

I know not whether it may be worth observing that the Houyhnhnms have no word in their language to express any thing that is evil, except what they borrow from the deformities or ill qualities of the Yahoos. Thus they denote the folly of a servant, an omission of a child, a stone that cuts their feet, a continuance of foul or unseasonable weather, and the like, by adding to each the epithet of Yahoo. For instance, *Hhnm Yahoo, Whnaholm Yahoo, Ynlhmndwihlma Yahoo,* and an ill-contrived house *Ynholmhnmrohlnw Yahoo.*

I could with great pleasure enlarge further upon the manners and virtues of this excellent people; but intending in a short time to publish a volume by itself expressly upon that subject, I refer the reader thither, and in the mean time, proceed to relate my own sad catastrophe.

10

I had settled my little economy to my own heart's content. My master had ordered a room to be made for me after their manner, about six yards from the house; the sides and floors of which I plastered with clay, and covered with rush mats of my own contriving; I had beaten hemp, which there grows wild, and made of it a sort of ticking; this I filled with the feathers of several birds I had taken with springes made of Yahoos' hairs, and were excellent food. I had worked two chairs with my knife, the sorrel nag helping me in the grosser and more laborious part. When my clothes were worn to rags, I made myself others with the skins of rabbits, and of a certain beautiful animal about the same size, called *nnuhnoh,* the skin of which is covered with a fine down. Of these I likewise made very tolerable stockings. I soled my shoes with wood which I cut from a tree and fitted to the upper leather, and when this was worn out, I supplied it with the skins of Yahoos dried in the sun. I often got honey out of hollow trees, which I mingled with water, or ate with my bread. No man could more verify the truth of these two maxims. *That nature is very easily satisfied;* and *That necessity is the mother of invention.* I enjoyed perfect health of body, and tranquillity of mind; I did not feel the treachery or inconstancy of a friend, nor the injuries of a secret or open enemy. I had no occasion of bribing, flattering, or pimping to procure the favour of any great man or of his minion. I wanted no fence against fraud or oppression; here was neither physician to destroy my body, nor lawyer to ruin my fortune; no informer to watch my words and actions, or forge accusations against me for hire; here were no gibers, censurers, backbiters, pickpockets, highwaymen, housebreakers, attorneys, bawds, buffoons, gamesters, politicians, wits, splenetics, tedious talkers, contro-vertists, ravishers, murderers, robbers, virtuosos; no leaders or followers of party and faction; no encouragers to vice, by seducement or examples; no dungeon, axes, gibbets, whipping posts, or pillories; no cheating shopkeepers or mechanics; no pride, vanity, or affectation; no fops, bullies, drunkards, strolling whores, or poxes; no ranting, lewd, expensive wives; no stupid, proud pedants; no importunate, overbearing, quar-relsome, noisy, roaring, empty, conceited, swearing compan-ions; no scoundrels, raised from the dust for the sake of their vices, or nobility thrown into it on account of their virtues; no lords, fiddlers, judges, or dancing-masters.

I had the favour of being admitted to several Houyhnhnms, who came to visit or dine with my master; where his Honour graciously suffered me to wait in the room, and listen to their discourse. Both he and his company would often descend to ask me questions, and receive my answers. I had also sometimes the honour of attending my master in his visits to others. I never presumed to speak, except in answer to a question; and then I did it with inward regret, because it was a loss of so much time for improving myself; but I was infinitely delighted with the sta-tion of a humble auditor in such conversations, where nothing passed but what was useful, expressed in the fewest and most significant words; where the greatest decency was observed, without the least degree of ceremony; where no person spoke without being pleased himself, and pleasing his companions; where there was no interruption, tediousness, heat, or difference of sentiments. They have a notion that when people are met together, a short silence doth much improve conversation: this I found to be true; for during those little intermissions of talk, new ideas would rise in their thoughts, which very much enlivened the discourse. Their subjects are generally on friendship and benevolence, or order and economy; sometimes upon the visible operations of nature, or ancient traditions; upon the bounds and limits of virtue; upon the unerring rules of reason, or upon some determinations to be taken at the next great assembly; and often upon the various excellencies of poetry. I may add without vanity that my presence often gave them sufficient matter for discourse, because it afforded my master an occasion of letting his friends into the history of me and my country, upon which they were all pleased to descant in a manner not very advantageous to humankind; and for that reason I shall not repeat what they said: only I may be allowed to observe that his Honour, to my great admiration, appeared to understand the nature of Yahoos in all countries much better than myself. He went through all our vices and follies, and discovered many which I had never mentioned to him, by only supposing what qualities a Yahoo of their country, with a small proportion of reason, might be capable of exerting; and concluded, with too much probability, how vile as well as miserable such a creature must be.

I freely confess that all the little knowledge I have of any value was acquired by the lectures I received from my master, and from hearing the discourses of him and his friends; to which I should be prouder to listen than to dictate to the greatest and wisest assembly in Europe. I admired the strength, comeliness, and speed of the inhabitants; and such a constellation of virtues in such amiable persons produced in me the highest veneration. At first, indeed, I did not feel that natural awe which the Yahoos and all other animals bear towards them; but it grew upon me by degrees, much sooner than I imagined, and was mingled with a respectful love and gratitude, that they would condescend to distinguish me from the rest of my species.

When I thought of my family, my friends, my countrymen, or human race in general, I considered them as they really were, Yahoos in shape and disposition, perhaps a little more civilized, and qualified with the gift of speech, but making no other use of reason than to improve and multiply those vices whereof their brethren in this country had only the share that nature allotted them. When I happened to behold the reflection of my own form in a lake or fountain, I turned away my face in horror and detestation of myself, and could better endure the sight of a common Yahoo than of my own person. By conversing with the Houyhnhnms, and looking upon them with delight, I fell to imitate their gait and gesture, which is now grown into a habit, and my friends often tell me in a blunt way, that I trot like a horse; which, however, I take for a great compliment. Neither shall I disown that in speaking I am apt to fall into the voice and manner of the Houyhnhnms, and hear myself ridiculed on that account without the least mortification.

In the midst of all this happiness, and when I looked upon myself to be fully settled for life, my master sent for me one morning a little earlier than his usual hour. I observed by his countenance that he was in some perplexity, and at a loss how to begin what he had to speak. After a short silence he told me he did not know how I would take what he was going to say; that in the last general assembly, when the affair of the Yahoos was entered upon, the representatives had taken offence at his keeping a Yahoo (meaning myself) in his family more like a Houyhnhnm than a brute animal. That he was known frequently to converse with me, as if he could receive some advantage or pleasure in my company; that such a practice was not agreeable to reason or nature, nor a thing ever heard of before among them. The assembly did therefore exhort him, either to employ me like the rest of my species, or command me to swim back to the place from whence I came. That the first of these expedients was utterly rejected by all the Houyhnhnms who had ever seen me at his house or their own: for they alleged that because I had some rudiments of reason, added to the natural pravity of those animals, it was to be feared I might be able to seduce them into the woody and mountainous parts of the country, and bring them in troops by night to destroy the Houyhnhnms' cattle, as being naturally of the ravenous kind, and averse from labour.

My master added that he was daily pressed by the Houyhnhnms of the neighbourhood to have the assembly's exhortation executed, which he could not put off much longer. He doubted it would be impossible for me to swim to another country, and therefore wished I would contrive some sort of vehicle resembling those I had described to him, that might carry me on the sea; in which work I should have the assistance of his own servants, as well as those of his neighbours. He concluded that for his own part he could have been content to keep me in his service as long as I lived; because he found I had cured myself of some bad habits and dispositions, by endeavouring, as far as my inferior nature was capable, to imitate the Houyhnhnms.

I should here observe to the reader, that a decree of the general assembly in this country is expressed by the word *hnhloayn,* which signifies an exhortation, as near as I can render it; for they have no conception how a rational creature can be compelled, but only advised or exhorted, because no person can disobey reason without giving up his claim to be a rational creature.

I was struck with the utmost grief and despair at my master's discourse, and being unable to support the agonies I was under, I fell into a swoon at his feet; when I came to myself he told me that he concluded I had been dead (for these people are subject to no such imbecilities of nature). I answered in a faint voice that death would have been too great a happiness; that although I could not blame the assembly's exhortation, or the urgency of his friends, yet, in my weak and corrupt judgment, I thought it might consist with reason to have been less rigorous. That I could not swim a league, and probably the nearest land to theirs might be distant above a hundred; that many materials, necessary for making a small vessel to carry me off, were wholly wanting in this country, which, however, I would attempt in obedience and gratitude to his Honour, although I concluded the thing to be impossible, and therefore looked on myself as already devoted to destruction. That the certain prospect of an unnatural death was the least of my evils; for supposing I should escape with life by some strange adventure, how could I think with temper of passing my days among Yahoos, and relapsing into my old corruptions, for want of examples to lead and keep me within the paths of virtue? That I knew too well upon what solid reasons all the determinations of the wise Houyhnhnms were founded, not to be shaken by arguments of mine, a miserable Yahoo; and therefore, after presenting him with my humble thanks for the offer of his servants' assistance in making a vessel, and desiring a reasonable time for so difficult a work, I told him I would endeavour to preserve a wretched being; and if ever I returned to England, was not without hopes of being useful to my own species by celebrating the praises of the renowned Houyhnhnms, and proposing their virtues to the imitation of mankind.

My master in a few words made me a very gracious reply, allowed me the space of two months to finish my boat; and ordered the sorrel nag, my fellow-servant (for so at this distance I may presume to call him) to follow my instructions, because I told my master that his help would be sufficient, and I knew he had a tenderness for me.

In his company my first business was to go to that part of the coast where my rebellious crew had ordered me to be set on shore. I got upon a height, and looking on every side into the sea, fancied I saw a small island towards the northeast: I took out my pocket-glass, and could then clearly distinguish it about five leagues off, as I computed; but it appeared to the sorrel nag to be only a blue cloud; for as he had no conception of any country beside his own, so he could not be as expert in distinguishing remote objects at sea as we who so much converse in that element.

After I had discovered this island, I considered no farther; but resolved it should, if possible, be the first place of my banishment, leaving the consequences to fortune.

I returned home, and consulting with the sorrel nag, we went into a copse at some distance, where I with my knife, and he with a sharp flint fastened very artificially after their manner to a wooden handle, cut down several oak wattles about the thickness of a walking staff, and some larger pieces. But I shall not trouble the reader with a particular description of my own mechanics; let it suffice to say that in six weeks' time, with the help of the sorrel nag, who performed the parts that required most labour, I finished a sort of Indian canoe, but much larger, covering it with the skins of Yahoos well stitched together, with hempen threads of my own making. My sail was likewise composed of the skins of the same animal; but I made use of the youngest I could get, the older being too tough and thick; and I likewise provided myself with four paddles. I laid in a stock of boiled flesh, of rabbits and fowls, and took with me two vessels, one filled with milk and the other with water.

I tried my canoe in a large pond near my master's house, and then corrected in it what was amiss; stopping all the chinks with Yahoos' tallow, till I found it staunch, and able to bear me and my freight. And when it was as complete as I could possibly make it, I had it drawn on a carriage very gently by Yahoos to the seaside, under the conduct of the sorrel nag and another servant.

When all was ready, and the day came for my departure, I took leave of my master and lady and the whole family, my eyes flowing with tears, and my heart quite sunk with grief. But his Honour, out of curiosity, and perhaps (if I may speak it without vanity) partly out of kindness, was determined to see me in my canoe, and got several of his neighbouring friends to accompany him. I was forced to wait above an hour for the tide, and then observing the wind very fortunately bearing towards the island to which I intended to steer my course, I took a second leave of my master; but as I was going to prostrate myself to kiss his hoof, he did me the honour to raise it gently to my mouth. I am not ignorant how much I have been censured for mentioning this last particular. For my detractors are pleased to think it improbable that so illustrious a person should descend to give so great a mark of distinction to a creature so inferior as I. Neither have I forgot how apt some travellers are to boast of extraordinary favours they have received. But if these censurers were better acquainted with the noble and courteous disposition of the Houyhnhnms, they would soon change their opinion.

I paid my respects to the rest of the Houyhnhnms in his Honour's company; then getting into my canoe, I pushed off from shore.

11

I began this desperate voyage on February 15, 1714-5, at 9 o'clock in the morning. The wind was very favourable; however, I made use at first only of my paddles; but considering I should soon be weary, and that the wind might chop about, I ventured to set up my little sail; and thus with the help of the tide I went at the rate of a league and a half an hour, as near as I could guess. My master and his friends continued on the shore till I was almost out of sight; and I often heard the sorrel nag (who always loved me) crying out, *Hnuy illa nyha majah Yahoo,* Take care of thyself, gentle Yahoo.

My design was, if possible, to discover some small island uninhabited, yet sufficient by my labour to furnish me with the necessaries of life, which I would have thought a greater happiness than to be first minister in the politest court of Europe; so horrible was the idea I conceived of returning to live in the society and under the government of Yahoos. For in such a solitude as I desired I could at least enjoy my own thoughts, and reflect with delight on the virtues of those inimitable Houyhnhnms, without any opportunity of degenerating into the vices and corruptions of my own species.

The reader may remember what I related when my crew conspired against me and confined me to my cabin. How I continued there several weeks without knowing what course we took; and when I was put ashore in the longboat, how the sailors told me with oaths, whether true or false, that they knew not in what part of the world we were. However, I did then believe us to be about ten degrees southward of the Cape of Good Hope, or about 45 degrees southern latitude, as I gathered from some general words I overheard among them, being I supposed to the southeast in their intended voyage to Madagascar. And although this were but little better than conjecture, yet I resolved to steer my course eastward, hoping to reach the southwest coast of New Holland, and perhaps some such island as I desired, lying westward of it. The wind was full west, and by six in the evening I computed I had gone eastward at least eighteen leagues, when I spied a very small island about half a league off, which I soon reached. It was nothing but a rock, with one creek, naturally arched by the force of tempests. Here I put in my canoe, and climbing up a part of the rock, I could plainly discover land to the east, extending from south to north. I lay all night in my canoe; and repeating my voyage early in the morning, I arrived in seven hours to the southeast point of New Holland. This confirmed me in the opinion I have long entertained, that the maps and charts place this country at least three degrees more to the east than it really is; which thought I communicated many years ago to my worthy friend Mr. Herman Moll, and gave him my reasons for it, although he hath rather chosen to follow other authors.

I saw no inhabitants in the place where I landed, and being unarmed, I was afraid of venturing far into the country. I found some shellfish on the shore, and ate them raw, not daring to kindle a fire, for fear of being discovered by the natives. I continued three days feeding on oysters and limpets, to save my own provisions; and I fortunately found a brook of excellent water, which gave me great relief.

On the fourth day, venturing out early a little too far, I saw twenty or thirty natives upon a height, not above five hundred yards from me. They were stark naked, men, women, and children, round a fire, as I could discover by the smoke. One of them spied me, and gave notice to the rest; five of them advanced towards me, leaving the women and children at the fire. I made what haste I could to the shore, and getting into my canoe, shoved off: the savages, observing me retreat, ran after me; and before I could get far enough into the sea, discharged an arrow, which wounded me deeply on the inside of my left knee (I shall carry the mark to my grave). I apprehended the arrow might be poisoned, and paddling out of the reach of their darts (being a calm day), I made a shift to suck the wound and dress it as well as I could.

I was at a loss what to do, for I durst not return to the same landing place, but stood to the north, and was forced to paddle; for the wind, though very gentle, was against me, blowing northwest. As I was looking about for a secure landing place, I saw a sail to the north-northeast, which appearing every minute more visible, I was in some doubt whether I should wait for them or no; but at last my detestation of the Yahoo race prevailed, and turning my canoe, I sailed and paddled together to the south, and got into the same creek from whence I set out in the morning, choosing rather to trust myself among these barbarians, than live with European Yahoos. I drew up my canoe as close as I could to the shore, and hid myself behind a stone by the little brook, which, as I have already said, was excellent water.

The ship came within half a league of this creek, and sent her longboat with vessels to take in fresh water (for the place it seems was very well known), but I did not observe it till the boat was almost on shore, and it was too late to seek another hiding place. The seamen at their landing observed my canoe, and rummaging it all over, easily conjectured that the owner could not be far off. Four of them well armed searched every cranny and lurking-hole, till at last they found me flat on my face behind the stone. They gazed awhile in admiration at my strange uncouth dress, my coat made of skins, my wooden-soled shoes, and my furred stockings; from whence, however, they concluded I was not a native of the place, who all go naked. One of the seamen in Portuguese bid me rise, and asked who I was. I understood that language very well, and getting upon my feet, said I was a poor Yahoo, banished from the Houyhnhnms, and desired they would please let me depart. They admired to hear me answer them in their own tongue, and saw by my complexion I must be a European, but were at a loss to know what I meant by Yahoos and Houyhnhnms, and at the same time fell a laughing at my strange tone in speaking, which resembled the neighing of a horse. I trembled all the while betwixt fear and hatred: I again desired leave to depart, and was gently moving to my canoe; but they laid hold of me, desiring to know what country I was of, whence I came, with many other questions. I told them I was born in England, from whence I came about five years ago, and then their country and ours were at peace. I therefore hoped they would not treat me as an enemy, since I meant them no harm, but was a poor Yahoo, seeking some desolate place where to pass the remainder of his unfortunate life.

When they began to talk, I thought I never heard or saw any thing so unnatural; for it appeared to me as monstrous as if a dog or a cow should speak in England, or a Yahoo in Houyhnhnm-land. The honest Portuguese were equally amazed at my strange dress, and the odd manner of delivering my words, which however they understood very well. They spoke to me with great humanity, and said they were sure the Captain would carry me gratis to Lisbon, from whence I might return to my own country; that two of the seamen would go back to the ship, inform the Captain of what they had seen, and receive his orders; in the mean time, unless I would give my solemn oath not to fly, they would secure me by force. I thought it best to comply with their proposal. They were very curious to know my story, but I gave them very little satisfaction; and they all conjectured that my misfortunes had impaired my reason. In two hours the boat, which went loaden with vessels of water, returned with the Captain's command to fetch me on board. I fell on my knees to preserve my liberty; but all was in vain, and the men having tied me with cords, heaved me into the boat, from whence I was taken into the ship, and from thence into the Captain's cabin.

His name was Pedro de Mendez; he was a very courteous and generous person; he entreated me to give some account of myself, and desired to know what I would eat or drink; said I should be used as well as himself, and spoke so many obliging things, that I wondered to find such civilities from a Yahoo. However, I remained silent and sullen; I was ready to faint at the very smell of him and his men. At last I desired something to eat out of my own canoe; but he ordered me a chicken and some excellent wine, and then directed that I should be put to bed in a very clean cabin. I would not undress myself, but lay on the bedclothes, and in half an hour stole out, when I thought the crew was at dinner, and getting to the side of the ship was going to leap into the sea, and swim for my life, rather than continue among Yahoos. But one of the seamen prevented me, and having informed the Captain, I was chained to my cabin.

After dinner Don Pedro came to me, and desired to know my reason for so desperate an attempt, assured me he only meant to do me all the service he was able, and spoke so very movingly, that at last I descended to treat him like an animal which had some little portion of reason. I gave him a very short relation of my voyage, of the conspiracy against me by my own men, of the country where they set me on shore, and of my three years residence there. All which he looked upon as if it were a dream or a vision; whereat I took great offence, for I had quite forgot the faculty of lying, so peculiar to Yahoos in all countries where they preside, and, consequently the disposition of suspecting truth in others of their own species. I asked him whether it were the custom in his country to *say the thing that was not*. I assured him I had almost forgot what he meant by falsehood, and if I had lived a thousand years in Houyhnhnm-land, I should never have heard a lie from the meanest servant, that I was altogether indifferent whether he believed me or no, but however, in return for his favours, I would give so much allowance to the corruption of his nature as to answer any objection he would please to make, and then he might easily discover the truth.

The Captain, a wise man, after many endeavours to catch me tripping in some part of my story, at last began to have a better opinion of my veracity, and the rather, because he confessed he met with a Dutch skipper, who pretended to have landed with five others of his crew upon a certain island or continent south of New Holland, where they went for fresh water, and observed a horse driving before him several animals exactly resembling those I described under the name of Yahoos, with some other particulars, which the Captain said he had forgot; because he then concluded them all to be lies. But he added that since I professed so inviolable an attachment to truth, I must give him my word of honour to bear him company in this voyage, without attempting any thing against my life, or else he would continue me a prisoner till we arrived at Lisbon. I gave him the promise he required, but at the same time protested that I would suffer the greatest hardships rather than return to live among Yahoos.

Our voyage passed without any considerable accident. In gratitude to the Captain I sometimes sat with him at his earnest request, and strove to conceal my antipathy to humankind, although it often broke out, which he suffered to pass without observation. But the greatest part of the day I confined myself to my cabin, to avoid seeing any of the crew. The Captain had often entreated me to strip myself of my savage dress, and offered to lend me the best suit of clothes he had. This I would not be prevailed on to accept, abhorring to cover myself with any thing that had been on the back of a Yahoo. I only desired he would lend me two clean shirts, which having been washed since he wore them, I believed would not so much defile me. These I changed every second day, and washed them myself.

We arrived at Lisbon, Nov. 5, 1715. At our landing the Captain forced me to cover myself with his cloak, to prevent the rabble from crowding about me. I was conveyed to his own house, and at my earnest request he led me up to the highest room backwards. I conjured him to conceal from all persons what I had told him of the Houyhnhnms, because the least hint of such a story would not only draw numbers of people to see me, but probably put me in danger of being imprisoned, or burnt by the Inquisition. The Captain persuaded me to accept a suit of clothes newly made; but I would not suffer the tailor to take my measure; however, Don Pedro being almost of my size, they fitted me well enough. He accoutred me with other necessaries all new, which I aired for twenty-four hours before I would use them.

The Captain had no wife, nor above three servants, none of which were suffered to attend at meals, and his whole deportment was so obliging, added to very good *human* understanding, that I really began to tolerate his company. He gained so far upon me that I ventured to look out of the back window. By degrees I was brought into another room, from whence I peeped into the street, but drew my head back in a fright. In a week's time he seduced me down to the door. I found my terror gradually lessened, but my hatred and contempt seemed to increase. I was at last bold enough to walk the street in his company, but kept my nose well stopped with rue, or sometimes with tobacco.

In ten days Don Pedro, to whom I had given some account of my domestic affairs, put it upon me as a matter of honour and conscience, that I ought to return to my native country, and live at home with my wife and children. He told me there was an English ship in the port just ready to sail, and he would furnish me with all things necessary. It would be tedious to repeat his arguments, and my contradictions. He said it was altogether impossible to find such a solitary island as I had desired to live in; but I might command in my own house, and pass my time in a manner as recluse as I pleased.

I complied at last, finding I could do no better. I left Lisbon the 24th day of November, in an English merchantman, but who was the master I never inquired. Don Pedro accompanied me to the ship, and lent me twenty pounds. He took kind leave of me, and embraced me at parting, which I bore as well as I could. During this last voyage I had no commerce with the master or any of his men; but pretending I was sick, kept close in my cabin. On the fifth of December, 1715, we cast anchor in the Downs about nine in the morning, and at three in the afternoon I got safe to my house at Redriff.

My wife and family received me with great surprise and joy, because they concluded me certainly dead; but I must freely confess the sight of them filled me only with hatred, disgust, and contempt, and the more by reflecting on the near alliance I had to them. For although since my unfortunate exile from the Houyhnhnm country, I had compelled myself to tolerate the sight of Yahoos, and to converse with Don Pedro de Mendez, yet my memory and imagination were perpetually filled with the virtues and ideas of those exalted Houyhnhnms. And when I began to consider that by copulating with one of the Yahoo species I had become a parent of more, it struck me with the utmost shame, confusion, and horror.

As soon as I entered the house, my wife took me in her arms and kissed me, at which, having not been used to the touch of that odious animal for so many years, I fell in a swoon for almost an hour. At the time I am writing it is five years since my last return to England: during the first year I could not endure my wife or children in my presence, the very smell of them was intolerable, much less could I suffer them to eat in the same room. To this hour they dare not presume to touch my bread, or drink out of the same cup, neither was I ever able to let one of them take me by the hand. The first money I laid out was to buy two young stone-horses, which I keep in a good stable, and next to them the groom is my greatest favourite; for I feel my spirits revived by the smell he contracts in the stable. My horses understand me tolerably well; I converse with them at least four hours every day. They are strangers to bridle or saddle; they live in great amity with me, and friendship to each other.

12

Thus, gentle reader, I have given thee a faithful history of my travels for sixteen years and above seven months; wherein I have not been so studious of ornament as truth. I could perhaps like others have astonished thee with strange improbable tales; but I rather chose to relate plain matter of fact in the simplest manner and style; because my principal design was to inform, and not to amuse thee.

It is easy for us who travel into remote countries, which are seldom visited by Englishmen or other Europeans, to form descriptions of wonderful animals both at sea and land. Whereas a traveller's chief aim should be to make men wiser and better, and to improve their minds by the bad as well as good example of what they deliver concerning foreign places.

I could heartily wish a law was enacted, that every traveller, before he were permitted to publish his voyages, should be obliged to make oath before the Lord High Chancellor that all he intended to print was absolutely true to the best of his knowledge; for then the world would no longer be deceived as it usually is, while some writers, to make their works pass the better upon the public, impose the grossest falsities on the unwary reader. I have perused several books of travels with great delight in my younger days; but having since gone over most parts of the globe, and been able to contradict many fabulous accounts from my own observation, it hath given me a great disgust against this part of reading, and some indignation to see the credulity of mankind so impudently abused. Therefore since my acquaintance were pleased to think my poor endeavours might not be acceptable to my country, I imposed on myself as a maxim, never to be swerved from, that I would *strictly adhere to truth;* neither indeed can I be ever under the least temptation to vary from it, while I retain in my mind the

lectures and example of my noble master, and the other illustrious Houyhnhnms, of whom I had so long the honour to be a
humble hearer.

—*Nec si miserum Fortuna Sinonem*
Finxit, vanum etiam mendacemque improba finget.[1]

I know very well how little reputation is to be got by writings
which require neither genius nor learning, nor indeed any other
talent except a good memory or an exact journal. I know likewise that writers of travels, like dictionary-makers, are sunk
into oblivion by the weight and bulk of those who come after,
and therefore lie uppermost. And it is highly probable that such
travellers who shall hereafter visit the countries described in this
work of mine, may, by detecting my errors (if there be any), and
adding many new discoveries of their own, justle me out of
vogue, and stand in my place, making the world forget that I
was ever an author. This indeed would be too great a mortification if I wrote for fame: but, as my sole intention was the
PUBLIC GOOD, I cannot be altogether disappointed. For who
can read of the virtues I have mentioned in the glorious
Houyhnhnms, without being ashamed of his own vices, when
he considers himself as the reasoning, governing animal of his
country? I shall say nothing of those remote nations where
Yahoos preside; amongst which the least corrupted are the
Brobdingnagians, whose wise maxims in morality and government it would be our happiness to observe. But I forbear des-
canting farther, and rather leave the judicious reader to his own
remarks and applications.

I am not a little pleased that this work of mine can possibly
meet with no censurers: for what objections can be made
against a writer who relates only plain facts that happened in
such distant countries, where we have not the least interest
with respect either to trade or negotiations? I have carefully

---

1. ["Though Fortune has made Sinon miserable, she has not made him untrue and
a liar."—Virgil, *Aeneid*.]

avoided every fault with which common writers of travels are often too justly charged. Besides, I meddle not the least with any party, but write without passion, prejudice, or ill will against any man or number of men whatsoever. I write for the noblest end, to inform and instruct mankind, over whom I may, without breach of modesty, pretend to some superiority, from the advantages I received by conversing so long among the most accomplished Houyhnhnms. I write without any view towards profit or praise. I never suffer a word to pass that may look like reflection, or possibly give the least offence even to those who are most ready to take it. So that I hope I may with justice pronounce myself an author perfectly blameless, against whom the tribes of answerers, considerers, observers, reflecters, detecters, remarkers, will never be able to find matter for exercising their talents.

I confess it was whispered to me that I was bound in duty as a subject of England to have given in a memorial to a Secretary of State at my first coming over; because whatever lands are discovered by a subject belong to the Crown. But I doubt whether our conquests in the countries I treat of, would be as easy as those of Ferdinando Cortez over the naked Americans. The Lilliputians I think are hardly worth the charge of a fleet and army to reduce them; and I question whether it might be prudent or safe to attempt the Brobdingnagians; or whether an English army would be much at their ease with the Flying Island over their heads. The Houyhnhnms, indeed, appear not to be so well-prepared for war, a science to which they are perfect strangers, and especially against missive weapons. However, supposing myself to be a minister of state, I could never give my advice for invading them. Their prudence, unanimity, unacquaintedness with fear, and their love of their country, would amply supply all defects in the military art. Imagine twenty thousand of them breaking into the midst of a European army, confounding the ranks, overturning the carriages, battering the warriors' faces into mummy by terrible yerks from their hinder hoofs. For they would well deserve the character given to Augustus: *Recalcitrat undique tutus.*[2] But instead of proposals for conquering that magnanimous nation, I rather wish they were in a capacity or disposition to send a sufficient number of their inhabitants for civilizing Europe, by teaching us the first principles of honour, justice, truth, temperance, public spirit, fortitude, chastity, friendship, benevolence, and fidelity. The names of all which virtues are still retained among us in most languages, and are to be met with in modern as well as ancient authors; which I am able to assert from my own small reading.

But I had another reason which made me less forward to enlarge his Majesty's dominions by my discoveries. To say the truth, I had conceived a few scruples with relation to the distributive justice of princes upon those occasions. For instance, a crew of pirates are driven by a storm they know not whither, at length a boy discovers land from the topmast, they go on shore to rob and plunder, they see a harmless people, are entertained with kindness, they give the country a new name, they take formal possession of it for their King, they set up a rotten plank or a stone for a memorial, they murder two or three dozen of the natives, bring away a couple more by force for a sample, return home, and get their pardon. Here commences a new dominion acquired with a title by *divine right*. Ships are sent with the first opportunity, the natives driven out or destroyed, their princes tortured to discover their gold, a free licence given to all acts of inhumanity and lust, the earth reeking with the blood of its inhabitants: and this execrable crew of butchers employed in so pious an expedition, is a *modern colony* sent to convert and civilize an idolatrous and barbarous people.

But this description, I confess, doth by no means affect the British nation, who may be an example to the whole world for their wisdom, care, and justice in planting colonies; their liberal endowments for the advancement of religion and learning; their choice of devout and able pastors to propagate Christianity;

---

2. ["He kicks backward, secure on every side."—Horace, *Satires*, II, i, 20.]

their caution in stocking their provinces with people of sober lives and conversations from this the mother kingdom; their strict regard to the distribution of justice, in supplying the civil administration through all their colonies with officers of the greatest abilities, utter strangers to corruption; and to crown all, by sending the most vigilant and virtuous governors, who have no other views than the happiness of the people over whom they preside, and the honour of the King their master.

But, as those countries which I have described do not appear to have any desire of being conquered, and enslaved, murdered, or driven out by colonies, nor abound either in gold, silver, sugar, or tobacco; I did humbly conceive they were by no means proper objects of our zeal, our valour, or our interest. However, if those whom it more concerns think fit to be of another opinion, I am ready to depose, when I shall be lawfully called, that no European did ever visit these countries before me. I mean, if the inhabitants ought to be believed; unless a dispute may arise about the two Yahoos, said to have been seen many ages ago in a mountain in Houyhnhnm-land, from whence the opinion is, that the race of those brutes hath descended; and these, for anything I know, may have been English, which indeed I was apt to suspect from the lineaments of their posterity's countenances, although very much defaced. But, how far that will go to make out a title, I leave to the learned in colony law.

But as to the formality of taking possession in my Sovereign's name, it never came once into my thoughts; and if it had, yet as my affairs then stood, I should perhaps in point of prudence and self-preservation have put it off to a better opportunity.

Having thus answered the only objection that can ever be raised against me as a traveller, I here take a final leave of all my courteous readers, and return to enjoy my own speculations in my little garden at Redriff, to apply those excellent lessons of virtue which I learned among the Houyhnhnms, to instruct the Yahoos of my own family as far as I shall find them docible animals; to behold my figure often in a glass, and thus if possible

habituate myself by time to tolerate the sight of a human creature; to lament the brutality of Houyhnhnms in my own country,
but always treat their persons with respect, for the sake of my
noble master, his family, his friends, and the whole Houyhnhnm
race, whom these of ours have the honour to resemble in all their
lineaments, however their intellectuals came to degenerate.

I began last week to permit my wife to sit at dinner with me,
at the farthest end of a long table, and to answer (but with the
utmost brevity) the few questions I ask her. Yet the smell of a
Yahoo continuing very offensive, I always keep my nose well
stopped with rue, lavender, or tobacco leaves. And although it
be hard for a man late in life to remove old habits, I am not altogether out of hopes in some time to suffer a neighbour Yahoo in
my company, without the apprehensions I am yet under of his
teeth or his claws.

My reconcilement to the Yahoo-kind in general might not be
so difficult, if they would be content with those vices and follies
only which nature hath entitled them to. I am not in the least
provoked at the sight of a lawyer, a pickpocket, a colonel, a
fool, a lord, a gamester, a politician, a whoremaster, a physician,
an evidence, a suborner, an attorney, a traitor, or the like; this
is all according to the due course of things: but when I behold
a lump of deformity and diseases both in body and mind, smit-
ten with *pride*, it immediately breaks all the measures of my
patience; neither shall I be ever able to comprehend how such
an animal and such a vice could tally together. The wise and
virtuous Houyhnhnms, who abound in all excellencies that can
adorn a rational creature, have no name for this vice in their
language, which hath no terms to express any thing that is evil,
except those whereby they describe the detestable qualities of
their Yahoos, among which they were not able to distinguish
this of pride, for want of thoroughly understanding human
nature, as it showeth itself in other countries, where that animal
presides. But I, who had more experience, could plainly observe
some rudiments of it among the wild Yahoos.

But the Houyhnhnms, who live under the government of reason, are no more proud of the good qualities they possess, than I should be for not wanting a leg or an arm, which no man in his wits would boast of, although he must be miserable without them. I dwell the longer upon this subject from the desire I have to make the society of an English Yahoo by any means not insupportable; and therefore I here entreat those who have any tincture of this absurd vice, that they will not presume to come in my sight. ∾

INTERPRETIVE QUESTIONS
FOR DISCUSSION

In portraying the Houyhnhnms as more civilized than humans, why does Swift make them lack hallmarks of human civilization— science, books, and love?

1. Why does Swift have the Houyhnhnms consider human vice to be unreasonable rather than immoral? (238–239, 242–243)

2. Why in the Houyhnhnm society are there no books or written learning and no use for the study of natural philosophy? Why do they lag behind humans in science and technology but outstrip them in poetry? (234, 265, 270–271)

3. Why do the Houyhnhnms value friendship and benevolence but not romantic or familial love? (266–267, 271)

4. Is isolation from other countries and ignorance of other peoples necessary for the success of the Houyhnhnm society?

5. Could the Houyhnhnms have developed their superior society without a rich bounty of nature? (250)

6. If reason among the Houyhnhnms strikes "with immediate conviction," why must their general assembly regularly debate the question of "whether the Yahoos should be exterminated from the face of the earth"? Why are the benevolent Houyhnhnms willing to consider genocide? (265, 268)

7. Are we meant to accept the Houyhnhnms' decision to expel Gulliver—an atypical Yahoo—as rational? (276–278)

8. Why are we told that the sorrel nag always loved Gulliver? (280)

Suggested textual analyses

Pages 238–239: beginning, "My master heard me," and ending, "so perfectly well understood among human creatures."

Pages 265–268: beginning, "As these noble Houyhnhnms," and ending, "shall breed another to supply the loss."

Why does living three years among creatures governed wholly by reason cause Gulliver to behave like a madman—to lose his reason—upon his return home?

1. Why does Swift model his ideal race on the horse rather than creating a more perfect kind of human being?

2. Why does Gulliver's experience with the Yahoos lead him to detest his own kind? Why does he come to think even of himself as a "miserable Yahoo"? (276, 278)

3. Why does Gulliver believe that he would prefer to live among barbarian Yahoos than among Europeans? (282)

4. Why does Swift make the "courteous and generous" and "wise" Don Pedro the person who reacquaints Gulliver with human society? Why doesn't this encounter alter his opinion that Europeans are Yahoos? (284–286)

5. Why, after learning virtue from the Houyhnhnms, must Gulliver be reminded by Don Pedro of his responsibility to his wife and children? (286)

6. Why does Gulliver's aversion to Yahoos continue upon his return to England, even though he is treated with great kindness and understanding? Why does he prefer the company of his horses and their groom to that of his wife and children? (287–288)

7. Why do Gulliver's attempts to emulate the Houyhnhnms impede his life rather than improve it?

8. In his rigid application of Houyhnhnm values to life in England, is Gulliver proving the Houyhnhnms' claim that Yahoos use reason only to aggravate their folly? (287–288)

Suggested textual analyses

Pages 274–278: beginning, "I had the favour of being admitted," and ending, "and proposing their virtues to the imitation of mankind."

Pages 283–288: beginning, "When they began to talk," and ending, "and friendship to each other."

Why is pride the single human vice that Gulliver will not tolerate?

1. Why does Swift make the Yahoos not just animals, but the most disagreeable of all animals, even to themselves? (223–224, 230, 241, 257)

2. Why does Swift suggest that the refinements of European society compound its barbarity instead of mitigating it? (250, 255, 274)

3. Why does Swift portray even government, law, and medicine as signs of degeneracy rather than of advanced civilization? (247–249, 251–254)

4. Why does Swift have Gulliver claim that his sole intention in writing about his travels is the public good? (289)

5. Why does Swift conclude his work with an attack on colonialism? Why does he suggest that some good might come from the Houyhnhnms visiting the Europeans, but not the other way around? (290–292)

6. Why does Gulliver admire the Houyhnhnms for not being proud of their good qualities? Why doesn't believing themselves to be "the perfection of nature" lead the Houyhnhnms to the human vice of pride? (234, 293)

Suggested textual analysis
Pages 290–294: beginning, "I confess it was whispered to me," to the end of the selection.

FOR FURTHER REFLECTION

1. Do the Houyhnhnms represent for you a perfect society? Would you, like Gulliver, want to live out your days among the Houyhnhnms?

2. Are human beings as irrational and evil as Swift portrays? Are we really just a bunch of Yahoos?

3. Is Swift's satire instructive or only a pessimistic complaint?

4. Is it only the power of the government to enforce the law that prevents people from being Yahoos?

5. Are friendship and benevolence higher virtues than love, as they are in Houyhnhnm society?

6. Would you want to be governed in a perfectly rational way by someone unaffected by passion? Do both passion and reason need to be moderated in dealing with human beings, or should reason be supreme?

POETRY

Derek Walcott

DEREK WALCOTT (1930–   ) was born
on the island of St. Lucia, studied at the
University of the West Indies, and has lived
extensively in Great Britain and the United
States. His first major volume of poetry,
In a Green Night, was published in 1962.
Omeros, Walcott's epic poem of almost
8,000 lines, was published in 1990. Two
years later, Walcott won the Nobel Prize for
literature; he was the first West Indian
writer to receive this honor.

The Schooner Flight

1 Adios, Carenage

In idle August, while the sea soft,
and leaves of brown islands stick to the rim
of this Caribbean, I blow out the light
by the dreamless face of Maria Concepcion
to ship as a seaman on the schooner *Flight*.
Out in the yard turning grey in the dawn,
I stood like a stone and nothing else move
but the cold sea rippling like galvanize
and the nail holes of stars in the sky roof,
till a wind start to interfere with the trees.
I pass me dry neighbour sweeping she yard
as I went downhill, and I nearly said:
"Sweep soft, you witch, 'cause she don't sleep hard,"
but the bitch look through me like I was dead.
A route taxi pull up, park-lights still on.
The driver size up my bags with a grin:
"This time, Shabine, like you really gone!"
I ain't answer the ass, I simply pile in
the back seat and watch the sky burn
above Laventille pink as the gown
in which the woman I left was sleeping,
and I look in the rearview and see a man
exactly like me, and the man was weeping
for the houses, the streets, that whole fucking island.

Christ have mercy on all sleeping things!
From that dog rotting down Wrightson Road
to when I was a dog on these streets;
if loving these islands must be my load,
out of corruption my soul takes wings.
But they had started to poison my soul
with their big house, big car, big-time bohbohl,
coolie, nigger, Syrian, and French Creole,
so I leave it for them and their carnival—
I taking a sea-bath, I gone down the road.
I know these islands from Monos to Nassau,
a rusty head sailor with sea-green eyes
that they nickname Shabine, the patois for
any red nigger, and I, Shabine, saw
when these slums of empire was paradise.
I'm just a red nigger who love the sea,
I had a sound colonial education,
I have Dutch, nigger, and English in me,
and either I'm nobody, or I'm a nation.

But Maria Concepcion was all my thought
watching the sea heaving up and down
as the port side of dories, schooners, and yachts
was painted afresh by the strokes of the sun
signing her name with every reflection;
I knew when dark-haired evening put on
her bright silk at sunset, and, folding the sea,
sidled under the sheet with her starry laugh,
that there'd be no rest, there'd be no forgetting.
Is like telling mourners round the graveside
about resurrection, they want the dead back,
so I smile to myself as the bow rope untied
and the *Flight* swing seaward: "Is no use repeating
that the sea have more fish. I ain't want her
dressed in the sexless light of a seraph,
I want those round brown eyes like a marmoset, and

till the day when I can lean back and laugh,
those claws that tickled my back on sweating
Sunday afternoons, like a crab on wet sand."
As I worked, watching the rotting waves come
past the bow that scissor the sea like silk,
I swear to you all, by my mother's milk,
by the stars that shall fly from tonight's furnace,
that I loved them, my children, my wife, my home;
I loved them as poets love the poetry
that kills them, as drowned sailors the sea.

You ever look up from some lonely beach
and see a far schooner? Well, when I write
this poem, each phrase go be soaked in salt;
I go draw and knot every line as tight
as ropes in this rigging; in simple speech
my common language go be the wind,
my pages the sails of the schooner *Flight*.
But let me tell you how this business begin.

2 *Raptures of the Deep*

Smuggled Scotch for O'Hara, big government man,
between Cedros and the Main, so the Coast Guard couldn't touch us,
and the Spanish pirogues always met us halfway,
but a voice kept saying: "Shabine, see this business
of playing pirate?" Well, so said, so done!
That whole racket crash. And I for a woman,
for her laces and silks, Maria Concepcion.
Ay, ay! Next thing I hear, some Commission of Enquiry
was being organized to conduct a big quiz,
with himself as chairman investigating himself.
Well, I knew damn well who the suckers would be,
not that shark in shark skin, but his pilot fish,
khaki-pants red niggers like you and me.
What worse, I fighting with Maria Concepcion,

plates flying and thing, so I swear: "Not again!"
It was mashing up my house and my family.
I was so broke all I needed was shades and a cup
or four shades and four cups in four-cup Port of Spain;
all the silver I had was the coins on the sea.

You saw them ministers in *The Express*,
guardians of the poor—one hand at their back,
and one set o' police only guarding their house,
and the Scotch pouring in through the back door.
As for that minister-monster who smuggled the booze,
that half-Syrian saurian, I got so vex to see
that face thick with powder, the warts, the stone lids
like a dinosaur caked with primordial ooze
by the lightning of flashbulbs sinking in wealth,
that I said: "Shabine, this is shit, understand!"
But he get somebody to kick my crutch out his office
like I was some artist! That bitch was so grand,
couldn't get off his high horse and kick me himself.
I have seen things that would make a slave sick
in this Trinidad, the Limers' Republic.

I couldn't shake the sea noise out of my head,
the shell of my ears sang Maria Concepcion,
so I start salvage diving with a crazy Mick,
name O'Shaughnessy, and a limey named Head;
but this Caribbean so choke with the dead
that when I would melt in emerald water,
whose ceiling rippled like a silk tent,
I saw them corals: brain, fire, sea-fans,
dead-men's-fingers, and then, the dead men.
I saw that the powdery sand was their bones
ground white from Senegal to San Salvador,
so, I panic third dive, and surface for a month
in the Seamen's Hostel. Fish broth and sermons.

When I thought of the woe I had brought my wife,
when I saw my worries with that other woman,
I wept under water, salt seeking salt,
for her beauty had fallen on me like a sword
cleaving me from my children, flesh of my flesh!

There was this barge from St. Vincent, but she was too deep
to float her again. When we drank, the limey
got tired of my sobbing for Maria Concepcion.
He said he was getting the bends. Good for him!
The pain in my heart for Maria Concepcion,
the hurt I had done to my wife and children,
was worse than the bends. In the rapturous deep
there was no cleft rock where my soul could hide
like the boobies each sunset, no sandbar of light
where I could rest, like the pelicans know,
so I got raptures once, and I saw God
like a harpooned grouper bleeding, and a far
voice was rumbling, "Shabine, if you leave her,
if you leave her, I shall give you the morning star."
When I left the madhouse I tried other women
but, once they stripped naked, their spiky cunts
bristled like sea-eggs and I couldn't dive.
The chaplain came round. I paid him no mind.
Where is my rest place, Jesus? Where is my harbour?
Where is the pillow I will not have to pay for,
and the window I can look from that frames my life?

3 *Shabine Leaves the Republic*

I had no nation now but the imagination.
After the white man, the niggers didn't want me
when the power swing to their side.
The first chain my hands and apologize, "History";
the next said I wasn't black enough for their pride.

Tell me, what power, on these unknown rocks—
a spray-plane Air Force, the Fire Brigade,
the Red Cross, the Regiment, two, three police dogs
that pass before you finish bawling "Parade!"?
I met History once, but he ain't recognize me,
a parchment Creole, with warts
like an old sea-bottle, crawling like a crab
through the holes of shadow cast by the net
of a grille balcony; cream linen, cream hat.
I confront him and shout, "Sir, is Shabine!
They say I'se your grandson. You remember Grandma,
your black cook, at all?" The bitch hawk and spat.
A spit like that worth any number of words.
But that's all them bastards have left us: words.
I no longer believed in the revolution.
I was losing faith in the love of my woman.
I had seen that moment Aleksandr Blok
crystallize in *The Twelve*.[1] Was between
the Police Marine Branch and Hotel Venezuelana
one Sunday at noon. Young men without flags
using shirts, their chests waiting for holes.
They kept marching into the mountains, and
their noise ceased as foam sinks into sand.
They sank in the bright hills like rain, every one
with his own nimbus, leaving shirts in the street,
and the echo of power at the end of the street.
Propeller-blade fans turn over the Senate;
the judges, they say, still sweat in carmine,
on Frederick Street the idlers all marching
by standing still, the Budget turns a new leaf.
In the 12:30 movies the projectors best
not break down, or you go see revolution. Aleksandr Blok

---

1. [Aleksandr Blok (1880–1921) was a Russian poet and dramatist. His poem *The Twelve* describes a band of Red Army soldiers, headed by a Christ figure, looting and killing on a march during the 1917–1918 St. Petersburg uprising.]

enters and sits in the third row of pit eating chocolate cone, waiting for a spaghetti Western with Clint Eastwood and featuring Lee Van Cleef.

4 The Flight, Passing Blanchisseuse

Dusk. The *Flight* passing Blanchisseuse.
Gulls wheel like from a gun again,
and foam gone amber that was white,
lighthouse and star start making friends,
down every beach the long day ends,
and there, on that last stretch of sand,
on a beach bare of all but light,
dark hands start pulling in the seine
of the dark sea, deep, deep inland.

5 Shabine Encounters the Middle Passage

Man, I brisk in the galley first thing next dawn,
brewing li'l coffee; fog coil from the sea
like the kettle steaming when I put it down
slow, slow, 'cause I couldn't believe what I see:
where the horizon was one silver haze,
the fog swirl and swell into sails, so close
that I saw it was sails, my hair grip my skull,
it was horrors, but it was beautiful.
We float through a rustling forest of ships
with sails dry like paper, behind the glass
I saw men with rusty eyeholes like cannons,
and whenever their half-naked crews cross the sun,
right through their tissue, you traced their bones
like leaves against the sunlight; frigates, barkentines,
the backward-moving current swept them on,
and high on their decks I saw great admirals,
Rodney, Nelson, de Grasse, I heard the hoarse orders
they gave those Shabines, and the forest

of masts sail right through the *Flight,*
and all you could hear was the ghostly sound
of waves rustling like grass in a low wind
and the hissing weeds they trailed from the stern;
slowly they heaved past from east to west
like this round world was some cranked water wheel,
every ship pouring like a wooden bucket
dredged from the deep; my memory revolve
on all sailors before me, then the sun
heat the horizon's ring and they was mist.

Next we pass slave ships. Flags of all nations,
our fathers below deck too deep, I suppose,
to hear us shouting. So we stop shouting. Who knows
who his grandfather is, much less his name?
Tomorrow our landfall will be the Barbados.

6 *The Sailor Sings Back to the Casuarinas*

You see them on the low hills of Barbados
bracing like windbreaks, needles for hurricanes,
trailing, like masts, the cirrus of torn sails;
when I was green like them, I used to think
those cypresses, leaning against the sea,
that take the sea-noise up into their branches,
are not real cypresses but casuarinas.
Now captain just call them Canadian cedars.
But cedars, cypresses, or casuarinas,
whoever called them so had a good cause,
watching their bending bodies wail like women
after a storm, when some schooner came home
with news of one more sailor drowned again.
Once the sound "cypress" used to make more sense
than the green "casuarinas," though, to the wind
whatever grief bent them was all the same,
since they were trees with nothing else in mind

but heavenly leaping or to guard a grave;
but we live like our names and you would have
to be colonial to know the difference,
to know the pain of history words contain,
to love those trees with an inferior love,
and to believe: "Those casuarinas bend
like cypresses, their hair hangs down in rain
like sailors' wives. They're classic trees, and we,
if we live like the names our masters please,
by careful mimicry might become men."

7 The Flight Anchors in Castries Harbor

When the stars self were young over Castries,
I loved you alone and I loved the whole world.
What does it matter that our lives are different?
Burdened with the loves of our different children?
When I think of your young face washed by the wind
and your voice that chuckles in the slap of the sea?
The lights are out on La Toc promontory,
except for the hospital. Across at Vigie
the marina arcs keep vigil. I have kept my own
promise, to leave you the one thing I own,
you whom I loved first: my poetry.
We here for one night. Tomorrow, the *Flight* will be gone.

8 Fight with the Crew

It had one bitch on board, like he had me mark—
that was the cook, some Vincentian arse
with a skin like a gommier tree, red peeling bark,
and wash-out blue eyes; he wouldn't give me a ease,
like he feel he was white. Had an exercise book,
this same one here, that I was using to write
my poetry, so one day this man snatch it
from my hand, and start throwing it left and right

to the rest of the crew, bawling out, "Catch it,"
and start mincing me like I was some hen
because of the poems. Some case is for fist,
some case is for tholing pin, some is for knife—
this one was for knife. Well, I beg him first,
but he keep reading, "O my children, my wife,"
and playing he crying, to make the crew laugh;
it move like a flying fish, the silver knife
that catch him right in the plump of his calf,
and he faint so slowly, and he turn more white
than he thought he was. I suppose among men
you need that sort of thing. It ain't right
but that's how it is. There wasn't much pain,
just plenty blood, and Vincie and me best friend,
but none of them go fuck with my poetry again.

9 *Maria Concepcion & the Book of Dreams*

The jet that was screeching over the *Flight*
was opening a curtain into the past.
"Dominica ahead!"
      "It still have Caribs there."
"One day go be planes only, no more boat."
"Vince, God ain't make nigger to fly through the air."
"Progress, Shabine, that's what it's all about.
Progress leaving all we small islands behind."
I was at the wheel, Vince sitting next to me
gaffing. Crisp, bracing day. A high-running sea.
"Progress is something to ask Caribs about.
They kill them by millions, some in war,
some by forced labour dying in the mines
looking for silver, after that niggers; more
progress. Until I see definite signs
that mankind change, Vince, I ain't want to hear.
Progress is history's dirty joke.
Ask that sad green island getting nearer."

Green islands, like mangoes pickled in brine.
In such fierce salt let my wound be healed,
me, in my freshness as a seafarer.

That night, with the sky sparks frosty with fire,
I ran like a Carib through Dominica,
my nose holes choked with memory of smoke;
I heard the screams of my burning children,
I ate the brains of mushrooms, the fungi
of devil's parasols under white, leprous rocks;
my breakfast was leaf mould in leaking forests,
with leaves big as maps, and when I heard noise
of the soldiers' progress through the thick leaves,
though my heart was bursting, I get up and ran
through the blades of balisier sharper than spears;
with the blood of my race, I ran, boy, I ran
with moss-footed speed like a painted bird;
then I fall, but I fall by an icy stream under
cool fountains of fern, and a screaming parrot
catch the dry branches and I drowned at last
in big breakers of smoke; then when that ocean
of black smoke pass, and the sky turn white,
there was nothing but Progress, if Progress is
an iguana as still as a young leaf in sunlight.
I bawl for Maria, and her *Book of Dreams*.

It anchored her sleep, that insomniac's Bible,
a soiled orange booklet with a cyclops' eye
center, from the Dominican Republic.
Its coarse pages were black with the usual
symbols of prophecy, in excited Spanish;
an open palm upright, sectioned and numbered
like a butcher chart, delivered the future.
One night, in a fever, radiantly ill,
she say, "Bring me the book, the end has come."
She said: "I dreamt of whales and a storm,"

but for that dream, the book had no answer.
A next night I dreamed of three old women
featureless as silkworms, stitching my fate,
and I scream at them to come out my house,
and I try beating them away with a broom,
but as they go out, so they crawl back again,
until I start screaming and crying, my flesh
raining with sweat, and she ravage the book
for the dream meaning, and there was nothing;
my nerves melt like a jellyfish—that was when I broke—
they found me round the Savannah, screaming:

All you see me talking to the wind, so you think I mad.
Well, Shabine has bridled the horses of the sea;
you see me watching the sun till my eyeballs seared,
so all you mad people feel Shabine crazy,
but all you ain't know my strength, hear? The coconuts
standing by in their regiments in yellow khaki,
they waiting for Shabine to take over these islands,
and all you best dread the day I am healed
of being a human. All you fate in my hand,
ministers, businessmen, Shabine have you, friend,
I shall scatter your lives like a handful of sand,
I who have no weapon but poetry and
the lances of palms and the sea's shining shield!

10 *Out of the Depths*

Next day, dark sea. A arse-aching dawn.
"Damn wind shift sudden as a woman mind."
The slow swell start cresting like some mountain range
with snow on the top.
                              "Ay, Skipper, sky dark!"
"This ain't right for August."
                              "This light damn strange,
this season, sky should be clear as a field."

A stingray steeplechase across the sea,
tail whipping water, the high man-o'-wars
start reeling inland, quick, quick an archery
of flying fish miss us! Vince say: "You notice?"
and a black-mane squall pounce on the sail
like a dog on a pigeon, and it snap the neck
of the *Flight* and shake it from head to tail.
"Be Jesus, I never see sea get so rough
so fast! That wind come from God back pocket!"
"Where Cap'n headin? Like the man gone blind!"
"If we's to drong, we go drong, Vince, fock-it!"
"Shabine, say your prayers, if life leave you any!"

I have not loved those that I loved enough.
Worse than the mule kick of Kick-'Em-Jenny
Channel, rain start to pelt the *Flight* between
mountains of water. If I was frighten?
The tent poles of water spouts bracing the sky
start wobbling, clouds unstitch at the seams
and sky water drench us, and I hear myself cry,
"I'm the drowned sailor in her *Book of Dreams*."
I remembered them ghost ships, I saw me corkscrewing
to the sea-bed of sea-worms, fathom pass fathom,
my jaw clench like a fist, and only one thing
hold me, trembling, how my family safe home.
Then a strength like it seize me and the strength said:
"I from backward people who still fear God."
Let Him, in His might, heave Leviathan upward
by the winch of His will, the beast pouring lace
from his sea-bottom bed; and that was the faith
that had fade from a child in the Methodist chapel
in Chisel Street, Castries, when the whale-bell
sang service and, in hard pews ribbed like the whale,
proud with despair, we sang how our race
survive the sea's maw, our history, our peril,

and now I was ready for whatever death will.
But if that storm had strength, was in Cap'n face,
beard beading with spray, tears salting the eyes,
crucify to his post, that nigger hold fast
to that wheel, man, like the cross held Jesus,
and the wounds of his eyes like they crying for us,
and I feeding him white rum, while every crest
with Leviathan-lash make the *Flight* quail
like two criminal. Whole night, with no rest,
till red-eyed like dawn, we watch our travail
subsiding, subside, and there was no more storm.
And the noon sea get calm as Thy Kingdom come.

11 *After the Storm*

There's a fresh light that follows a storm
while the whole sea still havoc; in its bright wake
I saw the veiled face of Maria Concepcion
marrying the ocean, then drifting away
in the widening lace of her bridal train
with white gulls her bridesmaids, till she was gone.
I wanted nothing after that day.
Across my own face, like the face of the sun,
a light rain was falling, with the sea calm.

Fall gently, rain, on the sea's upturned face
like a girl showering; make these islands fresh
as Shabine once knew them! Let every trace,
every hot road, smell like clothes she just press
and sprinkle with drizzle. I finish dream;
whatever the rain wash and the sun iron:
the white clouds, the sea and sky with one seam,
is clothes enough for my nakedness.
Though my *Flight* never pass the incoming tide
of this inland sea beyond the loud reefs
of the final Bahamas, I am satisfied

if my hand gave voice to one people's grief.
Open the map. More islands there, man,
than peas on a tin plate, all different size,
one thousand in the Bahamas alone,
from mountains to low scrub with coral keys,
and from this bowsprit, I bless every town,
the blue smell of smoke in hills behind them,
and the one small road winding down them like twine
to the roofs below; I have only one theme:
The bowsprit, the arrow, the longing, the lunging heart—
the flight to a target whose aim we'll never know,
vain search for one island that heals with its harbour
and a guiltless horizon, where the almond's shadow
doesn't injure the sand. There are so many islands!
As many islands as the stars at night
on that branched tree from which meteors are shaken
like falling fruit around the schooner *Flight*.
But things must fall, and so it always was,
on one hand Venus, on the other Mars;
fall, and are one, just as this earth is one
island in archipelagoes of stars.
My first friend was the sea. Now, is my last.
I stop talking now. I work, then I read,
cotching under a lantern hooked to the mast.
I try to forget what happiness was,
and when that don't work, I study the stars.
Sometimes is just me, and the soft-scissored foam
as the deck turn white and the moon open
a cloud like a door, and the light over me
is a road in white moonlight taking me home.
Shabine sang to you from the depths of the sea.

Derek Walcott

A Far Cry from Africa

A wind is ruffling the tawny pelt
Of Africa. Kikuyu,[2] quick as flies,
Batten upon the bloodstreams of the veldt.
Corpses are scattered through a paradise.
Only the worm, colonel of carrion, cries:
"Waste no compassion on these separate dead!"
Statistics justify and scholars seize
The salients of colonial policy.
What is that to the white child hacked in bed?
To savages, expendable as Jews?

Threshed out by beaters, the long rushes break
In a white dust of ibises whose cries
Have wheeled since civilization's dawn
From the parched river or beast-teeming plain.
The violence of beast on beast is read
As natural law, but upright man
Seeks his divinity by inflicting pain.
Delirious as these worried beasts, his wars
Dance to the tightened carcass of a drum,
While he calls courage still that native dread
Of the white peace contracted by the dead.

---

2. [The largest tribal group in Kenya. In the early 1950s, the Kikuyu led the bloody
   Mau Mau rebellion against British colonial rule.]

Again brutish necessity wipes its hands
Upon the napkin of a dirty cause, again
A waste of our compassion, as with Spain,
The gorilla wrestles with the superman.
I who am poisoned with the blood of both,
Where shall I turn, divided to the vein?
I who have cursed
The drunken officer of British rule, how choose
Between this Africa and the English tongue I love?
Betray them both, or give back what they give?
How can I face such slaughter and be cool?
How can I turn from Africa and live?

Derek Walcott

INTERPRETIVE QUESTIONS
FOR DISCUSSION

Why does Shabine leave Maria Concepcion, his family, and his home to become a sailor on the schooner *Flight*?

1. Why does Shabine feel that life on the islands had begun to "poison" his soul, but also that his soul "takes wings" out of the islands' corruption? (304)

2. What does Shabine mean when he says, "I have Dutch, nigger, and English in me, / and either I'm nobody, or I'm a nation"? (304)

3. After Shabine has left, why is Maria Concepcion all he can think about? Why does he know there will be for him "no rest" and "no forgetting"? (304)

4. Why does Shabine swear that he loved his children, wife, and home "as poets love the poetry / that kills them, as drowned sailors the sea"? (305)

5. When he takes up salvage diving, why does Shabine have a vision of the Caribbean choked with dead that causes him to panic and lands him for a month in the Seamen's Hostel? (306)

6. Why does the pain in his heart for Maria Concepcion and the hurt he has done to his wife and children cause Shabine to get "raptures"? Why does he see God "like a harpooned grouper bleeding" and hear a voice saying, "if you leave her, I shall give you the morning star"? (307)

7. Why does Shabine suggest that he has no resting place, no harbor, no pillow he will not have to pay for, and no window that frames his life? (307)

8. Why does Shabine refer to the white grandfather, who refuses to acknowledge him, as "History"? (308)

9. Why does Shabine no longer believe in the revolution? Why does he contrast the young men who die in the hills with those who have nothing better to do than go to the movies? (308)

10. Why does Shabine have a vision of the middle passage that includes great admirals as well as slave ships? Why does he find the vision beautiful as well as horrible? (309–310)

11. Why is Shabine's one theme "the flight to a target whose aim we'll never know,/vain search for one island that heals with its harbour/and a guiltless horizon"? (317) Are we meant to understand "flight" metaphorically as running away, taking wing, or both?

12. Why does Shabine think of the sea as both his first friend and his last? Why does he try to forget what happiness was? (317)

Why does Shabine find more hope and peace in poetry than in progress?

1. Why does Shabine tell the reader that the pages of his poem are going to be "the sails of the schooner *Flight*"? (305)

2. After he leaves, why does Shabine feel that he has "no nation now but the imagination"? Why does he say, "that's all them bastards have left us: words"? (307, 308)

3. Why is Shabine concerned about the correct name of the trees on the low hills of Barbados? Why does he compare them to wailing women and observe that "to the wind/whatever grief bent them was all the same"? (310–311)

4. To whom is Shabine speaking when he says, "I loved you alone and I loved the whole world"? Why does he say he has kept his own promise, "to leave you the one thing I own, / you whom I loved first: my poetry"? (311)

5. Why does Shabine regard the Vincentian's making fun of his poetry and his grief for his wife and children as a case "for knife"? Why do Shabine and Vince end up becoming best friends? (311–312)

6. Why does Shabine regard the fate of the Caribs of Dominica as proof that "Progress is history's dirty joke"? (312)

7. Why, in his madness, does Shabine scream that on the day he is "healed / of being a human" everyone's fate will be in his hand and he will scatter the lives of ministers and businessmen, though he has no weapon but poetry? (314)

8. Why, in the middle of the storm, is Shabine seized by a strength that restores to him his childhood faith? Why does his memory of singing in church "how our race / survive the sea's maw, our history, our peril" make him "ready for whatever death will"? (315–316)

9. Why does Shabine want nothing after the day that he sees "the veiled face of Maria Concepcion / marrying the ocean" and drifting away? Why does Shabine say, "I am satisfied / if my hand gave voice to one people's grief"? (316–317)

10. What does Shabine mean when he says, "Shabine sang to you from the depths of the sea"? (317)

In "A Far Cry from Africa," why does the poet feel he can neither embrace nor reject his African heritage?

1. What is the wind that is ruffling the tawny pelt of Africa? Why does the poet compare the Kikuyu to flies battening upon the bloodstreams of the veldt?

2. Why does the worm, "colonel of carrion," cry, "Waste no compassion on these separate dead"?

3. Why does the poet point out that the colonial policy justified by statistics and scholars is of no consequence to "the white child hacked in bed" or to "savages, expendable as Jews"?

4. Why does the poet contrast the "natural law" of the violence of beast on beast with the search of "upright man" for divinity through the infliction of pain?

5. What does the poet mean when he says that upright man "calls courage still that native dread / Of the white peace contracted by the dead"?

6. Why are we told that "brutish necessity wipes its hands / Upon the napkin of a dirty cause"?

7. Why does the poet describe the conflict between black and white as the gorilla wrestling with the superman? Why is this a "waste of our compassion, as with Spain"?

8. Why does the poet see himself as "poisoned" by the blood of his ancestors?

9. Why does the poet feel torn between "this Africa and the English tongue I love"? What would it mean to betray them both or give back what they give?

10. At the end of the poem, has the poet made the decision to "turn from Africa"? Is this decision one that he cannot make or one that he cannot avoid making?

FOR FURTHER REFLECTION

1. To what extent should race define who we are? Do people of mixed race have to create a new cultural, and personal, identity?

2. Is the imaginative flight of poetry a flight from reality? Is poetry as significant as political action in improving humankind?

3. Is a shared language critical to maintaining cultural identity? Is the language a person speaks a political statement?

4. Should each of us, regardless of our heritage, think of ourselves as being a nation, like Shabine, or is that too disorienting a concept?

5. Should people feel guilt over the crimes of their ancestors?

Questions for

A PASSAGE TO INDIA

E. M. Forster

E. M. FORSTER (1879–1970) was born
in London and educated at Cambridge
University. After leaving school, he decided
to devote his life to writing, and became
an influential novelist, essayist, and social
critic. Forster is also known for his literary
criticism, especially a series of Cambridge
lectures published under the title *Aspects
of the Novel*. Forster visited India in
1912–1913 and 1921. He documented his
experiences there six years after the end
of British colonial rule in *The Hill of Devi*
(1953). *A Passage to India* was published
in 1924.

NOTE: All page references are from the
Harcourt Brace & Company (Harvest)
edition of *A Passage to India*.

INTERPRETIVE QUESTIONS
FOR DISCUSSION

At the end of the novel, why can't Fielding and Aziz be friends, despite their ardent wish to be?

1. Why are Aziz and Fielding drawn to each other despite their cultural differences?

2. Are we meant to agree with Aziz when he says that "kindness, more kindness, and even after that more kindness" is "the only hope" for good relations between the British and the Indians? (126–127) Why is kindness more important to the Indians than truth? (272)

3. Why does Fielding's sense of honor lead him first to throw in his lot with Aziz against the British, and then to abandon Aziz in order to rescue his accuser, Adela? Why does Fielding feel that if "an attack was made on the girl by his allies, he would be obliged to die in her defence"? (210–212, 258–260)

4. Why does Fielding's boast of traveling light eventually begin to offend Aziz? When the two meet again two years after the trial, why does Fielding "not travel as lightly as in the past"? (131, 303–304, 355)

5. Why is Fielding "puzzled and worried" by Aziz' sexual snobbery? (268) Why does Fielding tell Aziz that the one thing he can't put up with in him is remarks like his suggestion that Adela is "an awful old hag" and wanted him to molest her? (281)

6. Why is Fielding horrified at the notion that Adela should pay Aziz twenty thousand rupees as compensation? (277) Why does Fielding try so insistently to talk Aziz out of suing Adela for damages? (279–281, 290)

7. Why does Aziz suspect Fielding of wanting to marry Adela for the money that would have gone to Aziz as compensation? Why does Aziz eventually persuade himself that the wedding has actually taken place? (310–313)

8. Why does Aziz forgive Mahmoud Ali and Godbole for letting him believe Fielding married Adela for her money, but tell Fielding that "it's as if you stole it"? (339, 342)

9. Why does Aziz choose to live in a Hindu state rather than in one run by the British, even though he doesn't understand Hindus either? (358) Why does Fielding, an atheist, tell Aziz, "There is something in religion that may not be true, but has not yet been sung. . . . Something that the Hindus have perhaps found"? (308)

10. At the end of the novel, why are we told that Fielding "had thrown in his lot with Anglo-India" and "was acquiring some of its limitations"? (358) Why does Fielding feel that "the British Empire really can't be abolished because it's rude," when before he thought it built upon sand? (289, 307, 360)

11. Why does Stella have a better understanding of how the Marabar is "wiped out" than Fielding does, but refuse to explain it to him? Why does Fielding say that Stella has ideas he doesn't share and, unlike Aziz and Adela and himself, is "after something"? (356–357)

12. Why does the author ask if "God si Love"—an echo of Mrs. Moore's quotation of John 4:8—is "the first message of India"? (53, 320, 324, 354)

Suggested textual analyses
Pages 302–313 (Chapter 31)

Pages 355–362 (Chapter 37)

Why does the author have a friendly expedition to the Marabar Caves result in a trauma to Adela—a misunderstanding that causes permanent damage to East-West relations in Chandrapore?

1. Why does Adela accuse Aziz of trying to molest her? Why does the author have Aziz' accuser be someone who is new to India and sympathetic to Indians?

2. Why are we told that before Adela's trauma in the cave she is thinking about her marriage to Ronny and wondering, "What about love?" Why does Adela decide that she and Ronny do not love each other, but that it doesn't matter? (168)

3. Why are we told that Adela admires Aziz' beauty, but feels no personal warmth toward him? (169)

4. Why is Aziz so shocked by Adela's innocent question about how many wives he has that he has to leave her alone momentarily? (169)

5. Why does Turton believe that "it's our women who make everything more difficult out here"? Why are we told that resentment lurks, "waiting its day," underneath Turton's chivalry toward Adela, and perhaps "in all chivalry"? (237)

6. Why does the alleged attack on Adela unleash so much hatred of Indians among the British? Why does it cause them to betray the very principle of justice they claim to be in India to maintain? (239–240)

7. Why do the British tend either to idealize Adela or to forget her altogether in their haste to condemn Aziz? (199, 203, 239–240)

8. Why does Adela decide that Aziz is innocent after all? Why does her recantation make the situation worse instead of better? (224–225, 255–256)

9. Why are Fielding and Adela the only people who have an interest in finding out what really occurred in the cave? Why does Adela tell Fielding, "I am up against something, and so are you"? (292)

10. Why is the story told so that both Fielding and Adela are ostracized by Anglo-Indian society? (271–273)

Suggested textual analyses
Pages 166–169 (from Chapter 15): from the beginning of the chapter to "and wondering with the other half about marriage."

Pages 180–184 (Chapter 17)

Why does Mrs. Moore come away from the Marabar Caves with an echo that begins to "undermine her hold on life," saying, "Everything exists, nothing has value"?

1. Why are we told that the odd, featureless caves in the Marabar represent an India "older than all spirit," and that they intimidated even Buddha, "who shunned a renunciation more complete than his own"? (136)

2. Is Mrs. Moore especially susceptible to the Marabar echo because of her natural sympathy with India and Indians?

3. Why does Mrs. Moore decide that there is no difference between love in a church and love in a cave? (224, 231)

4. What does Godbole mean when he says that when good or evil occurs, "it expresses the whole of the universe," and that "they are both of them aspects of my Lord"? (197–198) Why does the author have Mrs. Moore's vision of good and evil echo Godbole's? (227–228)

5. After her experience in the caves, why does Mrs. Moore refuse to help either Aziz or Adela? Why does even Christianity lose meaning for her? (166, 221–222, 227–228)

6. Why are we told that, after experiencing the cave and "hearing its voice," Mrs. Moore "had not entertained one large thought, she was actually envious of Adela"? Why does Mrs. Moore decide that "less attention should be paid to my future daughter-in-law and more to me, there is no sorrow like my sorrow"? (231)

7. Why does Aziz remain loyal to the memory of Mrs. Moore, even though she didn't help him? (350)

8. Why does Mrs. Moore's son have the same natural affinity with Aziz that she had? Why does Aziz say to him, as to her, ". . . you are an Oriental"? (349; cf. 21)

9. At the end of the novel, why do both Godbole and Aziz imagine that "Esmiss Esmoor" is reaching out to them? (326, 339–340)

10. Do the Marabar Caves reveal the truth about human existence in India, or render it even more confusing?

Suggested textual analyses

Pages 162–166 (from Chapter 14): from "The first cave was tolerably convenient," to the end of the chapter.

Pages 221–231 (from Chapters 22 and 23): beginning, "Oh, what of the echo?" and ending, "she rejected it irritably."

FOR FURTHER REFLECTION

1. Do some peoples and cultures need to be helped by more developed nations, or is it never justified for one culture to impose its values and customs upon another?

2. Why is sexuality often the focus of racial conflict?

3. Does the United States play a role in the world, politically and culturally, comparable to that of the British Empire in India? Are Americans guilty of the same self-righteous cultural imperialism?

4. Are Eastern and Western religious perspectives ultimately incompatible?

5. Are East and West doomed to never understand each other? Would achieving understanding mean the loss of what is distinctive in each culture?

Questions for

WIDE SARGASSO SEA

Jean Rhys

JEAN RHYS (1890–1979) was born in Dominica, one of the Leeward Islands in the Caribbean and a former British colony. Her parents, a Welsh doctor and a white West Indian, or Creole, woman sent her to England at age sixteen to attend school. Eventually, Rhys married the Dutch poet and journalist Max Hamer and moved to Paris, where she met a number of writers and artists, and received encouragement from Ford Maddox Ford to pursue a career as a writer. *Wide Sargasso Sea* is a reinterpretation of the story of the first Mrs. Rochester—the mad woman in the attic—of Charlotte Brontë's *Jane Eyre*.

NOTE: All page references are from the Norton Paperback edition of *Wide Sargasso Sea* (first printing 1982).

INTERPRETIVE QUESTIONS
FOR DISCUSSION

Why does growing up in emancipated Jamaica leave Antoinette vulnerable to a tragic marriage—and virtual enslavement—to the Englishman Rochester?

1. Why does Antoinette think of her Garden of Eden at Coulibri and the barriers of the cliffs, high mountains, and sea as things that make her safe from strangers? Why does she regard even negative aspects of nature—razor grass, ants, rain, and snakes— as "better than people"? (19, 27–28)

2. Why does Antoinette's mother reject her? (20, 26, 48)

3. Why, according to Christophine, are the new white people in the West Indies and their law worse—more cunning—than the slave owners? (26)

4. Why do the former slaves around Coulibri think of Antoinette and her family as "white niggers"? Why does being thought of in this way make Antoinette wonder "who I am and where is my country and where do I belong and why was I ever born at all"? (23–24, 42, 102)

5. Why is Antoinette's mother destroyed by the West Indian society she understands and appreciates, while her husband, who doesn't understand it, prospers? Why does she say, "They are more alive than you are, lazy or not, and they can be dangerous and cruel for reasons you wouldn't understand"? (32–33, 40)

6. As her family flees Coulibri, why is Antoinette taken completely by surprise when she runs to embrace Tia and Tia throws a rock at her? Why is looking at Tia's tear-covered face with her own blood-covered one like seeing herself in a looking glass? (45)

7. Why does Antoinette feel she must forget her mother and pray for her "as though she were dead, though she is living"? (55)

8. Why does Antoinette think of the convent as a "refuge, a place of sunshine and of death"? Why does she wonder if there is "no happiness" and, unable to wait for "all this ecstasy," pray for death? (56–57, 59)

9. Why does Antoinette have a recurring dream in which she associates marriage with hatred? Why does she think of this as a dream about hell? (59–60)

10. Why is Antoinette unable to pray or to cry at her mother's funeral? (61)

11. Why does Antoinette agree to marry Rochester regardless of her own better judgment and her Aunt Cora's warning? Why does she ask him if he can give her peace as well as happiness and safety? (78–79)

12. Why does Rochester, remembering Antoinette's "effort to escape" marriage, think that "she had given way, but coldly, unwillingly, trying to protect herself with silence and a blank face"? Why does he think, "If I have forgotten caution, she has forgotten silence and coldness"? (90–91)

Suggested textual analyses

Pages 17–23: from the beginning of the novel to "where I had been or what I had done."

Pages 56–61: from "This convent was my refuge," to the end of Part One.

Why does Rochester resolve to "break up" Antoinette, even though he succeeds in winning her love and making her—for the first time in her life—want to live?

1. Why does Rochester think that he has not bought Antoinette, but that "she has bought me, or so she thinks"? Why does he think she has "deceived" and "betrayed" him? (70, 164, 170)

2. Why does Antoinette reproach Rochester for making her want to live and beg him to tell her to die? Why does he do what she asks? (91–92)

3. Why is Rochester "thirsty" for Antoinette without loving her or feeling much tenderness for her? Why does he nonetheless experience a pang of rage and jealousy when Christophine suggests that Antoinette might remarry? (93, 159)

4. Why is Rochester "very rough" in his lovemaking with Antoinette? Why does he play a dangerous game in which desire, hatred, life, and death come "very close in the darkness," yet tell Antoinette—and himself—that she is safe? (94, 151)

5. Why is Rochester not surprised to get Daniel's letter accusing Antoinette and her mother of infamy and madness? (99) Why does Rochester come to believe that everyone knows the "truth" about his wife, but no one will tell it to him? (103–104)

6. Why does Christophine accuse Rochester of deliberately making Antoinette think he loves her and of wanting to "break her up" because he is jealous of her? Why does he admit to himself that "it was like that," but *not the way you mean*? (152–153)

7. Why does Rochester feel that he is the one who deserves pity—and revenge—for being "tied to a lunatic"? (164)

8. After his encounter with Amélie, why does Rochester have "not one moment of remorse"? (140) Why does he deliberately throw his dalliance with Amélie in Antoinette's face? (154)

9. Why does Christophine tell Rochester that he is neither the best nor the worst, but only someone who will not help Antoinette when she breaks up? (156)

10. Why does Rochester think he might be tender to Antoinette if she would only show her sorrow? Why can he imagine embracing her again as his "lunatic," his "mad girl"? (165–167)

11. As Rochester and Antoinette are preparing to leave the island for Jamaica, why does he "suddenly, bewilderingly" become certain that everything he has imagined to be true is false, that "only the magic and the dream are true"? (167–168)

12. Why does Rochester hate Antoinette for belonging "to the magic and the loveliness" of the island where they live? Why does he blame her for leaving him thirsty and think that all the rest of his life will be thirst and longing for what he had lost before he found it? (172)

Suggested textual analyses

Pages 92–95: beginning, "But at night how different," and ending, "red earth does not dry quickly."

Pages 167–173: from "He spoke politely enough," to the end of Part Two.

Why does Antoinette come to believe that she was brought to England to burn down Rochester's house?

1. Why does Rochester imprison Antoinette in his house in England instead of letting her go, as Christophine has urged?

2. When she is a child, why do hate and courage come to Antoinette at the same time? (49)

3. Why does Antoinette ask Rochester if her friend is right about London being "like a cold dark dream"? (80–81)

4. Why does Rochester think that the reality of life in Europe might disconcert, bewilder, or hurt Antoinette, but that it would not be reality for her? (94)

5. Why does Antoinette think she will be a different person in England? Why does she have foreknowledge of the bed she will sleep in and believe that in that bed she will dream the end of her dream? (111)

6. Once she is in England, why does Antoinette decide to say to Rochester "I give you all I have freely" in order to gain her freedom? Why does she decide to be "wise as serpents, harmless as doves"? (179)

7. Why does Antoinette, living in isolation with Grace Poole in Rochester's attic, eventually no longer know who she is? Why is she sure that she is not in England? (180, 181, 183)

8. Why does Antoinette attack Richard Mason when he says the word "legally"? (184)

9. On one of her forays downstairs in Rochester's house, why does Antoinette suddenly imagine she is in her Aunt Cora's room? Why does she knock down the candles and imagine that Christophine has saved her from the "ghost" by sending a wall of fire to protect her? (188–189)

10. Are we meant to see Antoinette's destruction of Rochester's house in England as an act of madness or of justice?

Suggested textual analysis
Pages 177–190 (Part Three)

FOR FURTHER REFLECTION

1. Does the story of Antoinette and Rochester reflect typical problems in gender relations? Is the notion of a clash of cultures a good way to understand certain kinds of conflict between men and women?

2. Why is place so important to our sense of self and well-being? Does place, more than race or ethnicity, form one's cultural identity?

3. Why is it often hard for people growing up in two cultures to find a home in either one?

4. Is Jean Rhys's Rochester consistent with the one created by Charlotte Brontë in *Jane Eyre*?

5. Does Rochester deserve to be pitied?

ACKNOWLEDGMENTS

All possible care has been taken to trace ownership and secure permission for each selection in this anthology. The Great Books Foundation wishes to thank the following authors, publishers, and representatives for permission to reprint copyrighted material.

Deep Play: Notes on the Balinese Cockfight, by Clifford Geertz. Copyright 1972 by *Dædalus: Journal of the American Academy of Arts and Sciences.* Reprinted by permission of *Dædalus: Journal of the American Academy of Arts and Sciences,* from the issue entitled "Myth, Symbol, and Culture," Winter 1972, Vol. 101, No. 1.

The Two Shores, from THE ORANGE TREE, by Carlos Fuentes. Translated by Alfred Mac Adam. Translation copyright 1994 by Farrar, Straus & Giroux, Inc. Reprinted by permission of Farrar, Straus & Giroux, Inc.

The Antheap, from AFRICAN STORIES, by Doris Lessing. Copyright 1951, 1953, 1954, 1957, 1958, 1962, 1963, 1964, 1965, 1972, 1981 by Doris Lessing. Reprinted by permission of Simon & Schuster.

"The Schooner *Flight*" and "A Far Cry from Africa," from COLLECTED POEMS 1948–1984, by Derek Walcott. Copyright 1986 by Derek Walcott. Reprinted by permission of Farrar, Straus & Giroux, Inc.

Cover photography: Robert Fujioka Studios, Mountain View, California

Cover and book design: William Seabright and Associates